PRIZING LITERATURE
The Celebration and Circulation
of National Culture

GILLIAN ROBERTS

Prizing Literature

The Celebration and Circulation of National Culture

UNIVERSITY OF TORONTO PRESS
Toronto Buffalo London

ISBN 978-1-4426-4271-3

Printed on acid-free, 100% post-consumer recycled paper with vegetable-based inks.

Library and Archives Canada Cataloguing in Publication

Roberts, Gillian, 1976–
    Prizing literature : the celebration and circulation of national
culture / Gillian Roberts.

(Cultural spaces)
Includes bibliographical references and index.
ISBN 978-1-4426-4271-3

1. Canadian literature (English) – Minority authors – History and
criticism.   2. Canadian literature (English) – 20th century – History
and criticism.   3. Citizenship in literature.   4. Literary prizes – Social
aspects – Canada.   I. Title.   II. Series: Cultural spaces

PS8089.5.I5R62 2011   C810.9'9206912   C2011-902650-3

The University of Toronto Press acknowledges the financial assistance to
its publishing program of the Canada Council for the Arts and the
Ontario Arts Council.

Canada Council   Conseil des Arts   ONTARIO ARTS COUNCIL
for the Arts   du Canada   CONSEIL DES ARTS DE L'ONTARIO

This book has been published with the help of a grant from the Canadian
Federation for the Humanities and Social Sciences, through the Aid to
Scholarly Publications Program, using funds provided by the Social
Sciences and Humanities Research Council of Canada.

University of Toronto Press acknowledges the financial support
for its publishing activities of the Government of Canada through the
Canada Book Fund.

For my parents, Delia and Jack,
and in memory of David Hewitt, Ada Murray, and Priscilla Roberts

Contents

Acknowledgments

This book, having had a lengthy gestation period, owes a great deal to a number of people. First and foremost, thanks are due to Lynette Hunter, my PhD supervisor at the University of Leeds, for her guidance, her support, and for never saying no to any of my ideas but always holding them to account, making this a better project, and me a better scholar. Thanks also to Shirley Chew, Graham Huggan, and Diana Brydon for their comments and questions. For financial assistance during my doctoral studies, thanks to the Social Sciences and Humanities Research Council, the British Council, and the University of Leeds.

This book has since followed me to three other institutions, the University of Western Ontario, Leeds Metropolitan University, and the University of Nottingham. Many thanks to colleagues in these departments, especially Jessica Schagerl, Susan Watkins, Sue Chaplin, Mary Eagleton, Ruth Robbins, and Susan Billingham for their support as this project evolved into its different incarnations. I owe countless friends on both sides of the Atlantic for their moral and intellectual support and their lively conversation: thanks especially to Catherine Bates, Lee Carruthers, Carmen Ellison, Corinne Fowler, Anna Greenwood-Lee, Caroline Herbert, Kaley Kramer, Nasser Hussain, Eric Langley, Donna McCormack, Jeffrey Orr, Edel Porter, David Stirrup, Charles Tepperman, Darrelle Villa, Abigail Ward, Jayne Waterman, Dominic Williams, Ingrid Young, Patricia Young, and Terence Young. A particular thank you to Catherine, Caroline, Jeff, Jayne, and especially Eric, for their attentive reading.

I would like to express my gratitude to Carol Shields for her hospitality, her time, and her encouragement, and to thank Don Shields and family and the Carol Shields Literary Trust for permission to quote from my interview with Carol here. At University of Toronto Press, thank you to Siobhan McMenemy and the anonymous readers for their much-appreciated advice. Some of the material in this book was published in a different form in the following: ' "Sins of Omission": *The English Patient*, THE ENGLISH PATIENT, and the Critics,' in *Essays on Canadian Writing* 76 (2002), pp. 195–215; 'Sameness and Difference: Border Crossings in *The Stone Diaries* and *Larry's Party*,' in *Canadian Literature* 191 (2006), pp. 86–102; 'Ethics and Healing: Hospital/ity and *Anil's Ghost*,' in *University of Toronto Quarterly* 76.3 (2007), pp. 962–76; and ' "The Greatest Hotel on Earth": Citizenship, Nationality, and the Circulation of Canadian Literature,' in *West Coast Line* 59, 42.3 (2008), pp. 146–60. Many thanks to the editors of these publications.

This book is about home, and being away from it. I must thank my family, particularly my parents, Delia and Jack, in Canada, and my expatriate brother, Jonathan, for their generosity, their good humour, and their patience.

PRIZING LITERATURE
The Celebration and Circulation
of National Culture

Introduction

In October 1992, after the announcement that Michael Ondaatje's novel *The English Patient* was joint winner of the Booker Prize with Barry Unsworth's *Sacred Hunger*, a *Toronto Star* editorial praised Ondaatje as a worthy recipient of the prize and, more specifically, a worthy Canadian:

> Michael Ondaatje has brought a rare honor to his adopted land by winning the Booker Prize that eluded such Canadian luminaries as Robertson Davies, Mordecai Richler and Margaret Atwood.
> The rare recognition, given to Commonwealth writers, befits this Canadian who presents his prose, poetry, plays and films against the backdrop of a global canvas.
> Born in Sri Lanka, educated in England and now a Canadian teaching international literature at York University, Ondaatje is a perfect model of modern Canada. ('Ondaatje's Honor' A22)

This editorial illustrates the intersection of national and literary interests: although the occasion of celebration is the Booker Prize, an award given outside Canada, it has a profound influence on the ways in which a writer can be considered integral to Canadian culture. Going on to list the other awards Ondaatje had won to date – the Governor General's Award, the Trillium Award, the W.H. Smith Award – the *Star* offers these prizes as evidence of Ondaatje's literary pedigree. But it also offers Ondaatje's *Canadian* credentials. Although the editorial acknowledges that Ondaatje's nation of origin is not Canada, it goes on to reinscribe Ondaatje's identity as Canadian. There is no mention of Ondaatje's having become a citizen; the reference to his 'now' being 'a Canadian' invokes this process while simultaneously writing it out, naturalizing Ondaatje's Canadianness as a personal development, rather than a legal question. Ondaatje's status as 'a perfect model of modern Canada' stems from both the evidence of his fitting into cultural norms, such as 'not [being] given to boasting – a very Canadian characteristic,' and, 'as most Canadians, volunteer[ing] his time and talent for the community' (in Ondaatje's case, as an editor) and from his exceptionality as a Canadian Booker winner (A22). Ondaatje moves from being a guest in Canada, as suggested by the metaphor of adoption, to encapsulating Canadian cultural success and values, not only occupying the Canadian host position, but also acting as Canadian culture's representative, an exemplary figure held up for emulation. Finally, the journalist credits Ondaatje, along with Atwood, Davies, and Richler, with sustaining Canadian identity in the face of 'the daily cultural onslaught from the United States' (A22), indicating that the values identified as Canadian intersect with the literary output of these writers, endorsing a literary and national citizenship based on a responsibility *to* and *for* a commitment to Canadianness.

Prizing Literature interrogates the relationships between national culture and hospitality, between celebration and accommodation, between writing, reading, and citizenship. In recent decades, Canadian literature has been particularly visible on the international stage. Since 1990, several Canadian writers have been internationally lauded, including Margaret Atwood, Austin Clarke, Rawi Hage, Lawrence Hill, Michael Ignatieff, Ann-Marie MacDonald, Alistair MacLeod, Yann Martel, Anne Michaels, Rohinton Mistry, Alice Munro, Michael Ondaatje, Mordecai Richler, and Carol Shields. These writers have been nominated for and/or have won such awards as the (Man) Booker Prize, the Commonwealth Writers' Prize, the IMPAC Dublin Award, the Man Booker International Prize, the Orange Prize, the Prix Médici (Etranger), and the Pulitzer Prize, among others. Such recognition of Canadian literature outside Canada has had consequences for Canadian literature's reputation both outside Canada and within it.

In the context of this phenomenon of international literary celebration, this book focuses on Michael Ondaatje, Carol Shields, Rohinton Mistry, and Yann Martel because of the negotiations their national identities have undergone in the wake of their celebration and international attention. Whereas Ondaatje, Shields, and Mistry immigrated to Canada as adults, Martel presents a different engagement with questions of nation through his Québécois background as well as the cosmopolitanism accorded him through his upbringing in several different countries.

Ondaatje's and Martel's Booker wins bookend a decade of increasing rec-ognition for Canadian writers whose cultural currency within Canada rose in accordance with celebration outside it. All three of Mistry's nov-els to date – *Such a Long Journey* (1991), *A Fine Balance* (1995), and *Family Matters* (2002) – have been nominated for the Booker Prize; *Such a Long Journey* also won the Governor General's Award for English-language fiction, and *A Fine Balance* won the Giller Prize. Shields's Booker nomina-tion for *The Stone Diaries* occurred in 1993, the year following Ondaatje's win, and her novel subsequently won the Pulitzer Prize in the United States. Both Ondaatje and Shields won the Governor General's Award for English-language fiction for these extranationally celebrated texts.

The complicated relationship between Canadian literature as circu-lated within Canada and Canadian literature as an international com-modity depends upon the external validation of Canadian cultural products and the writers who produce them. Extranational authori-ties preside over Canadian culture, and their aesthetic sanctioning of Canadian texts becomes translated into national success for Canada. For immigrant writers to win these external prizes is to increase the currency of Canadian literature outside the Canadian nation-state and to heighten the visibility and validity of Canadian literature within Canada; in taking on a representative status for the nation, such writ-ers undergo a reworking of their national identity and previous guest status.

Not merely incidental to the texts they celebrate, literary prizes sig-nify both on their own terms and in relation to the texts whose circula-tion and readership they function to increase. In *Paratexts: Thresholds of Interpretation*, Gérard Genette includes the literary prize in the category of 'factual' paratexts, which he otherwise leaves unexamined in his focus on 'peritext' and 'epitext,' those features produced and/or sanc-tioned by the publisher and author of a text. In contrast to the peritext or epitext, a factual paratext 'consists not of an explicit message (verbal or other) but of a fact whose existence alone, if known to the public, provides some commentary on the text and influences how the text is received' (7). In addition to Genette's sense of the prize's paratextual function, literary prizes and the larger discourse of celebration that sur-rounds them form a significant *intertext* for the reading of celebrated literature. As Tony Bennett writes: 'Just as, to bend Derrida, "*Il n'y a pas de hors-texte*," then so there is no outside of literature – no way of writ-ing about it that can be external to it in the sense of being unaffected by, or without consequences for, the way in which the field of literature is currently constituted' (5). Given that 'the seemingly extratextual world surrounding books . . . is also material for the construction of specific kinds of meaning' (Brouillette 2), *Prizing Literature* argues that what might otherwise be designated as 'outside' literature, namely the significance, influence, and implications of literary prizes, operates alongside, and in relation to, the texts themselves.

Literary prizes have come to accrue a particular significance to the constitution of contemporary Canadian literature. Prizes connected to the nation-state (through funding, for example) are most explicitly tied to national projects, and therefore suggest that winning texts, on some level, benefit the nation. However, prizes that are *not* bound up in national funding sources or concerns often attract national attention. A reading of works by prize-winning writers in relation to discourses of national celebration and corresponding issues of hospitality and citizenship effectively demonstrates the negotiations entered into by these celebratory projects and the frameworks through which we, the readers, are encouraged to approach these texts. Further, moments when texts resist or complicate recuperation into national discourses offer fruitful points for exploring the relationships between text and celebratory context. We are reminded that artists are 'licensed transgressors of liberal democratic nations' (Hunter 22), and that prize-winning writers may both contest the nation-state and be celebrated for doing so. The extent to which the four writers under discussion are allowed to transgress, and how such transgressions may or may not affect their alignment with the Canadian cultural host, will be discussed in later chapters.

Hospitality offers an enabling framework for discussing the configuration of national identity and belonging. Nation-state borders constitute the most obvious thresholds of belonging, of articulating distinctions between host and guest, citizen and foreigner. Mireille Rosello, probing 'the parallels between the immigrant and the guest, and between the state and the host,' points out that 'depicting immigrants as guests obscures the fact that the reason why they were "invited" had nothing to do with hospitality' (8, 9). Rosello therefore introduces the nation-state's interests in immigration as a complication to hospitality: '. . . if a nation invites immigrants because they are valuable assets, because it needs them for an economic or demographic purpose, that country is not being hospitable. At least not unconditionally, infinitely hospitable' (12). The categories of host and guest are circumscribed not only by legal issues, but also by perception, particularly of those who correspond to the dominant definitions of the host culture;

thus, borders are also internal to the nation-state, figurative thresholds that depend upon the hospitality or hostility offered by the host culture to its guests. Theorizing of hospitality has been particularly strong in France, where the hospitality metaphor is bound up in legislative discourse, for 'French legislation tends to prefer the use of the term "hospitality laws" to immigration laws' (Laachir 4). Writers such as Rosello and Jacques Derrida chiefly concern themselves with French and European in/hospitality. But hospitality discourse is also productive for examining Canada, a settler-invader colony whose population has depended largely on immigration, and whose own sense of self as a coherent host has been undermined since Canada's beginnings. My interest in hospitality therefore includes both Canada's gestures of hospitality towards immigrants and the attempts to forge a Canadian cultural host position.

As immigrant writers, Ondaatje, Shields, and Mistry have all, to varying degrees, exchanged their guest for host positions. More precisely, this exchange has been made for them, following their successes, by the Canadian cultural host. Texts welcomed into a national culture, and celebrated as part of that culture (particularly through national literary awards), can confer the status of host upon immigrant writers previously considered as guests. Hospitality functions here simultaneously in relation to national identity and through the vocabulary used to articulate responses to reading: to observe how a book has been *received* is to discuss the text as an object of hospitality, to assess the extent to which readers are hospitable to the work. Prizes form part of the text's reception; they also function to increase the opportunity for reception by promoting the circulation of celebrated texts, proliferating the possibilities of hospitality through readership. The welcoming of celebrated immigrant and ethnic-minority writers into the Canadian cultural host position must therefore coincide with a hospitality of reading and reception. For a writer such as Martel, whose French-Canadian identity and associations with cosmopolitanism complicate his place in English-Canadian literature, the celebration of his texts functions less to welcome him into the host position and more to *secure* his status as one of the hosts.

Hospitality discourse primarily concerns itself with the entitlements of 'strangers.' In 'Perpetual Peace,' Immanuel Kant focuses on hospitality as 'the right of a stranger not to be treated with hostility when he arrives on someone else's territory' (105). This right is conditional and depends upon the stranger's recognition of and compliance with the responsibility of a guest: '... he must not be treated with hostility, so long as he behaves in a peaceable manner in the place he happens to be in' (106). Thus, '*hospitality* is not to be understood as a virtue of sociability, as the kindness and generosity one may show to strangers who come to one's land or who become dependent on one's act of kindness through circumstances of nature or history; hospitality is a right that belongs to all human beings' (Benhabib 22). Yet Kant's vision of the rights of hospitality presupposes conditions whose very existence undermines hospitality itself. Building on Kant's work, Derrida explores the distinction 'between unconditional hospitality and ... the rights and duties that are the conditions of hospitality' (*Of Hospitality* 147), which constitute 'two, discontinuous and radically heterogeneous orders' (Honig 105). As Derrida points out, *absolute* hospitality cannot be circumscribed by rights or obligation, for it

> requires that I open up my home and that I give not only to the foreigner (provided with a family name, with the social status of being a foreigner, etc.), but to the absolute, unknown, anonymous other, and that I *give place* to them, that I let them come, that I let them arrive, and take place in the place I offer them, without asking of them either reciprocity (entering into a pact) or even their names. (25)

Distinguishing between degrees of hospitality, between legislated and absolute hospitality, Derrida examines the 'constant collusion between traditional hospitality, hospitality in the ordinary sense,' and power (55), identifying the host position as having been based on 'the *patron*, the master of the household ... [who] maintains his own authority *in his own home*' ('Hostipitality' 4).

The host is not always hospitable, and 'traditional' hospitality that depends upon the invitation of the host is not *absolutely* hospitable. This wavering of hospitality underpins the idea of the host culture and its power to accept or reject, of particular importance to a nation-state as relatively new as Canada, where the host culture undergoes constant explicit debate and revision. Canada's settler-invader history resonates with Kant's criticism of European colonial powers: '... the *inhospitable* conduct of the civilised states of our continent, especially the commercial states, the injustice which they display in *visiting* foreign countries and peoples (which in their case is the same as *conquering* them) seems appallingly great' (106). In particular, Kant criticizes European interference in 'America, the negro countries, the Spice Islands, the Cape, etc.

[which] were looked upon at the time of their discovery as ownerless territories; for the native inhabitants were counted as nothing' (106). The Canadian host position contains within it a legacy of colonial violence, as testified to by the history of Euro-Canadian treatment of 'native inhabitants.' The current dominant version of Canadianness depends upon the wresting of the host position from Aboriginal peoples by French and English colonizers and the subsequent defeat of the French by the English. Despite Canada's official bilingualism and official multiculturalism policy, the dominant construction of Canadianness is still white and anglophone. The extent to which the current dominant political and cultural host in Canada can be said to offer hospitality is compromised by its claim of the host position in the first place and the implications of hostility that precede this claim.

The binary opposition of hospitality and hostility is an unsettled one. Derrida uses the term 'hostipitality' to foreground the potential for slippage between hospitality and hostility, focusing on their etymological link: 'hospitality' has 'a troubled and troubling origin, a word which carries its own contradiction incorporated into it, a Latin word which allows itself to be parasitized by its opposite, "hostility," the undesirable guest [hôte] which it harbors as the self-contradiction in its own body' ('Hostipitality' 3). Although hostility is the inverse of hospitality, the two coexist, the border between them collapsed, thus complicating any sense of belonging. With respect to citizenship and national culture, the 'dichotomy' or 'hiatus' between 'citizenship and national belonging' (Kanaganayakam, 'Cool' 146) illustrates this 'hostipitality,' the legal invitation within borders tempered by the perpetuation of the cultural guest position for those who do not conform to the dominant host culture.

The hyphen that often accompanies and signals immigrant identity might also be viewed as a site of hostipitality. As Smaro Kamboureli notes, '... many Canadians reside within the space of the hyphen' (*Scandalous* 101), between one identity and another. The hyphen represents 'the problematic situating of the self as simultaneously belonging "here" and "there"' (Mishra 433), thereby constituting a space for negotiating guest and host status, the invitation and the reminder of the need for invitation: 'Sri Lankan-Canadian,' 'American-Canadian,' and 'Indo-Canadian,' for instance, not only trace and expose the movement from guest to Canadian host status, but also balance between guest and host through the space of the hyphen. 'French-Canadian,' according to official constructions of Canadianness, should correspond to a host status within Canada, yet it also indicates a kind of guest status within English-language national literature. The hyphen's hospitality depends on whether the hyphenate identity is claimed by the individual to whom it refers, or whether it is attributed by a representative of the (unhyphenated) Canadian host. The hyphenated space becomes a potential location of hostipitality, and the removal of the hyphen becomes both the ultimate act of hospitality (as in the *Toronto Star*'s proclaiming and celebrating Ondaatje's Canadian status) and the ultimate act of violence to identity, erasing 'there' (whether outside the nation-state, or within, as in Quebec) to insist upon 'here.' These concerns of hospitality and hostility, of recalibrating host and guest status, are integral not only to extratextual discussion of Ondaatje, Shields, Mistry, and Martel, but also to textual analyses in the context of their works' inter/national celebration and circulation.

The recruitment of the celebrations of the writers examined in this book for the Canadian national culture depends upon their Canadian citizenship, in both straightforwardly legal and less specifically cultural terms. In *Literary Celebrity in Canada*, Lorraine York argues that celebrity involves 'laying claims to various forms of citizenship and capital, ways of defining allegiance to human environments and characteristics of various kinds' (164). Of Ondaatje's success with *The English Patient*, in particular, York notes that citizenship becomes 'bound up with issues of national pride and achievement' (161–2). Indeed, citizenship not only plays a crucial role in the implications of literary prizes for a national culture, but it also intersects with the concerns of hospitality, indicating political membership in the host nation-state. A citizen, in theory, occupies the position of host, for 'citizen' is 'one of a pair of opposites,' the other being 'alien' (C.L. Smith 139), at best a guest, at worst an unwelcome foreigner. Citizenship implies the status of 'one of us' (Cairns 4), a designation conferred by the host culture. But distinctions between citizenship and nationality complicate, temper, and at times invalidate the assumption of hospitality; even a citizen of a nation-state can be unwelcome, treated as a guest within the borders of that nation-state, if s/he does not correspond to the cultural demands of the host. The works of Ondaatje, Shields, Mistry, and Martel each probe, to varying extents and in varying ways, the distinction between citizenship and nationality, exposing the degrees of belonging and *un*belonging, and the complication of national claims as perpetuated by host cultures.

Citizenship consists of a relationship between the individual and the state: it is 'a linking mechanism, which in its most perfect expression binds the citizenry to the state and to each other' (Cairns 4). This binding arises through 'an ensemble of rights and obligations' and the creation of 'a juridic identity that determines an individual's status within the political community' as 'citizenship ... ascribes to an individual as a legal personality' (B.S. Turner, 'Liberal' 23). But rights are not upheld in the same way for all individuals, as evidenced by the distinction between legal and cultural belonging. The terms of belonging are established not simply by law but also by the intersection of power interests within a community and the nation-state. The matching of citizenship with legal and cultural rights can be compromised by hostility to difference; these differences, as identified in texts by Ondaatje, Shields, Mistry, and Martel, include language, race, ethnicity, religion, and nationality. Shields, in particular, also identifies the different roles accorded male and female citizens, exposing the equation of public life with citizenship as having been traditionally gendered. The intersection of citizenship and hospitality therefore functions not only in relation to *new* citizens who have immigrated to the nation-state, but also to those who are *born* citizens who do not occupy the status of the powerful host.

The relationship between citizens (and indeed, non-citizens) and the spaces they inhabit configures what Eve Kosofsky Sedgwick terms the 'habitation / nation system,' defined as 'the set of discursive and institutional arrangements that mediate between the physical fact that each person inhabits, at a given time, a particular geographical space, and the far more abstract ... national identity, as signalized by, for instance, citizenship' (147–8). The relationship between nation and habitation not only arises in extratextual discussions and negotiations of the identities of Ondaatje, Shields, Mistry, and Martel, but it also features in the works of these writers, particularly through their migrant and travelling characters. Does a migrant belong to, or in, his/her location of habitation? Does s/he still belong to, or in, his/her nation of origin, once s/he has established habitation elsewhere? The degree to which hospitality is extended to the migrant, both in the new location of habitation and in the nation of origin (in the case of the *returning* migrant), underpins claims to belonging: both the claims of the migrant, and the ways in which s/he is claimed (or not claimed) by the nations of origin and habitation. Occupation is central to the habitation/nation dynamic: the power underpinning the occupation of a territory; the questions of belonging (and implied relations to power) arising from the situation of 'belonging' to one nation and occupying space in, inhabiting, another.

Sedgwick equates national identity with citizenship, but citizenship itself becomes complicated when an individual's nation of habitation does not match his/her nation of origin, or even the site of his/her citizenship. Characters in Ondaatje's, Shields's, Mistry's, and Martel's works at times display affiliations with nations outside their own, seeking (not always successfully) to transcend the limitations of nation-state borders variously through labour, cultural interest, attempts to seek personal refuge, the desire for a better life, and international political commitment.

Movement across state borders often corresponds with the interests of cosmopolitanism, sometimes identified as a 'detachment from the bonds, commitments, and affiliations that constrain ordinary nation-bound lives' (Robbins, Introduction 1). As Amanda Anderson notes, however, '. . . cosmopolitanism is a flexible term, whose forms of detachment and multiple affiliation can be variously articulated and variously motivated' (267). Although ideas surrounding cosmopolitanism date back to the Stoics and the Cynics, conceptions of cosmopolitanism relevant to the present, which can be traced to the Enlightenment, include 'the social outsider who becomes cosmopolitan because there are no satisfactory alternatives,' 'a choice of life style, involving frequent travelling and a refusal to be fully associated with one particular country, whilst tending to move in very similar social circles,' and 'membership of a particular profession or social group with interests that inherently transcend frontiers' (Carter 49). Not all cosmopolitanisms are as freely chosen as others, and those that are actively pursued may differ depending upon an emphasis on lifestyle, philosophy, or various kinds of transnational work. Where one individual's cosmopolitanism might be underpinned by 'rootlessness and lack of commitment' (49) to a home country, another's might be based precisely on commitment – to international justice, for instance.

Cosmopolitanism as an actively pursued lifestyle and worldview, which 'frequently advances itself as a specifically intellectual ideal, or depends on a mobility that is the luxury of social, economic, or cultural privilege' (Anderson 268), has made the concept a target of critique, especially where it 'suggest[s] an unpleasant posture of superiority toward the putative provincial' (Appiah xiii). Criticisms have emerged, for example, from the left, protesting against cosmopolitanism's indulgence in 'a privileged and irresponsible detachment' (Robbins, Introduction 4), and from postcolonial challenges concerned about cosmopolitanism being 'based on a false belief in the possibility of universalism' (Carter

9). Theorists have begun to supplement the term 'cosmopolitanism' in order to address such challenges – for example, James Clifford's notion of 'discrepant cosmopolitanisms' generated by 'specific, often violent, histories of economic, political, and cultural interaction' (108), Homi K. Bhabha's 'vernacular cosmopolitanism,' focused on pursuing the 'right to difference in equality' via 'political practices and ethical choices' (xvii), and Walter D. Mignolo's 'critical cosmopolitanism' that 'reconceive[s] cosmopolitanism from the perspective of coloniality' (723). Various kinds of cosmopolitanism surface in Ondaatje's, Shields's, Mistry's, and Martel's texts through characters that cross nation-state borders for diverging reasons. The overlaying of host and guest status in the experiences of these characters involves differently charged manifestations of cosmopolitanism, ranging from a less politically active cosmopolitanism to one that emphasizes global citizenship's rights and duties.

Of course, any discussion of Canadian literature and cosmopolitanism invokes A.J.M. Smith's mid-twentieth-century differentiation between the 'native' and 'cosmopolitan' tradition in Canada and its later rearticulation as 'a distinction between literary nationalism and colonialism' (Kokotailo 67). As the above discussion demonstrates, 'cosmopolitanism' offers an array of definitions and connotations, and is a great deal more complex than both Smith's use of it in this instance and the debate it has generated within Canadian literary criticism. In relation to writers such as Ondaatje, Shields, Mistry, and Martel, cosmopolitanism does not signify merely an 'abandoning [of] particulars in favour of universals' or an 'erasure of differences among places and peoples' (Bentley 257, 265), but rather a range of commitments, ideologies, and methods of seeking, enduring, or confronting displacements and connections across cultures. However, although Canadian literature has undergone dramatic shifts since Smith's initial elevation of cosmopolitan over native traditions, it is nevertheless worth recalling his distinction here because of the tensions between the national and the cosmopolitan that arise in relation to the international celebration of Canadian writers and its effect on those writers 'at home.' Smith's articulation of a preference for cosmopolitan literature, namely, international modernism, prompts questions about how taste might operate in relation to nation.

If, as Anderson argues, cosmopolitanism is often guilty of being 'insufficiently conscious of its investment in an elitist habitus' (275), how do national literary prizes attempt to configure habitus? French sociologist Pierre Bourdieu identifies habitus as the generator of taste, arguing that 'life-styles are ... the systematic products of habitus' (*Distinction* 172). The habitus, 'a set of dispositions which generates practices and percep- tions' that 'is sometimes described as a "feel for the game"' (R. Johnson 5), also 'connects "habitation" with "habit,"' making habitus a '"practice" of place' (Ashcroft 160). Whereas Bourdieu's sense of habitus privileges class, as he argues that 'class habitus' is 'the internalized form of class con- dition and of the conditionings it entails' (101), for Canadian literature and literary prizes, a sense of national habitus might be more fruitful in its connection of 'habitation' and 'habit,' engendered by the conditions of place. In relation to Canadian cinema, Charles Acland asserts, 'It would be wrong to suggest that there is a single, unified, national habitus, but there has been an attempt to situate a set of dispositions as central to a national character' (292). Although no 'single, unified, national habitus' operates *in practice* in Canada, national celebration of Canadian cultural products projects a unified habitus on the basis of shared nationhood. A national habitus rests on what we might consider national capital, rather than the economic, cultural, and academic capitals that are inte- gral to class habitus: a national habitus uses the nation as its currency, emphasizing the value of national cultural products precisely because of their nationality, and attempting to forge a national taste – a taste for the nation and its culture, whether considered 'cosmopolitan' in aesthetic terms or not. National habitus might be positioned as the legitimizing force behind national culture: if the Canadian public acquires a taste for Canadian culture, the Canadian hosts are thereby married to the nation's culture. Celebratory projects and institutions that support Canadian cul- tural production project a national habitus in order to attempt to estab- lish a national habitus that exists in practice. In other words, they must assume that an audience for Canadian culture exists in order to deliver it to them. In the context of celebrated immigrant and ethnic-minority writ- ers, national habitus also operates in relation to hospitality as 'hyphenate' writers are 'translated' into producers of a national culture whose cel- ebration encourages its consumption. Such writers contribute, wittingly or not, to the Canadian public's taste for Canadian culture while they are promoted for their contribution to the host culture *as* Canadians.

All the texts under examination in this book explore negotiations of identity, in Canada and elsewhere, and contribute to the surge of inter- national recognition for Canadian literature and its impact, 'at home,' on Canadian culture. Although all four writers have been made to rep- resent Canada, they have done so in very different ways, with different consequences; all of these writers have had their identities translated and recruited for various versions of the *Toronto Star*'s 'perfect model of modern Canada.' Ultimately, Ondaatje, Shields, Mistry, and Martel represent particular sites of challenges to dominant ideas of Canadianness that must be overcome in order to convert the international recognition of their work into currency for the nation to trade within both national and global cultural marketplaces.

1 Prizing Canadian Literature

The celebration of Canadian literature through the literary prize is hardly a new phenomenon. It has been a regular event since the establishment of the Governor General's Awards by the Canadian Authors' Association in 1936. But the high-profile, reasonably consistent international prizing of Canadian writers is relatively recent, its key moment being Michael Ondaatje's Booker Prize for *The English Patient* in 1992. Ondaatje was not the first Canadian to be nominated for the prize; indeed, only two years after the establishment of the Booker, Mordecai Richler appeared on its shortlist, in 1971 (*St. Urbain's Horseman*), and did so again in 1990 (*Solomon Gursky Was Here*). Until 1992, other Canadians who joined the ranks of Booker nominees included Brian Moore (*The Doctor's Wife*, 1976; *The Colour of Blood*, 1987; *Lies of Silence*, 1990); Alice Munro (*The Beggar Maid* [*Who Do You Think You Are?* in Canada], 1980); Robertson Davies (*What's Bred in the Bone*, 1986); Margaret Atwood (*The Handmaid's Tale*, 1986; *Cat's Eye*, 1989); and Rohinton Mistry (*Such a Long Journey*, 1991). Canadian writers, therefore, were not invisible on the international literary prize scene. But Ondaatje's Booker Prize shifted the momentum of Canadian literature's presence in the global cultural marketplace, and it was swiftly followed by Carol Shields's Pulitzer Prize for *The Stone Diaries*. Unsurprisingly, current Canadian literary criticism that grapples with 'the increasing exportability of our writers' (York 169) tends to identify the 1990s as a turning point for both the writers themselves and Canadian readers' awareness of Canadian literature's potential to travel outside the nation's borders. Ondaatje's and Shields's international prizes have everything to do with the increasing confidence in CanLit's 'exportability.' These celebrations generated outside the nation ultimately sold, and fed, the nation back to itself, as

Canadian readers were encouraged by external arbiters to cultivate a taste for their own nation's cultural products and to welcome their own culture and its consumption.

Literary prizes do particular kinds of work: they promote and perpetuate competing forms of valuing; not only are they competitions themselves, but they also compete with each other; and, in the context of national cultural celebration, they contribute to defining the parameters of the nation and its culture, particularly where immigrant writers are concerned. Cultural and economic capitals overlap in the workings of the literary prize, but prizes dedicated to national literature also reveal a national capital at work. The ideological implications that underpin national cultural celebrations in a Canadian context are essential to understanding the work that national prizes attempt, with varying degrees of success, and the borders of Canadianness that they draw. To this end, this chapter discusses three Canadian prizes – the Governor General's Award for English-language fiction, the (Scotiabank) Giller Prize, Canada Reads – and three extranational prizes – the (Man) Booker Prize, the Commonwealth Writers' Prize, the Pulitzer Prize – as a means of tracing the circulation of the nation and the relationship between the national and the global cultural marketplaces.

Literary prizes function explicitly to make aesthetic judgments about writing. In the process of shortlisting and selecting winning texts, prizes (and the juries who make decisions about them) infuse works of literature with cultural value. But cultural value is not the only value in play in the competition for literary prizes: more often than not, the recognition offered by literary prizes consists not only of an aesthetic anointing by the jury but also of a monetary prize; indeed, between literary prizes with similar catchment areas and mandates, the *amount* of money attached to the prize provides a point of competition in itself. The implication of literary prizes within forms of financial valuing increases when we consider that one of the knock-on effects of selecting a text for a prize shortlist, and especially the prize-winner itself, is the expected increase in sales for that text upheld by the prize jury as a worthy read. At this point various kinds of 'worth' intersect in the cultural marketplace where the reader finds herself encouraged to consume the text.

Despite the lofty claims that might be made – and indeed, *have* been made – on behalf of literary prizes, the aesthetic evaluation that constitutes the most obvious part played by literary prizes does not operate on its own. Prizes contribute to what James F. English and John Frow call 'the literary-value industry, that is, the whole set of individuals and groups and institutions involved not in producing contemporary fiction as such but in producing the reputations and status positions of contemporary works and authors, situating them on various scales of worth' (45). The very phrase 'literary-value industry,' combining as it does cultural and economic considerations, elite connotations embedded in 'literary' with debased connotations of mass production, embodies the intersection, if not the perceived clash, between 'scales of worth.' Similarly, literary prizes, ostensibly operating in the pursuit of highbrow cultural evaluation, always already invoke financial worth through the etymology of 'prize' itself: 'The word is traced to the Latin *pretium:* "price," "money"; akin to the Sanskrit *prati:* "against," "in return"' (English, *Economy* 76).

But while the word 'prize' might be considered to compromise the word 'literary' here, the cultural values that seem to inhere in the category of the literary are by no means stable. The 'literary' itself bears a 'contingent and shifting definition' (Squires, *Marketing* 6), one increasingly shaped and affected by various marketplace considerations and imperatives, including promotional activities such as marketing and celebration. If the 'literary' has traditionally been associated with cultural value, cultural value does not offer a neutral, transparent category. Rather, as English acknowledges, 'its production is always a social process. Neither can it emerge in a political vacuum, the participants uncolored by and indifferent to prevailing hierarchies of class, race, gender, or nation; its production is always politicized. And neither can it emerge in perfect independence of or opposition to the economic marketplace itself' (*Economy* 7).

There is no perfect state in which cultural value can operate autonomously. Neither is there a neutral position from which to judge and celebrate literature through the medium of the literary prize. As Graham Huggan writes, 'Far from offering tributes to an untramelled literary excellence, prizes bring the ideological character of evaluation to the fore' (118). If literary prizes contribute to 'constructing and reshaping notions of literary value and taste' (Squires, *Marketing* 15), the criteria that underpin 'good taste' are inescapably ideological, as the work of Pierre Bourdieu has demonstrated: 'Taste classifies, and it classifies the classifier' (*Distinction* 6). Drawing on Bourdieu's discussion of symbolic capital, English argues that the cultural prize functions both 'as a piece of objectified symbolic capital (the sort of hard credential or qualification that is "to cultural capital what money is to economic capital")' and 'as an instrument of exchange and conversion with its own particular rules of operation' ('Winning' 110).

One process of conversion effected by the literary prize is that of popularization, which might initially appear to be at odds with symbolic capital and the cultural respectability it entails. But the literary prize, operating within 'a broad range of motivations and implications,' engages not only in the celebration of literary excellence but also in the promotion of particular authors and texts, the attraction of media attention to literary production, and the 'support [of] the consumption of literature generally' (Squires, *Marketing* 97). Sarah M. Corse argues that literary prizes explicitly function to 'encourage the current elite version of literary aesthetics, otherwise known as rewarding "good" writing' (100), but this claim seeks to divide symbolic from economic value in the prize's privileging of elite aesthetics over the category of the bestseller. Corse contends that prize-judging in itself ensures such a division, because prize-winners 'are not chosen by popular ballot, but by panels of "experts," experts with vested interests in the maintenance of a system which ... strongly differentiates between high-culture literature and popular-culture literature' (102). Yet popularization forms part of the mandate of prizes, regardless of what aesthetic category the texts themselves might be seen to occupy, for even prizes devoted to 'highbrow' literature play an 'evident [if] non-formalised role in popularising the literary' (Squires, 'Book Marketing' 76). In attempting to celebrate aesthetic excellence, literary prizes also function to suggest to readers that they consume the texts that offer such aesthetic excellence, thereby merging literary and economic value. Thus, Corse's analysis does not account for the intermediary position in which the literary-value industry can place celebrated authors: 'somewhere between literary success and mass-market best-seller' (York 24), a position that all four of the writers with whom this book is concerned – Michael Ondaatje, Carol Shields, Rohinton Mistry, and Yann Martel – arguably occupy.

In Canadian cultural celebration, the nation itself features as part of the goal of attempted popularization. According to English, cultural prizes 'are the single best instrument for negotiating transactions between cultural and economic, cultural and social, or cultural and political capital – which is to say that they are our most effective institutional agents of *capital intraconversion*' (*Economy* 10). More precisely in the context of Canadian culture, the 'political capital' belongs to the status of the national culture itself, the extent to which it is considered worthy of celebration and consumption. The celebration of Canadian culture presents particular issues in the process of capital intraconversion because of the role that the state plays in supporting national culture and its reasons for doing so: namely, the concern about the dominance of non-Canadian cultural products in Canadian cultural consumption and the assumption that Canadian culture cannot rely on the marketplace for financial viability, partly because of a perceived disjunction between Canadian culture and popular consumption. Acknowledging that his analysis of the economy of prestige is largely based on 'British and American contexts' (*Economy* 26) of celebration, English focuses on two dominant English-language cultural sites. Despite challenges to hegemonic constructions of British and American identity and culture, particularly from racial and ethnic minorities excluded from orthodox definitions, British and American culture have not been subject to the same *kind* of sustained anxiety that Canadian culture has.

Alongside the conflicting yet overlapping elements of symbolic and economic capital more generally at work in literary prizes, there is a kind of national capital that functions in Canadian literary prizes and in Canadian responses to extranational prizes that anoint Canadian literature. If cultural evaluation is always ideological, Canadian literature itself has been part of an ideological project at least since the establishment of the Canada Council for the Arts in 1957 on the recommendation of the Massey Report, which 'issued the first clear warning about the dangers of dependence upon American culture' (Litt 3) and argued that the state should take on responsibility for national cultural development. With government funds, the Canada Council has sustained both the production of Canadian literature, among other cultural forms, through grants to both individual writers and to publishers, and the celebration of Canadian literature through its administration of the Governor General's Awards since 1959. If 'policies of national culture are ideological attempts to bring certain visions of nation and citizenship into existence' (Acland 288), part of this citizenship, invoked in relation to state-sponsored national culture, must involve the consumption of national cultural products; however, 'the cry that there is no Canadian culture' (281) has not been completely silenced despite the Council's efforts, and the Massey Commission's anxiety about American influence resonates five decades later.

It is not the case, of course, that there is no Canadian culture, but it *is* the case that a perceived absence of a national culture in Canada has long been in evidence. As Bonnie H. Erickson noted in a study of taste in the Toronto business community, although 'prosperous Canadians have traditionally preferred the work of dead male foreigners for their conspicuous consumption' (261), in particular, 'being a Canadian novelist seems to be a greater handicap than being alive or a woman' (263). Erickson's study was published the year before Ondaatje's Booker Prize win, the event that seems to have infused Canadians' sense of their literature's 'exportability' and viability in a global cultural marketplace. But Erickson's findings indicate that celebratory projects such as literary awards in Canada must operate ideologically in terms of winning consent of the Canadian public to the idea of the nation, and to a sense that national culture is worthy of consumption. Indeed, the Canada Council's role in both supporting and celebrating the arts constitutes what we might consider an attempt to forge a national habitus. If habitus, as Bourdieu argues, is the generator of taste, what might a national habitus look like? How would taste 'functio[n] as . . . a "sense of one's place"' (Bourdieu, *Distinction* 466) in national terms? A national habitus would presumably apply to all members of a nation, indicating a disposition *towards* the nation and its cultural products on the basis of nationality.

If a national *habitus* indicates a disposition towards the consumption of national cultural products, the notion of national *capital* suggests that nationality becomes a kind of currency in the cultural marketplace. The addition of national capital to the collision of the symbolic and the economic reinforces the literary prize's function as a tool of popularization: not only do literary prizes support the consumption of literature in general terms, but in the Canadian context, they also specifically promote the consumption of Canadianness alongside the idea that Canadian culture can profitably trade in the currencies of both symbolic and economic capital. Consumption exceeds the simple purchasing of literary texts, or even the reading of them, for as John Frow writes, 'In its most literal sense, consumption is an incorporation, a swallowing up of the external world' (49). Canadian literary prizes thereby attempt to render the Canadian public more hospitable to Canadian literature, to match the contours of the 'host culture,' so to speak, with the national identity of the public by encouraging the consumption of Canadianness.

In Canada, the Governor General's Award, the (Scotiabank) Giller Prize, and Canada Reads all work on some level to win the consent of the Canadian public to the valuing of Canadian literature, and to the idea that CanLit is worthy of celebration. These prizes also grapple with the competing values of symbolic, economic, and national capital, but in different configurations, and with different claims made by and for each prize. Ultimately, all three participate in capital intraconversion, but specifically, in the case of the Governor General's Award, the Giller, and Canada Reads, the ultimate conversion arises from the conjunction of the symbolic and economic with the valuing of the nation.

The Governor General's Award for English-Language Fiction

Originally established by the Canadian Authors' Association, the Governor General's Literary Awards have been aligned with the state since their administrative shift in 1959 to the Canada Council (the same year French-language prizes were added). These awards now encompass seven categories – fiction, non-fiction, drama, poetry, children's literature (text), children's literature (illustration), and translation – in both official languages. Although the Bank of Montreal has co-sponsored the awards since 1988, this additional financial backing has not been reflected through a change of name. The retention of the awards' name, 'redolent of British royalty,' insists upon the link with the state, a link that has, historically, led to controversy through the refusal of the award by Québécois writers in the 1960s and 1970s, as well as by Leonard Cohen in 1969, when, standing in solidarity with these writers, he 'became the only English-language author to refuse an award' (Abley, 'Booby Prize' 52).

English argues that 'far from posing a threat to the prize's efficacy as an instrument of the cultural economy, scandal is its lifeblood' (*Economy* 208). Refusals to accept the Governor General's Award might be considered scandalous, though the award has also participated, as with most other, if not all, literary prizes, in 'the most common and generic scandals[, which] concern . . . the judges' dubious aesthetic dispositions, as betrayed by their meager credentials, their risible lack of habitus, or their glaring errors of judgment' (190). But 'scandals' involving a partly state-funded prize resonate somewhat differently than English suggests. Granted, media complaints about shortlists and final winners do, at least, draw attention to the prize under attack, allowing the prize to benefit from what English terms 'journalistic capital' (208). But an award aligned with the state also invites complaints from journalists (and indeed readers) who double as aggrieved citizens and taxpayers. In the case of the Governor General's Award for English-language fiction, in particular, several accusations have been made over the course of the prize's history about its seeking to implement particular political agendas under the guise of celebrating literature.

In recent decades, critics of the Governor General's Award have often assumed that the juries have an agenda involved in constructing the Canadian nation and its culture. Not only have juries been accused of elitism (McClelland 8) – an accusation that should not be surprising, given the taste implications of artistic judgment – but they have also been criticized for being 'politically correct, [for] bending over backward to encourage small regional presses' (Ross, 'Striking' C10), for putting too great an emphasis on 'concern for social issues' (Ross, 'Tale' C7), and for 'climbing onto another CanLit bandwagon, multiculturalism' (Yanofsky, 'Don't Bet' I3). Echoing the Canada Council's guidelines for jury composition for peer-assessment review of grant applications, which recommend diversity of professional role, artistic practice, language, region, gender, age, ethnicity, race, and representation of Aboriginal artists (see Canada Council, 'Peer' n.p.), the Governor General's Literary Awards juries 'are chosen from the three main regions of the country – one from the west, one from central Canada, one from the east – but there are all kinds of other criteria to take into account too: age, sex, ethnicity, literary schools of thought' (Yanofsky, 'Picking' J3). Complaints about the Governor General's Awards' consideration of factors conventionally seen as 'non-literary' reveal an irritation that is perhaps rooted in conflicting views of the nation, or perhaps based on the fact that aesthetic judgment within the context of a state-sponsored prize has been articulated in relation to nation in the first place.

A 2002 article by Noah Richler in the *National Post* clearly expresses this discontent with the Governor General's Award for failing to privilege both aesthetic achievement and potential economic capital. Richler complains,

> I am . . . sorry the GG administration doesn't take a clearer stand on what it perceives its mandate to be in the fiction category. Obviously, . . . the GG jury feels a responsibility to embrace the full map of Canada. It wants to throw light on authors working in neglected pockets of Canada . . . There's nothing wrong with any of this – but why not state the difference? Why not say, 'We are the Canadian prize. We know what literary excellence is, but it is not our sole criterion. We will moderate it because we are here to recognize the full diversity of all the territories and peoples of this diverse country and have to do it in five books.' ('We Are Looking' AL1)

According to Richler, the Governor General's Awards' English-language fiction juries concern themselves too deeply with mapping

the parameters of Canadianness. Richler entreats these juries to ann-
ounce, 'There are other prizes to tell you what the Best Big Book is, but
that is not what our job is' (AL1), suggesting that the Best Big Book is
a transparent category, carrying no cultural assumptions, and having
no impact on or responsibility to the construction of the nation.

Richler's equation between award-winning fiction and Best Big Book
presupposes a certain degree of economic capital, both before and after
the prize announcement. Carol Shields's remarks about judging the
Governor General's Award are not only informative but also significant
for the ways in which they intersect with Richler's claims, yet diverge
from the spirit of his complaint: 'I think one of the things they look for
in that jury – I've only done it once – they look for something that has
changed the novel form into something different. I certainly am interested in that, what book has changed the way we think of novels, what
a novel can be' (Personal interview). Shields emphasizes the symbolic
capital of Governor General's Award–winning fiction, with an implicit
privileging of aesthetic experimentation and therefore a link to the
field of restricted production. Certainly, journalists have described the
Governor General's Award as making 'bold but flaky' selections (Ross,
'Heads-up' D10), though this boldness has occasionally been expressed
more charitably, as in Paul Gessell's claim that 'Governor-General's
Awards juries have historically plucked books out of obscurity for
their fiction shortlists' ('Just One' C5) and 'often include emerging
authors who experiment and live beyond the shadow of the CN Tower'
('Toronto' D1). Significantly, both Michael Ondaatje and Carol Shields
first attracted Governor General's Award notice through some of the
most experimental works of their careers: Ondaatje won a Governor
General's Award for *The Collected Works of Billy the Kid* (1970), a text
so difficult to categorize that a new category – 'Prose and Poetry' –
was invented to celebrate it; and Shields received her first Governor
General's Award nomination for *Swann* (1987), widely viewed as a
departure from her previous writings, particularly in terms of that novel's play with form.

Although Richler might disagree, national literary prizes, by virtue of the fact that they celebrate literature included on the basis of
its nationality, *are* partly responsible for constructing a national literature, and, by implication, the boundaries of the nation itself. It is not
just aesthetic difference that can be negotiated through a national cultural prize, but also the national identity of celebrated writers. On the
one hand, a national prize can secure the Canadianness of expatriate

writers, as seen in recent years through the Governor General's Awards for novelists Douglas Glover (*Elle*, 2003) and Kate Pullinger (*Mistress of Nothing*, 2009), long-time residents of New York State and London, England, respectively. On the other hand, in terms of negotiating the boundaries of Canadianness, the hospitality, and host position, of national prizes becomes especially clear with respect to immigrant and ethnic-minority writers. According to the state, all Canadian citizens are Canadian, part of the legal host. But the cultural host is not the same as the legal host; citizenship is not the same as national belonging. Thus, *legally* Canadian writers, having immigrated from elsewhere (and, indeed, Canadian writers who were born in Canada but are primarily associated with ethnic-minority identities), are in some sense *declared* Canadian, part of the cultural host, through national prize recognition and the parameters of eligibility. For example, writing about Rohinton Mistry, Ranu Samantrai claims that 'Mistry's work has been acknowledged as legitimate by no less an authority than the committee that grants the Governor General's Awards, Canada's highest literary prizes' (34). Samantrai credits this award with providing Mistry's writing 'the status of Canadian literature' (34). The national prize works here to erase Mistry's guest status, to affirm host status, and to encourage hospitality amongst the rest of the host population, particularly those conforming to more dominant definitions of Canadianness. This encouraged hospitality actually seeks to erase the *need* for hospitality: if Mistry is no longer considered a guest, but one of the hosts, he is thereby afforded the status of 'one of us,' a cultural and national status to match his legal host position. Canadian culture expands through redefinition of who *qualifies* as host, and attempts to marry the category of citizenship to definitions of the nation. In this way, national prizes interpolate the status of citizenship *into* the status of the cultural – not just legal – host position.

Any national prize for which Canadian citizens are eligible can forge this connection between citizenship and the cultural host position. But Samantrai implies, in discussing Mistry's entry into the contemporary canon of Canadian literature, that the Governor General's Awards, in particular, carry national weight because of their link to the state. Indeed, the Governor General's Awards likely attract the criticism they do because of their status as 'a tax-based government program' (R. Martin 102), whose name reminds Canadians of the relationship between state and celebration. And yet, as Dionne Brand and M. Nourbese Philip have argued, the apparatuses of the state that work to support the production and dissemination of Canadian literature often exclude writers from the host position. Philip's essays frequently expose and interrogate the racism of the Canadian arts funding and publishing system, which is more hospitable to the aesthetic experiments of white writers than to writers of colour who challenge our received ideas of literature. Although the market is often used as an excuse for why more challenging works are not published, as Philip points out, 'Market forces do not determine the publishing activity of those publishing houses receiving subsidies; if they did, these houses would not be in business' (160).

Similarly, Brand argues that African-Canadian artists have been failed by such institutions as the Canada Council, Ontario Arts Council, and government departments responsible for multiculturalism: 'The black community cannot depend upon, cannot trust these institutions to maintain or nurture our cultural expression in Canada. Those institutions should be asking themselves what it is precisely that they maintain and nurture, if particular communities are not funded or are underfunded. And they should be asking themselves: what is Canadian culture?' (Interview 275). As much as the 'various "para-statal" bodies, including the CBC, the NFB, the Canada Council, provincial and metropolitan arts councils,' should be accountable to the Canadian public, funded as they are with public money, a Canadian 'culture . . . organised around "whiteness"' (Bread 159) only addresses the needs of the white Canadian public. Despite the Canada Council's concerns about racial diversity on its grant juries, underfunding of African-Canadian literature persists, allowing, as Brand argues, the contours of Canadian culture to remain undisturbed. Further, Brand's own experiences of sitting on the jury for the Governor General's Award for poetry demonstrates the ways in which the guidelines for representativeness do not adequately address the assumptions behind dominant aesthetics. As Brand notes, 'I fill two of the spaces for the "marginalized." I am a woman and I am Black' (166). Finding herself in complete disagreement with the other two (white, male) jurors, Brand 'take[s] on [her] "inclusion" on this jury and others, not as a task of assimilation into Euro-centric values but as contesting those very values and widening the sets of cultural forms that come to stand for Canadian culture' (167); yet she is advised that the jury's goal is to come to a consensus, despite her sense that a genuine consensus is impossible. Brand's frustration echoes her criticism elsewhere of self-congratulatory quotas on the part of writing organizations in Canada:

... the Writers' Union and PEN ... seem to feel that you can quantify culture into six per cent of this and two per cent of that. These demographic
figures are trotted out in hasty self-defence to deny charges of racism. This
approach assumes that the contradictions of Canadian culture can be han-
dled by putting them into discrete and isolated packages. Further, it assumes the ongoing dominance of white culture as justifiable and having no
responsibility to change its fundamental stance. (Interview 275)

In Brand's analysis, the diversity and contradictions of Canadian culture are not allowed truly to redefine the shape of the host position, or
to devise 'a new Canadian poetics' (*Bread* 167), but are instead parcelled
out as individual units of difference.

As Brand's and Philip's contentions demonstrate, not every immigrant writer is as readily translated – or converted – into the Canadian
host position as Mistry, Ondaatje, or Shields. Philip argues that Canadian publishers posit 'the Canadian audience as narrow-minded, provincial and unable to read and enjoy anything but work written *by*
white writers, with the odd dash of ethnic literary spice proffered by
one or two carefully chosen writers' (163), suggesting, perhaps, that
Ondaatje and Mistry might be two such writers. For her part, Brand
won a Governor General's Award in the English-language poetry category, for *Land to Light On*, in 1997. This victory, and its implication of
her insertion into state-recognized national culture, does not discount
her critique of the institution of the Canada Council and the systemic
racism experienced by African-Canadian and other ethnic-minority artists, or her analysis of the falsity of 'consensus' on Governor General's
Award juries that posit unity where perhaps none exists. As Smaro
Kamboureli argues, the success of some ethnic-minority Canadian writers '[does] not necessarily imply either that ethnicity has become an
integral part of the literary canon or that Canadians have finally come
to terms with the diversities inherent in Canada' (*Making* 81). Brand's
Governor General's Award demonstrates that national prizes constitute sites of struggle, wherein definitions of the nation and national
cultural aesthetics undergo challenges, even if those challenges might
be hegemonically absorbed. Brand's Governor General's Award may
well lend political capital to the prize itself, perhaps operating like the
Writers' Union and PEN in Brand's critique, as evidence that exoner-
ates the prize or organization of racism. At the same time, by virtue of
Brand's winning the prize, she has been, through that act, interpolated
as Canadian.

If the Governor General's Awards have been criticized in some quarters for 'politically correct' agendas, such politics are by no means straightforward in relation to this national cultural institution. The complaint that multiculturalism features too prominently in this award's selection of texts might be countered with the sustained criticism of Canadian official multiculturalism, itself an institutionalized attempt to 'recognize ethnic differences, but only in a contained fashion, in order to manage them' (Kamboureli, *Scandalous* 82). The gap between the perception of the Governor General's Award in media coverage and the critique of the institution that sustains it underscores the national prize as site of struggle. But again, the link between the Governor General's Award and the state attracts particular forms of media criticism that its rival, the Giller Prize, has not.

The (Scotiabank) Giller Prize

As English notes, 'Every prize that declares or betrays a social agenda opens the door to new prizes claiming greater purity of aesthetic judgment' (*Economy* 60). The perception of the Governor General's Award's 'agenda' in attempting (if not, as Brand and Philip argue, succeeding) to represent the multiplicities and contradictions of the Canadian nation adequately has indeed prompted claims about the aesthetic purity of the Giller Prize. Real estate mogul Jack Rabinovitch established the award in 1994 in memory of his late wife, journalist Doris Giller, and funded the prize, its presentation, and its promotion himself, until the co-sponsorship agreement with Scotiabank in 2005. Apart from the difference between state and private sponsorship (despite their corporate co-sponsorship), the Governor General's Awards and the Giller Prize also diverge in terms of structure. Whereas the Governor General's literary awards now comprise seven categories in both official languages, the Giller is just one prize, for best English-language fiction (though, since 2006, translations from French-language Canadian fiction have also been eligible). The Giller has attempted to distinguish itself from the Governor General's Awards in terms of philosophy and mandate, priding itself on taking into consideration no factors other than 'excellence – in writing, judging, and promotion,' and rejecting 'some of the contortions other prizes go through to ensure every kind of regional, gender and ethnic balance. Instead, the Giller prize juries are selected from among the very best writers and critics in Canada, based not on any criterion other than proved expertise through past writing' (J. Simpson A18).

The Giller's declared exclusive focus on 'excellence' harks back to Matthew Arnold's vision of criticism, whose 'business is ... simply to know the best that is known and thought in the world' (270). Arnold's insistence on criticism's 'disinterestedness,' on its 'keeping aloof from what is called "the practical view of things,"' and its 'steadily refusing to lend itself to any of those ulterior, political, practical considerations about ideas' (270) resonates in the Giller's passing literary judgment while avoiding any acknowledgment of socio-cultural context. It is unsurprising that a literary prize should claim that it privileges aesthetic criteria; however, given that cultural value cannot exist in a vacuum, attempts to construct the Giller in opposition to the Governor General's Awards on the basis of a 'pure' contest are disingenuous. Canada's national cultural policy, which supports the Canada Council and the Governor General's Awards, does not, by definition, promote a 'disinterested' concern for the arts. But regardless of whether or not the Giller declares an interest in ideas of nation when selecting juries, the prize does present a vision of Canadian literature. The visibility of a select group of works chosen by an awards jury contributes to constructing the contemporary national literature for the reading public. To claim that 'excellence' occupies a neutral position, carrying no further implications, effaces the role of literary prizes in relation to the national literature, regardless of any one prize's attempt to claim to judge its winner 'on merit alone' (Posner, 'The Giller Prize' R1). As Jennifer Scott and Myka Tucker-Abramson argue, invocations of 'excellence' and 'best' in Giller Prize discourse are anything but 'non-ideological,' particularly given the implications of 'the "big business" of corporate sponsorship' of the prize itself (15, 16).

In terms of its shortlists and winners, the Giller gained a reputation, five years into its history, 'for being "blue chip conservative" in its choices' (Ross, 'Heads-up' D10), particularly in contrast to the Governor General's Award. The fact that the 'Giller Prize is generally considered to be the one to embrace the stars – the household names of Canadian letters' (Gessell, 'Year' C21) gives the impression of offering 'more [of] an industry prize, where long-term efforts get acknowledged' (quoted in Renzetti C1). Revisiting Richler's invocation of Best Big Book, it seems that implicit in his critique of the Governor General's Award for not selecting this kind of text is that the Giller Prize makes such a work its celebratory focus. The phrase 'There are other prizes to tell you what the Best Big Book is,' which Richler attributes to the imagined confession of the Governor General's Award's administration, suggests that the rival Giller should be equated with that kind of celebration. Shields's description of judging the Giller Prize fits this characterization: 'I think the Giller wants, really, to pick the best book of the year, the highest quality book of the year, and that tends to be tied up in sales, I suppose, somewhat, at least that's what I hear' (Personal interview). Shields exposes the *lack* of 'pure' aesthetic consideration in selecting Giller-celebrated texts by emphasizing the economic capital that underpins Giller choices. Although there are exceptions, such as 2010 winner Johanna Skibsrud's *The Sentimentalists*, published by the small Gaspereau Press, the 'Big-ness' of the Giller winner, or its publisher, might be said to already be somewhat determined by the Giller's shortlist fee, currently at $1,500 per title, which can exclude smaller 'publishers [who] might not be able to afford' the cost (Henighan 84), resulting in 'Canada's major publishing houses ... influenc[ing] the outcomes of literary prizes by virtue of having the resources to promote their wares' (Dobson 166). If the 'best-ness' of Giller choices relates in some way to sales figures, perhaps the Giller is closer to the reading public, celebrating texts with which Canadian readers may be more familiar. Such texts are commercially viable, and lend themselves more easily to popularization. Broadcaster Carolyn Weaver has argued that whereas 'the Governor-General's are about literary heritage,' in contrast, 'the Giller winner should be the novel that just grabs people, the one book clubs want to read. Commercial consideration *should* come into play' (quoted in Posner, 'Giller Prize' R1). The Giller's philosophy appears to echo Weaver's views, given the prize's website's privileging of sales figures and prize money in 'a cynical slippage that naturalizes equivocations between art and market' (Scott and Tucker-Abramson 14).

While the Giller claims not to have a philosophy other than support of artistic excellence, it projects a unitary vision in its structure. The Giller is constructed through exclusion. Rabinovitch has declared of the Giller presentation, 'I invite my friends ... I don't have anyone I don't want' (quoted in Cameron 42), asserting the host's power to invite and to refuse entry. Rabinovitch has also been involved in choosing the jury; many jurors, such as Mordecai Richler (a friend of Rabinovitch who assisted in 'building the Prize's creative template' ['Jack Rabinovitch' 1]), David Staines, Jane Urquhart, and Margaret Atwood, have served more than once over the prize's history (and both Richler and Atwood have been winners). Notably, these jurors are based in central Canada. Indeed, Gessell articulates the diverging projections of nationhood extrapolated from the Governor General's Award and the Giller: 'The ... GG's tend to be more "national" if one defines that word as meaning more representative of the literary voices, both young and old, one finds in Canada. The Giller tends to define "national" as meaning what's good for Toronto's top clique of writers is good for the country' ('Toronto' D1). If Toronto equals the nation in the Giller's practice, the prize *does* implicate itself in constructing the nation, albeit by privileging Toronto as the nation's representative.

GG vs. Giller: Prizing Promotion

In 2000, an unprecedented degree of overlap between the two prizes arose in the awards' shortlists and winners: Ondaatje won the Governor General's Award for *Anil's Ghost*, which shared the Giller Prize with David Adams Richards's *Mercy among the Children;* Richards was also nominated for the Governor General's Award; and Eden Robinson was nominated for both prizes for *Monkey Beach*. In another overlap, Margaret Atwood, nominated for the Governor General's Award for *The Blind Assassin*, was on the Giller jury. These strong connections were read by some as a compromise on the part of the Governor General's Award, as the 2000 shortlist was accused of having taken 'a sharp turn towards the Establishment' (Gessell, 'Year' C21), as though, through the overlapping shortlist, the Governor General's Award appeared to be *just like* the Giller.

The winner of both the Governor General's Award and the Giller Prize in 2001 was Richard B. Wright's *Clara Callan*, continuing the overlap of taste. But since 2001, the prizes have selected different winning texts, despite the fact that some degree of overlap in nominations between the two prizes tends to be the norm (since 2001, only the 2005 shortlists have featured no shared nominations whatsoever). The tendency towards some shortlist overlap demonstrates that these prizes and the perceived differences between them are dynamic, rather than static. The Governor General's Award does grant prizes to household names – Ondaatje won his fifth in 2007 for *Divisadero*, tying him with Hugh MacLennan's record – as well as lesser known writers; and the Giller has gone to first-time author Vincent Lam in 2006 for *Bloodletting and Miraculous Cures* as well as to the likes of Ondaatje, Atwood, Richler, and Munro, although Atwood's status as Lam's 'booster' (Dobson 166) suggests the link between Giller and household names was maintained in his case. Public denunciations by jurors of the rival shortlist have emphasized the differences between the prizes: witness

1998, for example, when Giller juror David Staines dismissed the Governor General's shortlist as 'embarrassing – again,' to which Governor General's Award juror Susan Swan responded, 'To allow a tweedy Poo-Bah like David Staines to define the country's literary tastes would keep us in the wooden tracks of 19th-century traditional realism forever' (quoted in Renzetti C1). Despite the aspersions cast on the integrity of each prize, such incidents actually help both awards accrue journalistic capital through the apparent scandal that illegitimate taste offers.

Despite the recurrence of overlapping shortlists, the circumstances of each prize and the conditions under which they are promoted present discrepancies in journalistic capital. The Canadian media have consistently discussed the Giller, as an award and an event, in terms of excess and lavishness, anointing the Giller in recent years as English-language Canadian literature's 'most prestigious literary award' (Atkinson WP5), leaving the Governor General's Award with the distinction of 'the country's oldest literary prize' (Posner, 'No Giller' R1). Despite the now ubiquitous refrain in literary prize coverage declaring the Giller's prestige, no justification accompanies this claim. Through the prize's media-friendliness, promotional campaign, and the discourse of excess that surrounds the prize, it seems that journalistic capital, in this case, *determines* prestige. In economic terms, the Giller exceeds the Governor General's Award in the prize money itself. The Giller is currently worth $50,000, compared to the Governor General's $25,000 for each of its fourteen literary awards. Further, Jeffrey Simpson writes that 'the Giller prize has definitely eclipsed the Governor General's Awards in the retailers' eyes' (A18), due to the former's extensive publicity, 'which includes newspaper ads, posters and shelf stickers . . . It is the kind of publicity . . . that no publisher can afford' (Cameron 42).

Criticisms of the Governor General's Awards' lack of publicity have been ongoing for several decades. In 1960, Robert Weaver complained that the awards 'had about as much prestige as an invitation to address a ladies' book club' (29), lamenting the 'very little publicity about them' (31). In 1981, however, R.P. Bilan criticized attempts to attract publicity for the awards: ' . . . the presentation has been turned into a literary equivalent of the Academy Awards. There are now nominees, they are announced ahead of time, and then everyone gathers for the opening of the letters. This attempt to create hoopla *guarantees* that the awards will be given; publicity is now more important than real distinction' (32). Bilan's concern that 'the award has become apparently automatic, mandatory' (32) suggests a desire to return to the 1960s, when no English-language fiction award was given in 1962, 1965, and 1967. To make the awards 'automatic, mandatory,' and perhaps ritualistic, indicates a focus on the awards as an entity unto themselves, rather than a focus on the works being judged.

But Bilan's call to 'eliminate the Hollywood atmosphere' (32) was never answered. Changes to the timing of the Governor General's Awards in 1991 met with approval with respect to marketing and publicity. The shift in shortlist announcement from the beginning of the following year to the fall of the year in question was 'intended to maximize the awards' promotional value – they were established to promote Canadian literature, after all – and take advantage of the pre-Christmas book-buying season' (Kirchhoff C16). Integral to an award's 'promotional value' is its ability to popularize the literature being celebrated. Bourdieu argues that 'annual literary prizes perfor[m] a function analogous to that of fashion "collections"' (*Field* 100). Prizes not only attempt to popularize the works, but they also render more visible a selection of that year's literature (the shortlist, as well as the longlist, adopted by the Giller in 2006) before announcing the winner. Shortlist and longlist announcements are designed not only to sell a larger number of books, but also to create anticipation about the outcome of the literary contest.

Bilan's reference to the Academy Awards is apt, considering they were also established to promote a cultural industry. While the televised Oscar presentation relies on an easier analogy between media, the Academy Awards constitute a point of reference for all cultural prizes. For literary awards, to expect a glamorous presentation is a different matter, as the medium being celebrated is not a spectacle in itself. Canadian writers are most often visible to the public through readings, not through mass-mediated events. But the less likely transition from print product to television celebration has arisen on the Canadian literary prize scene. The Giller has been surrounded by discussions of glamour since its inception: as Alice Munro once described the occasion, 'We all wear glitzy clothes and pretend that it's the Academy Awards' (quoted in Ross, 'Tale' C7). Indeed, media coverage of the Giller ceremony in recent years has included information about the dinner menu (Stoffman, 'Vassanji' F1), glamorous clothing (Govani AL2), and a pre-Giller ceremony makeover for Susan Swan, complete with Botox treatment (Atkinson WP5). The presentation itself now airs live on Bravo!, BookTelevision, and CTV's website, with additional broadcasts at later dates on CTV and Star! Whereas the Scotiabank Giller ceremony features 'musical fanfares and video dramatizations' (MacSkimming 372), as well as Canadian screen actors among its presenters, in contrast, the Governor General's Awards have been criticized for their 'bland afternoon ceremony,' where 'winning authors and publishers are notified in advance' (Ross, 'Tale' C7).

The clearest mark of 'success' for a literary prize is the book sales it generates. In 1991, fifty-five years after the establishment of the Governor General's Awards, Val Ross stated that the 'awards now have a positive impact' ('Awards' C1). Ross equated this 'positive impact' with book sales, and it was not until the change in timing of the short-list announcement to before Christmas that this success became evident. Conversely, the Giller Prize very quickly became associated with significant marketing success, and its influence on sales demonstrates a 'Midas touch' (MacSkimming 372) much greater than that of the Governor General's Award. According to BookNet data, the Giller is the most effective Canadian prize at translating its celebration of texts into sales, with twice the impact of the Governor General's Award ('Giller Winner' C 9). Both the Giller and the Governor General's Award, by virtue of their function to celebrate Canadian literature, participate in the circulation of literary, national, and economic value. Despite this shared function, however, they are perceived to emphasize different values, and to trade with varying degrees of success in each of these forms of capital.

Canada Reads

Launched in 2002, the Canada Reads competition, sponsored by the CBC, is the most recent addition to high-profile Canadian literary celebration. Canada Reads diverges from the Governor General's Award and the Scotiabank Giller Prize in that it does not limit its shortlist to texts published in the previous year. Instead, any text in Canadian literary history might be selected for consideration. Literary prizes have generally been credited with the power to bestow 'precanonical' status (Corse 100) or to enact 'mid-term canon formation' (Squires, *Marketing* 2), but Canada Reads, through its inclusion of texts regardless of their publication date, also reproduces the more established canon in some of its shortlist selections, both testing the canon against popular consumption and updating it.

This popularization embedded in Canada Reads arises in a further divergence from the Governor General's Award and the Giller through its celebrity judges. Although the Canada Reads panels frequently feature at least one writer, they have also included popular musicians, actors, and former politicians, who are required to defend a text from a shortlist selected by 'a small jury of literary aficionados – including people from outside the CBC' ('The Panel' n.p.).The winner is declared through a process of elimination that 'adapt[s] a *Survivor*-type format' (Fuller and Rehberg Sedo 6), and the elimination discussions are broadcast on CBC radio, with an accompanying program on CBC television.

Despite these distinctions between Canada Reads and the national literary prizes, if the literary prizes attempt to create a taste for Canadian cultural products, and implicitly attempt to forge community through the celebration of national culture, Canada Reads makes these aims explicit, seeking to select a text 'that the nation should read together' (S. Martin, 'Just' R3) in what has been described as an 'attempt to create a huge trans-Canadian book club' (Fuller and Rehberg Sedo 6). In this way, the national cultural celebration of Canada Reads is the most overt in its attempt to create and sustain a national habitus. The state is indirectly involved in this attempt through the CBC's government funding. Perhaps unsurprisingly, in newspaper coverage of Canada Reads, dissenting voices have invoked taxpayers' money in their critique (see C. Woodcock C5).

If the national literary prizes constitute attempts to popularize the literature upon which they confer cultural value, Canada Reads is clearest in its efforts to do so. Where the Scotiabank Giller populates its gala dinner with Canadian entertainment celebrities, incorporating them into the prize ceremony, Canada Reads' format and its selection of celebrities as judges more obviously connects the project with the popular. As Fuller and Rehberg Sedo describe the format of Canada Reads, 'An aural medium borrows a TV-game-show-cum-reality-TV format, which has been franchised and reproduced around the world, in order to promote explicitly a nation-wide shared act of reading and learning about a "national" cultural product – Canadian Literature' (10). Canada Reads thereby exposes a tension between the desire to popularize Canadian literature through a format borrowed from American popular culture and the CBC's history of 'cultural authority as arbiter of literary quality, as a promoter of Canadian literature, and as a nation-building institution' (6); the lowbrow status of *Survivor* meets the CBC's usual association with highbrow literary culture. At the same time, the celebration of literature through the nomination of a group of texts collides with the explicit rejection of elimination of all but one title, as books are voted out of the competition. If shortlists, for Canada Reads and other prizes, offer a selection of possible winning texts as worthy of the reading public's attention, the *Survivor*-type format claws back the recognition of the shortlist through the process of the panel singling out all but the winning text to be discarded.

Canada Reads attempts to construct a national habitus and a vision of Canadian culture. Criticism often returns to the notion of the state's involvement in the project and a resentment of the attempt to impose a national habitus. Following the selection of *In the Skin of a Lion* as winner of the inaugural 2002 competition, the *Toronto Sun*'s Connie Woodcock implicitly critiqued the national habitus attempted by Canada Reads: 'As with many things the CBC does, its little book contest was the perfect way to make most Canadians feel nearly illiterate and utterly inadequate, if not downright excluded' (C5). Woodcock identifies the novel as an 'elitist' (C5) work (though admits to not having read it), one whose popularization through the tool of Canada Reads is at odds with the text itself. Others have suggested a class exclusion that intersects with Woodcock's critique of a faulty national habitus. Scott Feschuk, in the *National Post*, ridicules Canada Reads and its selection of Ondaatje's text by stating, 'Listen, I'd love to opine at great and profound length about the Canada Reads competition on CBC radio, but I'm taking my car in for a tune up this afternoon and I've got to at least skim the winner, Michael Ondaatje's *In the Skin of a Lion*. If I don't, it'll be all awkward just standing there as the boys down at the garage probe the novel's thematic complexities' ('My Canada' AL6). In this way, the explicit aim of Canada Reads clearly draws more fire than the celebration of national literature that arises from the Governor General's Awards and the Giller. The fact that Canada Reads was established to select a book for the nation to read together, a premise that has been considered 'somewhat totalitarian' (Gordon, 'Once' A18), exposes the problems of trying to create a national habitus.

Canada Reads both depends upon and perpetuates an 'increase in interest in bestselling literary fiction' (Fuller and Rehberg Sedo 7), although poetry has also featured in the competition. The attempt to increase sales alongside an interest in the category of the literary has prompted media criticism of a perceived disconnect between winning texts and popular taste and a rejection of the national habitus projected by Canada Reads. Fuller and Rehberg Sedo ask, 'Who is interpellated by the program as the "Canada" that "Reads"'? (16). Clearly, readers such as Woodcock and Feschuk refuse to be hailed as the Canadian Readers the project attempts to attract. In contrast, academic criticism of

Canada Reads has focused to varying degrees on the program's reductive methods of discussion and its limitation of the national literature. Although Canada Reads in its first year only offered Anglo-Canadian texts, subsequent years have included French titles translated into English (and Radio Canada has had a French-language version of the competition, *Le Combat des Livres,* since 2004). Yet Fuller and Rehberg Sedo note that Canada Reads' projection of the nation remains 'problematically, if predictably conservative (bilingual and uncritically multicultural)' (7). This conservatism extends to the choices of shortlisted titles, for, as they note, these selections 'favour a handful of highly commodified texts and writers' (7), texts that have already been bestsellers or rendered canonical through inclusion on university reading lists, and writers who already bask in the glow of international recognition. Further, several of the nominated texts have already been national or international prize-winners before they find their way onto the Canada Reads shortlist. Whereas the Governor General's Awards have sometimes been criticized for choosing obscure writers, Canada Reads, in contrast, has taken the opposite approach, 'introducing' to Canadian readers texts with which they should, on the whole, already be familiar. In this sense, Canada Reads projects a national culture that is already part of the mainstream national imagination.

Unlike the Governor General's Awards and the Giller Prize, Canada Reads is itself a substantial text through the broadcasting of the on-air elimination discussions. In this way, Canada Reads is not simply the sum of its nominees; rather, the celebrity judges feature prominently in the text of Canada Reads and are a highly visible (or, indeed, audible) component of the competition itself. Discussion of the nominated texts unfolds within the context of Canada Reads' popularization project. For Laura Moss, this context limits the possibilities of on-air analysis, particularly when politically engaged readings are considered. As she argues, Canada Reads 'celebrates the shortlisted novels rather than engaging critically with them'; the fact that 'the level of discussion rarely goes beyond character development, plot, or emotional response to the texts' means that 'the politics of the novels . . . is lost' ('Canada' 8). Of course, without being privy to Governor General's Award or Giller jury deliberations, we cannot know whether the national prize selection processes engage with the political implications of Canadian texts either. But given that Canada Reads is not just a prize, but also 'a mass reading event' (Fuller and Rehberg Sedo 9), the on-air discussions provide, according to Moss, an inadequate model of reading for the nation.

Because the discussions are presented as part of the Canada Reads text, these reading practices are foregrounded in ways that do not arise with more conventional literary prizes.

Canada Reads is not as 'high on prestige' as other prizes, lacking their cultural capital through its overt popularization, but in wielding a tremendous amount of national as well as economic capital, its 'economic and cultural spin-off is enormous' (Moss, 'Canada' 8). As Fuller and Rehberg Sedo note, 'sales figures alone' demonstrate that Canada Reads succeeds in 'creat[ing] new readers of CanLit' (7). Canada Reads is a limited host, inviting the nation's readers to be hospitable to authors and texts with whom they may largely be familiar already, but in economic and popular terms, it does host a successful celebration. Whereas Moss entreats the CBC to take more responsibility for the fact that the 'game' it plays cannot be divorced from its 'cultural, social, and economic consequences' ('Canada' 10), Canada Reads' paratextual elements demonstrate an expansion of the celebratory project beyond what the CBC chooses to broadcast. In particular, the website discussions can exceed the limitations of the on-air format, offering a 'potential for creative resistance' by 'opening up spaces where dominant ideologies and social formations can be contested' (Fuller and Rehberg Sedo 7, 24–5). The discursive aspects of the competition, the fact that the debates of the celebrity judges are aired in the first place, potentially invites further discussion and dissension.

Canada Reads is limited, and, indeed, its executive producer, Talin Vartanian, has proudly declared on a number of occasions that the program is 'not pointy-headed smart,' 'not intellectual' (quoted in Hanson C8), 'not a highbrow debate' (quoted in R. Caldwell R7), as though rigorous debate is itself a kind of limitation for the Canadian reader. However, there is no reason to suppose that the celebrity judges of Canada Reads interpellate listeners and readers to such an extent that they must replicate the judges' discussions or opinions, for Canada's Readers engage in 'a range of reading practices, not all of which are determined by the on-air discussions or by the medium of expression' (Fuller, 'Listening' 22). Neither is there reason to suppose that all readers who take note of the Canada Reads shortlist and winner listen to the debates at all. Although prizes, including Canada Reads, work to popularize the texts they offer to the reading public, those texts may not do the same work in the hands of a reader that they have in those of the prize jurors or panellists.

With its association with the CBC, and in its very name, Canada Reads trades in the currency of national capital, much more explicitly so than the Scotiabank Giller Prize. The contest's popularization, through its celebrity judges, media format, and the on-line discussions that accompany the selection process, suggests that Canada Reads confers much less symbolic value upon its winning texts and their authors than it might economic value. But some of the media critiques of Canada Reads and its positing and/or shaping of national habitus curiously omit any mention of the other national literary prizes that perform the same function, even if only implicitly. Every Canadian literary prize seeks to select texts for the nation to read together, and to interpellate Canadian readers as Canadians who presumably want to consume their own nation's culture.

Guest Authorities in the Host Culture

Part of Fuller and Rehberg Sedo's illustration of Canada Reads' limitations includes the fact that many of the shortlisted authors have international reputations. Implicit in this observation is that, despite the number of Canadian literary prizes, Canadian readers have their literature vetted for them by external authorities. As Lorraine York demonstrates in her study of the history of Canadian literary celebrity, the implications of this external vetting are hardly new in Canadian culture, and long predate Ondaatje's Booker Prize. Rather, as York points out, extranational prizes won by Martha Ostenso and Mazo de la Roche in 1925 and 1927, respectively, testify to Canadian culture seeking validation from outside the nation (61–2). But some forms of external validation are more 'valid' than others, particularly those that are strongly rooted in specific national literary cultures. Although the Booker and Pulitzer prizes are neither generated nor administered within the Canadian nation-state, they have had a considerable impact on both the celebration of Ondaatje, Shields, Mistry, and Martel specifically and the status of Canadian literature in Canada itself. These prizes wield an enormous authority *over* Canadian culture, creating a taste for it within Canada even though it is not their mandate to do so. The effectiveness of these extranational prizes at generating a taste for Canadian culture complicates the circulation of cultural power within the nation-state.

The (Man) Booker Prize

The Booker Prize was established in 1968 and first awarded in 1969. It was sponsored by Booker McConnell (later Booker plc), but established by Jonathan Cape editor Tom Maschler, who envisioned a British prize that would have as much influence on the reading public as the Prix Goncourt in France (Maschler 20). The Booker's centrality to current prize discourse is attested to by the fact that, seventeen years after its inception, 'Le Figaro referred to the Goncourt as the "French Booker"' (Caine 13), thereby inverting the status of model from the Goncourt to its British emulation. The Booker is open to writers in English from the Commonwealth and the Republic of Ireland.

Booker Prize administration shifted in 1971 to the National Book League (now Booktrust), and again in 2002 to the Booker Prize Foundation, when the Man Group took over the prize's sponsorship, and the award was renamed the Man Booker Prize. But the history of Booker itself presents some problems for its postcolonial cultural project. As Graham Huggan notes, Booker's nineteenth-century status as a company 'initially formed ... to provide distributional services on the sugar-estates of Demerara' demonstrates 'a history in contradiction with its current reputation as a postcolonial literary patron' (107, 106). As much as Booker 'has been eager to downplay its nineteenth-century colonial past' (107), the prize's British administration, in contrast to its wide-ranging catchment area, gives the impression of a colonial authority presiding over postcolonial texts. Indeed, the relationship between the prize's administration and its catchment area requires some scrutiny. Richard Todd views the Booker Prize as a celebration of 'fiction in Britain' (7), explaining that '"the novel in Britain" ... now includes fiction from Australia, New Zealand, Canada, South Africa, Nigeria, the Caribbean, and many other areas of the English-speaking world which is published in Britain' (8). But Todd's emphasis on the Booker's relationship with 'the novel in Britain,' regardless of the national identities of the writers who may produce the fiction published and consumed in Britain, is telling for what it does not acknowledge. Put simply, despite the fact that all countries of the Commonwealth as well as the Republic of Ireland fall within Booker Prize geographical eligibility, 'most of the judges, ... and crucially, the seat of judgment remain British' (Huggan 111).

The disjunction between catchment area and site of celebration places non-British writers in an awkward position where hospitality is concerned. The Booker situates Britain as the host, gathering literature from all other eligible countries under the umbrella of what Todd considers to be novels in Britain, or what might be termed 'British literary culture' (Showalter 11). Booker's celebration is limited in a number of ways. Firstly, like the Giller, the Booker demands a fee from publishers for promotion, with the result that the 'advertising budget required for eligibility [has] tended to freeze out first novels and works by fringe publishers, keeping the prize squarely in the commercial sector of the book trade' (Sutherland 11). Secondly, despite its catchment area, the Booker Prize does *not* play host to national literatures of the Commonwealth and Ireland, for considerable editing of these literatures occurs in the process of eligibility: nominations and winners are chosen from books 'published in the UK' (Caine 14). Only a selection of each eligible country's literature falls within the Booker's 'international' literary celebration. Characterizations of the Booker Prize as 'Britain's most prestigious literary award' (Finkle 92), particularly when they emerge from outside Britain, significantly demonstrate how the prize is defined by its site of administration. Thus, as Huggan contends, the structure of Booker Prize judgment and celebration 'reinforc[es] the earlier, now largely discredited view that farflung Commonwealth fictions should be referred for validation' (111) to the former imperial centre and its literary culture. If Britain plays the role of host to Booker-anointed texts, this hospitality, coupled with the role of judgment, underscores British cultural power.

Despite its British base, the Booker, by virtue of its catchment area, has an international presence and significance, and it means different things in different locations. English argues that the Booker's dominance on the international literary prize scene has been cultivated through the prize's visibility, particularly the discourse of 'scandal' that frequently surrounds the prize. He not only cites the specific scandals of anti-Booker speeches by John Berger in 1972 and J.G. Farrell in 1973, but also considers scathing British journalism surrounding the prize as contributing to this framework of scandal. As English argues, '... the charge of fundamental, irremediable illegitimacy ... keeps the prize a focus of attention, increasing its journalistic capital, *and* speeds its accumulation of symbolic capital, or cultural prestige' ('Winning' 115). According to this logic, even Booker 'failures,' such as Keri Hulme's *The Bone People* (1985) and James Kelman's *How Late It Was, How Late* (1994) with their relatively poor sales, contribute to this increase of journalistic and then symbolic capital. Similarly, Huggan argues that the Booker's ascendancy has been carefully constructed as the prize has 'acquired and cultivated a mythology of its own. Much of this has to do, of course, with careful media management. Newspaper coverage was solicited, and granted, from the beginning; but probably the crucial step was taken in 1981, when the Prize's final award-ceremony was first televised on BBC' (107). Televised spectacle of the prize announcement has no doubt increased public access to information about the award and the prize's accompanying 'razzmatazz' (Craddock 15), part of the process of popularization whereby the Booker event 'exemplifie[s] the intertwining of the restricted and extended subfields of the cultural market, as the ceremony for an elite literary award bec[o]me[s] material for London media and celebrity gossip mills' (Brouillette 70). But the Booker's status as a 'watchable event' primarily affects British readers and viewers, as does the British media's hyper-critical responses to the prize. Since other countries, like Canada, will not have had access to the Booker ceremony via television, the televised ceremony makes little or no difference to the prize's clout; neither will the British media responses travel as far as the Booker judgment. Similarly, the betting that precedes the prize announcement, while generating suspense and excitement in Britain, will not have the same impact elsewhere. The Booker is therefore a different kind of event for most of its catchment area.

What, then, is Canadian literature's relationship to the Booker Prize? In financial terms, the prize money offered by the Booker, currently at £50,000 following the change in sponsorship to the Man Group, is considerably more than that offered by either the Governor General's Awards or the Scotiabank Giller. After his Booker Prize win for *The English Patient* in 1992, Michael Ondaatje declared, 'The Booker is more important in Canada than the Governor General's Awards, which is a shame, really' ('Ondaatje' A1). The implication of deferring to British taste arises in refrains of 'Britain's most prestigious literary award.' Frank Davey views 'the [Canadian] media's excitement over Michael Ondaatje's Booker Prize' as attesting to an absence of '"national" power . . . in Canadian literature' (*Canadian* n.p.). Indeed, the importance of Booker recognition to Canadian literature is evidenced by such statements as Paul Gessell's, following the 2002 Man Booker shortlisting of Martel, Mistry, and Shields: 'Canada has scored an impressive showing' and 'Canada has actually won the Booker' ('Canada's Grand' C7). These declarations posit the nation-state as a whole speaking for both the 2002 nominees and the previous winning writers (Ondaatje and Atwood), and claims these victories *as* national victories, but which had to be conferred from without. As Canadian publisher Louise Dennys stated, Ondaatje's Booker 'made an enormous difference to the psyche of the Canadian book trade' (quoted in McGoogan, 'Patient' B7). Her emphasis on the *psyche*, rather than the *economics*, of Canadian publishing indicates the importance of the Booker win for perceptions of

Canadian literature, even in Canada itself. In other words, Canadian culture was not only legitimated through British judgment, but also became more easily popularized for Canadians.

Part of this validation of Canadian culture likely stems from the expanded geographical eligibility of the Booker Prize, and its conferral of cosmopolitan status. Canadian Booker-winners receive more attention than winners of Canadian prizes because, unlike the Governor General's Award, the Booker does not take into account a construction of the Canadian nation. This lack of Canada-centrism has two significant implications for perceptions of Canadian literature within Canada: first, Canada, having 'won' the Booker, will have 'beaten' all other eligible countries, thereby increasing the validation of Canadian literature; second, by not actively promoting a single national literature, the Booker might be considered by some to be more 'purely' artistic than the Governor General's Award, as the Giller claims to be. The fact that the Booker makes Canadian authors internationally celebrated suggests that they have somehow 'transcended' their Canadian context, even as such prizes won by Canadians lend some kind of cultural power to Canada itself. The Booker's own cosmopolitanism (with its wide geographical range alongside its rooting in the metropolitan centre of London) becomes transferred onto Canada and its literature because CanLit is seen to travel well. Its exportability, the willingness of outsiders to consume CanLit, increases its value at home.

The Commonwealth Writers' Prize

In 1987, two decades after the establishment of the Booker Prize, the Commonwealth Foundation instituted the Commonwealth Writers' Prize. Like the Governor General's Awards, the Commonwealth Writers' Prize is part of an ideological project, albeit one that functions above the level of the nation-state. The Commonwealth Foundation describes itself as 'an intergovernmental organization, resourced by and reporting to Commonwealth governments, and guided by Commonwealth values and priorities' (Commonwealth Foundation, 'About Us' n.p.). Despite its status as a supranational entity, the Commonwealth is here attributed a kind of unitary identity, as the above description implies a synchronicity of 'values and priorities' amongst Commonwealth countries. These priorities include a concern to 'promote arts and culture' as part of the Foundation's 'mandate . . . to strengthen civil society' through 'democracy and good governance, respect for human rights and gender equality, poverty eradication and sustainable, people-centred development' (n.p.). Despite a similar catchment area to the Booker, the Commonwealth Writers' Prize clearly diverges from its rival in terms of the role it is seen to play amongst the countries represented and its connection, even at one remove, to government.

The function of the prize itself, as described by the Foundation, is 'to encourage and reward the upsurge of new Commonwealth fiction and ensure that works of merit reach a wider audience outside their country of origin'; further, 'the objectives of the prize are to promote new voices, reward achievement, encourage wider readership and greater literacy, thereby increasing appreciation of different cultures and building understanding between cultures' (Commonwealth Foundation, 'Commonwealth Writers' Prize' n.p.). Although funded by the Foundation and administered by the Book Trust, the prize also receives support from the Australia-based Macquarie Group Foundation, 'the philanthropic arm of the Macquarie Group,' which itself is 'a diversified international provider of banking, financial, advisory and investment services' (n.p.).

Like the Man Booker Prize, then, the Commonwealth Writers' Prize receives support from a finance company; also like the Man Booker, the Commonwealth Writers' Prize's administration is based in London. However, the hosting of the prize judging and ceremony is not fixed: it rotates every two years between Commonwealth countries. The prize's international judging involves multiple steps, and the prize has been praised as 'a model of complex multi-national administration' (Tonkin 33) and described as 'the most complicated literary competition in the world' (quoted in Kee 8). The catchment area of the Commonwealth is divided into four regions: Canada and the Caribbean; Southeast Asia and the South Pacific; South Asia and Europe; and Africa. Each region holds two competitions: one for Best Book, and another for Best First Book, both of which win £1,000. Regional winners are then entered into the overall competitions for Best Book and Best First Book, with prize money of £10,000 each.

Because the first round of the competition is based at the regional level, texts are initially judged within their regional contexts (though each such 'region' contains within it a multitude of national and cultural differences). Unlike the Booker, however, the Commonwealth Writers' Prize does not make London the perpetual seat of judgment. Crucially, texts need not have been published in Britain at all. Diana Bailey, project officer of the prize, has argued that 'that encourages small publishers to take part. In some cases, particularly in Africa, regional winners have only had a few hundred copies of the book printed' (quoted in Tracey 9). In this sense, the Commonwealth Writers' Prize is more hospitable than the Booker, both in its inclusion of titles not published in Britain and in its widening of the judging process beyond British jurisdiction.

However, despite the fact that the Commonwealth Writers' Prize has been credited with 'probably encompass[ing] the broadest range of styles, voices and concerns of any literary prize outside the Nobel' ('Rohinton Mistry in Line'), the prize has nowhere near the same impact as the Booker. Given the similarity of their catchment areas (with the absence of Ireland for the Commonwealth prize constituting the only difference), the Commonwealth Writers' Prize is frequently, perhaps inevitably, compared to the Booker. Certainly, despite the Commonwealth Writers' Prize's mandate to increase the audience of Commonwealth literature across national boundaries, the prize does not have the Booker's sales impact (see Abley, 'Author's Intent' JI; Ong, 'Hear'). Many have observed that the Commonwealth Writers' Prize receives particularly scant attention in Britain, partly because 'British fiction has a very marginal place' in the Commonwealth competition (English, 'Everyone's' 3) and partly because, conversely, 'the literature [the prize] promotes receives little attention in Britain' (Trilling). For instance, Lawrence Hill's *The Book of Negroes* (2007), winner of the 2008 overall prize, has accrued a 'perpetually best-selling' status (Barber A1) in Canada, but has hardly registered in the U.K., despite positive reviews. Asked to recommend a 'Christmas read' by the *Guardian* in 2009, Naomi Klein notes that whereas 'in [her] city of Toronto, [she] see[s] its yellow cover everywhere – perched on laps in doctors' offices, propped up on tables in cafes, dissolving the minutes on street cars and in airport lounges,' Canada's 'rare national conversation' about its own racist history in the midst of transatlantic slave trade and beyond has not been matched in the U.K., where the novel 'could stand a visit to a few more doctors' offices' (quoted in Hooker 2). Although much of the attention on Hill's book in Canada has no doubt been due to its selection as Canada Reads' winning text in 2009, the Commonwealth Writers' Prize has been credited with 'boost[ing] the book's sales past the 100,000 mark in Canada'; however, sales were already healthy prior to the Commonwealth prize announcement (Wagner E6).

Although the Commonwealth Writers' Prize's status differs depending on location – Boyd Tonkin notes, for example, 'the gap between its relative obscurity at home and its glamour and glory abroad' (33) –

there is a possibility that Britain's relative lack of involvement in the prize, in contrast to the Booker, somehow makes the Commonwealth Writers' Prize less prestigious. Certainly, 'prestige' is far less frequently associated with the Commonwealth Writers' Prize than with the Booker in media coverage. This lack of prestige extends to marketing: for instance, the strapline on the cover of Faber and Faber's paperback edition of Mistry's *A Fine Balance*, his second overall Commonwealth Writers' Prize–winning novel, declares that Mistry has been 'three times shortlisted for the Booker Prize,' but no mention is made of the novel's actual win of the Commonwealth prize. A Booker shortlisting clearly trades more successfully than a Commonwealth victory in literary and economic capital. Indeed, the fact that the prize amounts for the Commonwealth Writers' Prize are much smaller than the Booker's suggests that monetary valuing and literary valuing converge in how readers are encouraged to consume winning texts.

The focus on the Commonwealth itself likely appears somewhat outdated, with the association incapable of lending the kind of legitimacy to literary texts that the explicitly privately funded Booker can. As an intergovernmental body, the Commonwealth Foundation perhaps has too large a task in the attempt to create a taste for supranational ties based largely on the former British Empire. Indeed, the prize's political implications have often arisen in its relatively short history. In 2001, Indian writer Amitav Ghosh demanded that his novel *The Glass Palace* be withdrawn from consideration on the grounds that the Commonwealth Writers' Prize is open only to works in English, thus 'exclud[ing] the many languages that sustain the cultural and literary lives of [Commonwealth] countries' ('Commonwealth'). In withdrawing *The Glass Palace* from competition, Ghosh stated that his novel 'is eligible for the Commonwealth Prize partly because it was written in English and partly because I happen to belong to a region that was once conquered and ruled by Imperial Britain. Of the many reasons why a book's merits may be recognized these seem to me the least persuasive' ('Commonwealth').

Although Ghosh's rejection of his nomination for the prize has been viewed as 'an act of political refusal [that] becomes a gateway to authorial self-definition and to career development and promotion' (Brouillette 72), Ghosh is not the only writer to resist the prize's political implications. Further controversy has focused on the fact that overall Commonwealth Writers' Prize winners are invited to meet the Queen. Despite the relatively egalitarian nature of the prize's judging process, and the emphasis on rotating the host position of the prize, it seems that the final prize is inextricably bound up in imperial history and a stark power imbalance: that of subjects, from all regions of the Commonwealth, bowing before their monarch. Some writers, such as the British Caryl Phillips and Mark Haddon in 2004, have refused to meet the Queen. The Australian Peter Carey sparked controversy when it appeared he had rejected this meeting after his prize in 1998, though he had only stated he could not make the date suggested to him, and did meet the Queen at a rearranged time. However, the republican Australian's delay in his meeting with the monarch prompted criticism from London's *Evening Standard*, which castigated Carey for not bestowing upon the Queen the same 'great affection' she has 'for Australia,' and described Carey as a 'chippy Antipodea[n]' ('Republican' 10). In 2005, British writer Andrea Levy compromised by meeting the Queen, but 'refus[ing] to curtsy' (Jaggi 4). Canadian media reports of Hill's meeting with the Queen have enjoyed emphasizing his adoption of a pedagogical role in informing her that his novel was based on an actual historical document in the U.K.'s National Archives, 'creating the ironic situation of the British monarch learning about British history from a Canadian' (Zajac A3). In contrast, Hill's fellow Canadian Austin Clarke described winning the Commonwealth Writers' Prize in 2004 as 'the most gratifying moment of [his] life,' and, as 'a self-confessed "old colonial,"' considered his meeting with the Queen to be part of the honour the prize bestowed upon him (Freeman R1).

In many ways, the Commonwealth Writers' Prize is contradictory: more wide-ranging than the Booker in terms of eligibility and judging, but still ultimately referring back to the imperial centre. And despite its range of competition, the Commonwealth Writers' Prize's function at times seems limited to 'pic[king] up the slack' of the Booker shortlist, 'with the result that it is seen unofficially as a sort of consolation prize for not getting the Booker' (Ong, 'Booker'). Although Commonwealth victories for Canadian literature have celebrated D.Y. Béchard (Best First Book, 2007), Bonnie Burnard (Best First Book, 1989), Clarke (Best Book, 2004), Hill (Best Book, 2008), Ann-Marie MacDonald (Best First Book, 1997), Mistry (Best Book, 1992 and 1996), Mordecai Richler (Best Book, 1990), Keri Sakamoto (Best First Book, 1999), and Tim Wynveen (Best First Book, 1998), along with countless other Canadian regional victories for Canada and the Caribbean, the Booker Prize remains the ultimate guest authority in Canada. The fact that fewer Canadian texts are eligible for the Booker, due to its regulation concerning British publication, does not detract from the Booker's greater influence on Canadian culture. With its perpetual British seat of judgment, the Booker also betrays its imperial implications, interpellating Canadian writers as both old and new colonials even as it celebrates them, and especially as it confers its legitimacy upon them.

The Pulitzer Prize

The Pulitzer Prize presents a different kind of influence on Canadian literature, primarily because Canadian writers are not meant to be eligible. Whereas the Booker Prize and Commonwealth Writers' Prize exclude writers of the United States, the Pulitzer Prize is a U.S.-specific award. Prior to the establishment of the Man Booker International Prize in 2005 (a kind of 'lifetime achievement' award, given every two years, for which writers of any nationality are eligible), debates about the possibility of the Man Booker Prize expanding to include American authors often involved the response by those rejecting expansion that 'the US Pulitzer Prize is restricted to Americans' ('Hands' 12). In fact, this analogy between the Booker and the Pulitzer is not apposite, for Britain has British-specific awards, such as the Costa (formerly Whitbread) Book Awards. With respect to Canadian literature, the Pulitzer is an extranational award that complicates notions of representative Canadian literature in relation to the work of Carol Shields. The fact that the Pulitzer is an American award presents particular effects on perceptions of Canadian literature within Canada, especially in the context of the cultural hostipitality between Canada and the United States.

First awarded in 1917, the Pulitzer Prizes were established by Joseph Pulitzer, a self-made millionaire who was born in Hungary and emigrated to the United States in 1864. A newspaper owner, Pulitzer helped found and fund Columbia University's college of journalism (the university is also the site of Pulitzer Prize administration). The Pulitzer Prizes are awarded in several categories of journalism, and in music, biography, fiction, non-fiction, history, drama, and poetry. As Corse notes, the Pulitzer is 'the most visible literary award in the United States . . . , in large part because most Pulitzers are for newspaper writing, which ensures extensive media coverage of the Pulitzer announcements' (105). Despite the publicity afforded the Pulitzer Prize for fiction, and some characterizations of the prize as 'America's most legitimate book prize' (English, 'Winning' 122) or 'the greatest of America's literary prizes' (Hohenberg 59), the Pulitzer's credibility has been frequently undermined by critics, contesting its symbolic value. Whereas there have been Booker 'failures,' their implications for Booker taste do not involve the wholesale undermining of judgment throughout Booker history that is evident in criticism of the Pulitzer Prize.

Part of the lack of credibility of the Pulitzer Prize for fiction throughout its history stems from the prize's original terms, which stipulated that the award would be given 'annually, for the American novel published during the year which shall best present the wholesome atmosphere of American life and the highest standard of American manners and manhood. $1000' (quoted in Stuckey 263). As W.J. Stuckey points out, 'wholesome' did not appear in Pulitzer's own version of these terms, but was changed from 'whole,' 'presumably' by Nicholas Murray Butler, then president of Columbia University (7). This change had considerable consequences for the prize's terms of judgement: 'wholesomeness' as a criterion 'ma[d]e it more difficult for [the] best jurors to exercise their own judgment, and would encourage the rest to play it safe and pick books that would not offend "respectable" taste' (7). The award's terms changed periodically: for the 1929 prize, for example, 'wholesome' was replaced with 'whole,' as Pulitzer had originally intended (9). But as J. Douglas Bates argues, Butler's 'Puritan tastes resulted in years of controversial awards . . . that do not accurately represent the best or even "distinguished examples" of American writing' (122).

John Hohenberg, administrator of the Pulitzer Prizes and secretary of the Pulitzer board from 1954 to 1976, writes, 'Perhaps the most persistent attack on the prizes came from those who regarded them as a collection of largely middle-class prejudices that sought to avoid the unpleasant aspects of American life in order to stress conformity to the ways of our elders' (158). With less interest in sounding diplomatic, William Gass condemns the Pulitzer for 'tak[ing] dead aim at mediocrity and almost never miss[ing]; the prize is simply not given to work of the first rank, rarely even to the second' (3). Common in critiques of the Pulitzer Prize is the fact that both Ernest Hemingway and William Faulkner were given awards well past their most deserving works: Hemingway won the Pulitzer in 1953 for *The Old Man and the Sea*, Faulkner in 1955 for *A Fable* and in 1963 for *The Reivers*. Bates views these belated awards as an attempt by the Pulitzer Board to 'pla[y] catch-up,' but contends, 'By then, irreversible damage had been done to the prizes. Not only had the best works of Hemingway and Faulkner been slighted, but several of the era's greatest writers were ignored altogether. Besides Thomas Wolfe, these included F. Scott Fitzgerald, Theodore Dreiser, and Flannery O'Connor' (123).

The Pulitzer Prize therefore offers an expression of Americanness, as the earlier years of the award's terms indicate, but which has been largely rejected in retrospect, indicating that Pulitzer winners for much of the prize's history have not tended to wield 'precanonical' weight. As Stuckey claims, 'With some notable exceptions, the Pulitzer prize novels ... constitute a body of fiction distinct from novels now commonly regarded as the major novels of the period, not entirely popular and therefore not to be dismissed, but not serious enough to deserve the kind of interests accorded even the work of minor novelists' (259). Stuckey's characterization of these novels as having made 'a significant if negative contribution to the history of American fiction' (262) is echoed by perceptions of the award 'as a badge of middlebrow mediocrity rather than a mark of excellence' (Cryer II 6).

Pulitzer-winning novelists in recent decades have included John Updike, Alice Walker, Toni Morrison, and Philip Roth, writers with more assured canonical status than most Pulitzer winners. But if, as a whole, the Pulitzer winners do not constitute a body of work that continues to be validated through canonical authority, what do we make of the excitement in Canada surrounding Shields's win for *The Stone Diaries*? Although the *Winnipeg Free Press* declared that this prize 'catapult[ed] [Shields] into [a] select club of great authors' (Prokosh and Rosborough C8) such as Hemingway and Faulkner, these authors did not win for their best works. However, excitement generated in Canada by *The Stone Diaries'* Pulitzer Prize speaks to an external validation of Canadian culture, and a conferral of cultural power. Although the novel's Booker nomination and Governor General's Award win helped increase sales, the Pulitzer is most credited with the novel's bestseller status. Not only did the novel's sales increase exponentially – 'what we usually sell in a month we sold in a week' (quoted in Archer, 'Unstoppable' 29) – but the translation of celebration into consumption within Canada was also attributed to the fact that the Pulitzer is an American prize: 'You just know the only reason a lot of these people are buying the book is because of the American media attention' (quoted 29). Declarations that 'it's the prizes and accolades from abroad that are, as usual, causing Canadians to sit up and take notice,' indicating 'the residue of a colonial mentality' (Kalman Naves I1), refer most immediately to the Booker Prize, but they apply equally to Shields's Pulitzer Prize and a neocolonial mentality in Canada with regards to the United States.

Given the omnipresence of American culture in Canada, and the imbalance of power between the two countries that positions Canada

as subordinate to the United States, the sanctioning of Canadian culture through Shields's Pulitzer Prize and its celebration in Canada is
both symptomatic and a redressing of this power imbalance. The
Pulitzer functions as a guest authority in relation to Canadian culture,
but because it is specifically an American prize, the Canadian celebration of this external sanctification operates within the larger hostipitality of Canada-U.S. relations. Further, the general direction of cultural
exchange shifted somewhat: rather than American culture infiltrating
Canadian culture, the success of *The Stone Diaries* and its celebration in
the United States reversed the direction of cultural flow, with a Canadian
text (as perceived by the Canadian reading public) becoming integral to
American culture. Shields thereby accrued the status of a guest-host
on either side of the Canada-U.S. border, a position that would become
pivotal to the negotiation of her identity and celebration.

The Canadian appropriation of Shields's Pulitzer Prize demonstrates the role that literary celebration plays not only in competitions
between writers but also in competitions between national cultures. If
the cultural prize is 'a form of play, of competitive struggle, a "cultural
game,"' this game fulfils some serious functions: it provides 'a means
of positing an "us" and an "our" around which to rally some group of
individuals, as well as a means of raising the status of that self-avowed
community within the symbolic economy of all such groups' (English,
Economy 50, 51). In Shields's case, despite the threat that the Pulitzer
potentially posed to the Canadian 'us' and our claim to Shields, this
threat was rejected in favour of the implications for 'raising the status' of CanLit via the extranational prize. The Pulitzer became a game
at which Canadians could win, both specifically, through Shields, and
more generally through Canada's reinforcement of its claims to the
author herself.

Literary prizes are not merely reflections and celebrations of the literatures they celebrate. Rather, they are entities unto themselves, carrying
as many cultural implications as the works they celebrate, and forming
a cultural frame in which the works are consumed and read. In the context of Canadian culture, the anointing of celebrated texts offers a form
of hospitality, particularly with respect to writers who were not born
in Canada and ethnic-minority writers, a legitimation of their contribution to Canadian culture and of the authors' joining the host position.
But as Philip and Brand remind us, not every ethnic-minority writer
in Canada is as easily absorbed into mainstream prizes' projections of
Canadianness. It is precisely for this reason that subsequent chapters of

this book examine the ways in which the identities of Ondaatje, Shields, Mistry, and Martel have been configured and reconfigured, and what factors have determined their positioning in relation to the nation.

The boundaries of Canadian culture are shaped, and reshaped, through competing national literary prizes and their projects of celebration and promotion. If the Governor General's Awards provide a cultural vision for the nation, celebrate that nation, and attempt to win the consent of the public, their success (or failure) has been measured by the (un)detectable influence on the public. In this sense, the 'success' of an award is related to publicity and commercial profit, categories in which the Scotiabank Giller Prize, without its overt attempts to construct the nation, has been more successful; yet the inevitable national capital that infuses the CBC-sponsored Canada Reads suggests that excising discussions of nationhood from literary celebration is not necessary for the conversion of national into economic capital.

In closing their borders in terms of national eligibility, all three Canadian prizes ultimately argue for the validity of celebrating national culture. But prizes located outside Canada's borders, especially the Man Booker and Pulitzer Prizes, have also been appropriated in the negotiation of Canadian hospitality, in different but more effective ways than the Canadian prizes. The lack of prestige associated with the Commonwealth Writers' Prize indicates that Canadians prefer their guest authorities to be firmly attached to national cultures that have long dominated our own, exemplifying A.J.M. Smith's definition of colonialism as 'a spirit that gratefully accepts a place of subordination, that looks elsewhere for its standards of excellence' (14). Significantly, the Scotiabank Giller has recently included non-Canadian writers on its jury – for instance, the American Russell Banks in 2009 and the American Claire Messud and British Ali Smith in 2010 – suggesting both a new manifestation of the Giller's desire to distance itself from national celebration and the colonial mentality that Smith described more than six decades ago. Outside Canada, hospitality shown to Canadian writers by the Booker and the Pulitzer and their British and American literary cultures reinforces the construction of Canadian culture, and has a significant impact on the consumption practices of the Canadian reading public. Regardless of the status of external prizes within their own literary cultures, they are translated when they come in contact with a Canadian culture that is grateful for the recognition. The significance of these prizes is refashioned to celebrate Canadian culture and to attempt to forge public consent to the idea of Canadian culture and the nation itself.

2 The 'Sri Lankan Poet, Domiciled in Canada': Michael Ondaatje's Territories, Citizenships, and Cosmopolitanisms

Although it has been nearly two decades since its publication, Michael Ondaatje is still best known as the author of the Booker Prize–winning *The English Patient*, or, alternatively, the author of the novel that was adapted into the multiple Academy Award–winning film of the same title. If this novel has become, by default, representative of Ondaatje's oeuvre, it is both misleading and telling at once, for Ondaatje's body of work has covered a vast amount of geographical ground, genres, and preoccupations, rarely returning to the same setting. And yet *The English Patient*'s eclectic grouping of main characters marooned together at the end of the Second World War in a Tuscan villa, comprised of two Canadians of different ethnic backgrounds, an Indian Sikh, and a Hungarian posing as an Englishman, does illustrate the range of Ondaatje's literary territory, which has also included nineteenth-century Queensland (*the man with seven toes*, 1969), the Wild West geography of Billy the Kid (*The Collected Works of Billy the Kid*, 1970), cornet player Buddy Bolden's New Orleans (*Coming through Slaughter*, 1976), early-twentieth-century Toronto (*In the Skin of a Lion*, 1987), Sri Lanka as a site of family history and civil war, and a poetic setting of cultural history (*Running in the Family*, 1982; *Anil's Ghost*, 2000; *Handwriting*, 1998), and most recently a combination of various U.S. locations and France throughout a twentieth century punctuated by warfare (*Divisadero*, 2007).

Non-Canadians are often surprised to learn that Ondaatje, who immigrated to Canada at the age of nineteen, is a Canadian writer. Granted, only *In the Skin of a Lion* expresses an overt Canadianness in its geographical and historical setting, but it seems Ondaatje's own Canadianness has been repeatedly contested, qualified, assessed, and affirmed in international and Canadian media coverage. The stakes of these identity negotiations have been particularly high since Ondaatje became the first Canadian Booker Prize winner in 1992. But it is clear that every Canadian prize Ondaatje has won (and he won plenty in the years before *The English Patient* captured the Booker jury's attention, and has also won plenty since) has, in some sense, participated in situating Ondaatje within Canadian literature and negotiated his cultural belonging.

Just as Ondaatje's citizenship has been debated and defended, so three of his prize-winning novels – *In the Skin of a Lion, The English Patient,* and *Anil's Ghost* – focus on issues of citizenship, habitation and nation, and cosmopolitanism. Despite the disparate geographies these novels inhabit, each illustrates how access to power is manifested in access to space, right to habitation, and claims to belonging by demonstrating hierarchies of entitlement, increments of power, and degrees of distance from or proximity to the powerful host position. By exploring the workings of power through national identity and race, Ondaatje exposes the political and cultural power of the host position and distinguishes between claims of legitimacy through the interests they uphold.

While these texts question the boundaries of the host position within communities, cities, and nations, Ondaatje's own Canadian awards have claimed Ondaatje for Canadian culture, naming him one of the hosts. Conversely, his international celebration has inserted him into larger contexts that might threaten to overwhelm his Canadianness. *In the Skin of a Lion*'s City of Toronto Book Award, Trillium Prize, Governor General's Award nomination, and Canada Reads selection, *The English Patient*'s Governor General's Award, Commonwealth Writers' Prize (Canada and the Caribbean), and Booker Prize, and *Anil's Ghost*'s Governor General's Award and Giller Prize demonstrate various municipal, provincial, national, and international contexts and locations of Ondaatje's identity. The Canadian prizes also generate a particular tension between celebration, critique, and containment, as the awards sponsored by various levels of Canadian governments uphold texts that are often critical of the structures that offer their support and sanctification, all the while asserting Ondaatje's cultural belonging in Canada. Ondaatje's international celebration offers another tension altogether: that between the bolstering of Ondaatje's host position in Canada – for he contributes to Canadian cultural legitimacy through international recognition – and the unsettling of this host position through this international recognition's *failure* to 'recognize' or underscore Ondaatje's Canadianness, privileging the Sri Lankan half of his hyphenate identity. The anxiety caused by this lack of overt Canadianization of Ondaatje in an international context – mirroring, perhaps, an absence of overt Canadianness in many if not most of Ondaatje's texts – prompts a negotiation of Ondaatje's belonging to Canadian culture *by* Canadian culture in an attempt to convert Ondaatje's success into the nation's.

Drawing Lines: Competing Claims to the Host Position

In the Skin of a Lion, The English Patient, and *Anil's Ghost* all probe the making of territory from spaces that are, to varying degrees, underpinned by claims to power, claims that distinguish host from guest, legitimate presence from illegitimate. In *In the Skin of a Lion's* narrative of Canada's early-twentieth-century development, the power of ownership coincides with the power of ethnic-majority belonging in the formation of a host position that excludes labourers and those considered foreign. The novel provides an early example of this exclusion when the Finnish loggers whom Patrick watches on their way to work warm their hands on the cows they walk past: 'They must do this gently, without any sense of attack or right. They do not own this land as the owner of the cows does' (7). Although Patrick is Canadian, his place within the nation is obscured by official history and geography: 'He was born into a region which did not appear on a map until 1910, though his family had worked there for twenty years and the land had been homesteaded since 1816' (10). Critics have commented that this passage highlights a geographic silencing (Heble, 'Putting' 239; Hutcheon 94; Davey, *Postnational* 142), but the basis of claim to belonging is also important: to privilege Patrick's family's labour as the premise of their claim underscores the fact that they do not quite share in the host position, and are not masters of their house.

In the novel's Toronto sections, the narratives of the Public Works projects overseen by Commissioner Harris demonstrate how the labourers who build these structures are denied access to them. A wealthy municipal official, Harris embodies the powerful Canadian host, the master of the Canadian house under construction, and represents the official version of the construction stories. Free indirect discourse periodically conflates the narrative voice with Harris's public perspective and its dominant capitalist view. During the construction of the water-filtration plant, Harris is described as 'providing jobs as he had in the building of the Boor Street Viaduct'; however, this official rationalization of his contribution to the city is complicated by the acknowledgment that 'Harris was building it for himself. For a stray dream he'd always had about water' (110). Despite the magnificence of Harris's dreams for the city, his 'monocular urban vision' (Spinks 138) occludes the labour required to bring them into being. Harris 'envision[s] . . . a lower trestle' for trains, and 'want[s] giant water mains' to transport water (29), but leaves the physical construction to others. Whereas the labourers are, in fact, building the city, they have no authority over the Public Works, a fact which throws the degree to which these structures are indeed public into question. Harris takes credit for the bridge and waterworks, for having 'bullied' (29) them through and for the final result. When Patrick seeks to blow up the waterworks near the end of the novel, he finds Harris there in his 'dressing-gown' (221), 'sip[ping] his brandy' (238), as though it is Harris's space in both public and private senses. Meanwhile, the state's repressive apparatus forcibly and coercively denies the labourers' claims at both the bridge and the waterworks: previously integral to its construction, the workers are excluded from commemoration on the viaduct by its status as a political territory, having to resist 'officials who guar[d] the bridge' (27) in order to honour their co-workers who have died; later, the militarized zone that the waterworks becomes prevents the meetings of the immigrant labourers from continuing to take place there.

The official use of these structures colludes with the exclusive construction of the nation, as Ondaatje's choices of naming suggest: the bridge workers travel in a flatbed truck where 'written in yellow over the green door is DOMINION BRIDGE COMPANY' (25); descriptions of the bridge include 'the Dominion Steel castings' (30); and years later, at the waterworks, Patrick 'lay[s] a charge with its electric detonator over the plaque that says Dominion Centrifugal Pump' (233). The reappearance of 'Dominion' in the context of labour and commerce reveals the intersection of power interests, as 'the interests of capital . . . are coterminous with the state's interest in monitoring the mobility of immigrant labourers' (Mason 68). The Dominion of Canada benefits from the construction of Public Works in Toronto, from the mistreatment of labourers, many of them foreign-born. By 1939, 'over 10,000 foreign-born workers [have] been deported out of the country' (*Skin* 209), no longer useful to the state. If these labourers have been 'invited' by Canada to assist in its construction, this invitation does not signal a genuine hospitality, as Mireille Rosello has pointed out (see Introduction). Temporary and limited, this hospitality, not hospitable at all, results in the expulsion of foreigners once they become surplus to economic requirements.

Whereas *In the Skin of a Lion* centres on the city in its examination of the nation, the spatial focus of *The English Patient* in its present-day narrative offers a much smaller scale through the villa. While nation-states vie for territory during the Second World War, the villa community, comprised of Hana, the patient, Caravaggio, and Kip, ostensibly offers an international space. The villa's space has been appropriated by different territories and powers, giving way to different hosts: '. . . it was . . . an old nunnery, taken over by the Germans, then converted into a hospital after the Allies had laid siege to it' (28). As a makeshift hospital, the villa presents a site of hospitality, but the fact that it is a war hospital suggests a redefinition through territoriality. That 'hospital' and 'hospitality' share the Latin *hospitalis* ('hospitable' in English) indicates that a hospital is a place of hospitality, and hospitality a form of healing. This reading of the hospital diverges from a Foucauldian perspective that underscores patients as impoverished 'object[s] of clinical observation' (*Clinic* 101) who repay debts to society by offering their sick bodies up to medical experimentation. Although Foucault's analysis here focuses on late-eighteenth-century French society, the notion of 'the modern hospital . . . [as] the place where patients can be studied in isolation from each other and where new types of medical knowledge and curing techniques can be applied' (Wallenstein 31) demonstrates that 'the spatial ordering of knowledge and power' persists in the present. Crucially, however, in *The English Patient* healing does not take place within the space of hospitals, but rather at sites initially devised for other purposes: 'nunneries and churches' (92) and 'bathing cabins along the beach that tourists had rented at the turn of the century' (95) are recruited as spaces of healing. Yet the hospitality of healing is also complicated by the fact that these are *war* hospitals, the term itself embodying a contradiction between the most extreme manifestation of hostility, on the one hand, and hospitality through healing, on the other: the primary function of a war hospital is to restore the bodies of soldiers whose purpose is to kill the enemy. In the novel's present-day action, the villa is no longer a hospital, the Allied forces having moved on. Hana refuses to leave the villa, though she acknowledges its rightful inhabitants: 'Till the nuns reclaimed it she would sit in this villa with the Englishman' (52). Hana insists that the war is over (41) and '[gets] out of her nurse's uniform' (52), despite being 'told it would be like desertion' to stay with the patient, and that 'the war is not over everywhere' (41). Regardless of her rejection of the war, however, Hana's presence in the villa depends upon her status as part of the Allied forces, which allows her to act as the host.

The ostensibly harmonious co-existence between the characters at the villa reveals, on closer inspection, a delineation of degrees of legitimacy in the villa and their diverging relations to power. Hana tries to emulate a civilian status through her rejection of the war and her insistence throughout the text that 'it does not matter who [the patient] is' (166) or what side he was on as she continues to take care of him. Her use of the villa and the surrounding land implies a desire for settled domesticity: 'In one soil-rich area beside the house she began to garden with a furious passion ... In spite of the burned earth, in spite of the lack of water. Someday there would be a bower of limes, rooms of green light' (43). These efforts not only contribute to Caravaggio's sense that 'it [is] Hana's house ... He notice[s] her civilization in the small wildflowers, the small gifts to herself' (58), but they also acknowledge the authority Hana now wields: among the villa inhabitants, she is in charge, and attempts to regulate the activities within and access to the villa while she herself takes liberties with the space. Some of her activity attempts to be reconstructive, such as her gardening, clearing filth out of rooms, or rebuilding a damaged staircase with books from the villa library (13). But she also occupies different spaces in the villa at various times, 'preferr[ing] to be nomadic in the house with her pallet or hammock, sleeping sometimes in the English patient's room, sometimes in the hall, depending on temperature or wind or light' (13).

If the house is Hana's, the patient is the most obvious recipient of hospitality through her medical care. Although she does ask him, 'Who are you?' (5), Hana's insistence that his identity does not matter exemplifies Derrida's characterization of absolute hospitality: 'Let us say yes *to who or what turns up,* before any anticipation, before any *identification,* whether or not it has to do with a foreigner, an immigrant, an invited guest, or an unexpected visitor' (*Of Hospitality* 77). Caravaggio, an honorary 'uncle' (48) to Hana, has come specifically in search of Hana – 'I came because of the girl. I knew her father' (252) – though his family guest status alters somewhat when he begins to suspect the patient is Almásy.

The last to arrive, Kip is most consistently positioned as a guest, separate from the others and subject to their hospitality: 'some kind of loose star on the edge of their system,' Kip 'enters the house only when invited in, just a tentative visitor' (75). Hana's regulation of the villa space often involves a desire to censure Kip, sometimes due to safety concerns – 'Kip's unnerving habit of leaping down the stairs one hand halfway down the rail had to be stopped. She imagined his feet travelling through air and hitting the returning Caravaggio in the stomach' (220) – but also because Kip's movement challenges her tacit authority: she is 'put out that the sapper ha[s] strolled casually into [the patient's room], seem[s] able to surround her, be everywhere' (88). Kip's sleeping in his military-issued tent emphasizes Hana's host position, for after their relationship begins, Hana 'feels displaced out of Canada during [the] nights' (128) she spends with him, suggesting she feels more at home in the villa, and that she has, in fact, made the villa a Canadian space, rather than a truly international one.

In *Anil's Ghost*, Ondaatje moves from the context of international warfare to one of civil war in Sri Lanka. Anil, a returned migrant, potentially wields the means of undermining her home country's government. Derrida's discussion of 'hostipitality' illustrates the link between hospitality and hostility, a blurring that characterizes Anil's presence in her nation of origin, as she is 'invited' by the Sri Lankan government, attempting 'to placate trading partners in the West' (16), as part of a human rights investigation that the government has no real wish to accommodate. This 'accommodation' is literal, in many ways: the Bandarawela caves, where she and Sarath discover the skeleton 'Sailor,' their piece of evidence of human rights abuses perpetrated by state forces, is 'a government-restricted archaeological site' (52). When Anil attempts to present her findings at the Armoury Auditorium, the space itself becomes hostile: '. . . they must have turned off the air-conditioning thirty minutes into the evidence, an old device to distract thought' (272). Sarath must perform hostility towards his colleague in order to keep her safe, partly by reminding her that the 'international authority' that employs her 'has been invited here by the government . . . That means you do work for the government here' (274). Ultimately, Anil suffers physical violence as a result of her investigation – 'I can't walk. I was . . . in there . . .' (282) – wholly undermining the hospitality implicit in an invitation.

Anil has also received a compromised hospitality on her visit to her Tamil ayah, Lalitha. During this visit, Lalitha's granddaughter takes on the role of host and regulator of Anil's belonging, or lack thereof, and language becomes paramount in this negotiation. Anil has had 'her last conversation in Sinhala' (145) with Lalitha, when Anil was studying in London. Because Anil no longer speaks Sinhala, there is 'a lost language between them' (22); meanwhile, Lalitha speaks to her grand-daughter in Tamil, and 'seem[s] embarrassed' (23) to be doing so. This disjunction of languages between Anil, Lalitha, and the granddaughter operates in a politicized context that designates 'a strange kind of alien language as the language of the other, but then of course, and this is the strange and troubling part, the other as the nearest neighbour' (Derrida, *Monolingualism* 37). An important division between the characters emerges: Anil cannot speak the language of her hosts, since she has never been able to speak Tamil, can 'understand only a few words' (23); the language she once had in common with Lalitha is the politically dominant Sinhala; but the fact that Anil has also lost this official language further removes her from Sri Lankan life, underscoring her outsider position. For her part, Lalitha does not speak Sinhala here, emphasizing in her conversation with her granddaughter that their family's preferred language is Tamil.

Lalitha's granddaughter speaks to Anil in English, thereby acting hospitably, but she also uses this common language between them to reinforce Anil's outsider position:

'You have parents here?'
'They're dead. And my brother left. Just my father's friends are still here.'
'Then you don't have any connection, do you?'
'Just Lalitha. In a way she was the one who brought me up.' Anil wanted to say more, to say that Lalitha was the only person who taught her real things as a child.
'She brought *all* of us up,' the granddaughter said. (23–4)

This last line might be read positively to suggest an inclusive unity between Tamil and Sinhalese, effected by Lalitha's care of children in both groups. But the granddaughter appears not to offer genuine hospitality, 'barely look[ing] at Anil after the first shaking of hands' (23). She emphasizes Anil's lack of filiative connection to Sri Lanka, and undermines rather than reinforces Anil's claim to an affiliative connection, possibly concerned about the political implications of Anil's presence in their home. The granddaughter recasts Anil's relationship with Lalitha as not unique, and based on a class imbalance: while it was Lalitha's job to care for Anil, she also cared for her own family. Although Lalitha's weeping at Anil's presence, and asking her grand-daughter to take a photograph of Lalitha and Anil together, suggests that Anil has not misread her relationship to Lalitha, Lalitha's grand-daughter's version overrides any other, through the benefit of language. This scene ultimately demonstrates the slipperiness of Anil's position: she is welcome, and yet not welcome; family, in an affiliative capacity, but not in a filiative one; Sri Lankan, but an unwelcome guest in her own country.

Citizenship, Nation, and Habitation

All three of these novels are concerned with the parameters of citizenship: *In the Skin of a Lion*, set exclusively in Canada, probes the distinction between Canadian citizenship and national belonging; *The English Patient* examines the significance of citizenship when nation and habitation diverge in the context of international warfare; and *Anil's Ghost*'s civil-war setting alters the stakes of wartime citizenship and explores the implications of Anil's attempts to reconcile her host and guest status in her home country.

In the Skin of a Lion takes place in the early twentieth century, when 'there effectively *was* no Canadian citizen, in statute or substance,' for, prior to the National Citzenship Act of 1947, 'native-born Canadians were first and foremost subjects of the British Empire, and their paramount allegiance was to the Queen or King. This colonial status, and the privileges and duties it bestowed, was indistinguishable from those enjoyed by individuals around the world' (Menzies, Chunn, and Adamoski 21). But despite the apparent anachronism of discussions of Canadian citizenship in relation to *In the Skin of a Lion*'s historical setting, ideas about citizenship, and legal and cultural belonging in Canada, are integral to this text. If citizenship 'links individuals to the state by reinforcing the idea that it is "their" state' (Cairns 4), not everyone in this novel is recognized by the state or encouraged to identify with it.

Ondaatje juxtaposes the narratives of Nicholas Temelcoff, a Macedonian-born immigrant, and Patrick, the Canadian-born protagonist, to illustrate the nuances of claiming and refusing to claim Canadianness. Both men work on Public Works projects in Toronto, offering personal narratives of labour in contrast to Harris's erasure of labour from his visions of the city, and both men are interpellated into different versions of Canadian identity. Nicholas and Patrick occupy opposite trajectories, as Nicholas seeks to learn English to facilitate his entry into the cultural host, whereas Patrick sheds his linguistic privilege by choosing to affiliate with Nicholas's community.

Nicholas has been perceived as a 'recluse' (47) while working on the bridge, where his 'daredevil' (34) labour is exceptional and somewhat glamorous. He does have a sense of cultural community, however, outside the context of this labour. The Ohrida Lake Restaurant simulates 'an old courtyard of the Balkans' (37), recoding the city space as Macedonian in this location. In some parts of Ontario, Nicholas is more of a guest than in others: he is part of the host culture at a sub-municipal level, within his own community; but elsewhere, he has been a guest, particularly during his stay in Sault Ste Marie, where he is determined to learn English, without which 'he would be lost' (46), a perception that indicates the pressures to conform to the dominant linguistic host. Nicholas's continued attempts to learn English while he works on the bridge, 'sing[ing] various songs' (42) as he labours, demonstrate once again the intersection of cultural and economic power.

By the time Patrick meets Nicholas, Nicholas has left the bridge labour behind and opened a bakery, with few reminders of his bridge experience until the re-emergence of a newspaper photograph that Patrick discovers at the public library: 'Patrick's gift, that arrow into the past, shows him the wealth in himself, how he has been sewn into history' (149), a history that, according to Harris's version, does not exist, despite the fact that the Commissioner has 'watche[d] [Nicholas] often' (42) while the bridge was under construction. At the same time, the text offers a more public characterization of Nicholas and his place in Toronto, in Canada: 'Nicholas Temelcoff never looks back. He will drive the bakery van over the bridge with his wife and children and only casually mention his work there. He is a citizen here, in the present, successful with his own bakery. His bread and rolls and cakes and pastries reach the multitudes in the city' (149). Julie Beddoes claims that Nicholas, an 'independent and entrepreneurial' character, 'represent[s] conventional immigrant success stories,' rendering the text's 'championing of the marginalized and the ignored . . . equivocal' (210). But the text undermines this official description by underscoring its correspondence to dominant ideas of immigrant success that require assimilation, abandonment of personal history, and contribution to the economy in its assessment of the immigrant's invitation to join the Canadian host.

In this passage, marking the novel's only use of the word 'citizen,' the narrative voice is consonant with Nicholas as he has been hailed as 'successful immigrant': 'He is a citizen here' expresses his official legitimacy within Canada, writing over any prior status of 'alien.' The novel portrays many kinds of citizen (of towns, cities, and countries), without ever using that term; thus, the official legitimation of Nicholas's position as citizen demonstrates how Nicholas has been declared 'one of us' (Cairns 4) in Canada, and therefore part of the legal host, regardless of whether he is viewed as such by the ethnic majority. Patrick's showing Nicholas the photograph of himself, 'that arrow into the past,' reveals there are other things for Nicholas to claim than nation-state citizenship, for 'now he will begin to tell stories' (*Skin* 149). Rather than suggesting that 'access to storytelling' depends upon 'his participation in the logics of capital – that is, [through] ownership' (Dobson 109), this invitation to storytelling implies that the official narrative of Nicholas as 'citizen' is inadequate, that he is *not* simply an immigrant 'success' story. His stories of the bridge will puncture the official version, just as the text's earlier depiction of Nicholas's labour, of the catalogue of scars which that labour has left on his body (37), has already thrown Harris's dreamlike vision into question.

Whereas Nicholas has to acquire the status of citizen in Canada, Patrick does not, but his association with the Eastern European immigrant community seemingly overturns his privilege: 'The southeastern section of the city where he now lived was made up mostly of immigrants and he walked everywhere not hearing any language he knew, deliriously anonymous. The people on the street, the Macedonians and Bulgarians, were his only mirror. He worked in the tunnels with them' (112). Patrick is both their mirror and 'their alien' (113), suggesting a 'distanced sense of community' (Hutcheon 96). In 'belong[ing] to the central racial and gender group that controls Canadian life' (Hutcheon 94) and having 'easy access to spoken English' (Davey, *Post-national* 142), Patrick corresponds to the dominant cultural host position. But at the tannery, he keeps 'his true name and voice from the bosses at the leather yard, never [speaks] to them or answer[s] them' (*Skin* 136), appropriating the status of immigrant and guest not just to Toronto, where he is 'an immigrant to the city' (53) upon his arrival from Bellrock, but to Canada as well. His ability to 'pass' as an immigrant stems from both his rejection of linguistic advantage and his appearance, with his 'Finnish suit' and 'Macedonian-style moustache' (113).

When Patrick is a guest at Kosta's house, 'Alice speaks with her friends, slipping out of English and into Finnish and Macedonian. She knows she can be unconcerned with [Patrick's] lack of language, that he is happy' (*Skin* 132–3). Simone Vauthier argues, 'The lesson is clear: on the margins of Canadian society, English, the majority language, becomes a minority language; and the whole idea of socio-cultural centrality is undermined' (72). But Patrick is 'happy' in his lack of language because he can afford to be; he has no sense that without language he will be 'lost,' and his guest status is limited to the parts of Toronto where he prefers to live and socialize. When he first meets Kosta and his neighbours on the street, making friends at the market stalls, he is embraced as a 'guest of honour' (114). Patrick is 'immensely comfortable' at Kosta's, enjoying 'the irony of reversals' rather than suffering a sense of exclusion (133).

For all his 'passing' as an immigrant, Patrick's co-workers (if not his employers) recognize him as belonging to the dominant definition of Canadian background and culture. The tannery workers 'kno[w] little more than each other's false names or true countries. *Hey Italy! . . . Hey Canada!* A wave to Patrick' (135). Ajay Heble argues that 'Patrick does manage, through a process of interpellation, to become a signifier for the nation as a whole'; further, 'if Patrick *is* Canada, at least for this brief moment, then Ondaatje's point . . . is that the immigrants whom he describes are *also* Canada' ('Putting' 242). But if the scene suggests that 'even a Canadian can be an ex-centric here' (Hutcheon 98), there are clear distinctions between Patrick's position and that of the immigrants of non-British background. Patrick may be ex-centric through class, but he is much closer to the centre than his immigrant co-workers who identify him as 'Canadian.' If Patrick is interpellated into his Canadian identity, this complicated hailing involves not his identification as Canadian by the dominant structures of Canadian life, but rather by individuals at the margins who have been subject to dominant ideology and excluded from its definitions of Canadianness. Patrick has been identified as 'the unmarked Canadian citizen' (Lundgren 20) by those who do not presume to claim Canadianness for themselves, and would not recognize themselves if *they* were to be hailed as 'Canadian.'

The issue of who 'gets' to be Canadian functions on several levels, as *In the Skin of a Lion* emphasizes the fracture between citizenship and national belonging, between legal entitlement to live in Canada and acceptance by the cultural host. Although the novel includes multiple ethnicities within its representation of Canadianness, this representation diverges from the public definition of those in power. The Finnish and Macedonian conversations at Kosta's house are forbidden outdoors: 'Police Chief Draper . . . has imposed laws against public meetings by foreigners. So if they speak this way in public, in *any* language other than English, they will be jailed. A rule of the city' (*Skin* 133). Patrick does not have to worry about such censure. Although he is a labourer whose usefulness to the dominant class may vary, he is still protected by his status in Canada and, indeed, by his ignorance of any language other than English. A born citizen, with linguistic and cultural connections to the dominant view of Canadianness, he will always be acceptable, as a Canadian, to those who officially define Canadian public life.

Within the international setting of *The English Patient*, the examination of Canadianness figures less prominently than in *In the Skin of a Lion*. Although Hana's upbringing in the earlier novel unfolds within the Eastern European immigrant community, her Canadianness is unqualified here, with no invocation of the ethnic and linguistic complexity of her childhood. More concerned with what happens to nationality and citizenship for individuals displaced outside the nation-state, *The English Patient* highlights the disjunction between location and national identity, invoking Eve Kosofsky Sedgwick's idea of the 'habitation / nation system' that negotiates people's immediate geography in relation to their identity. D. Mark Simpson argues that the habitation / nation system approximates 'the conceptual dynamics on offer' at the villa: 'Physical facts of habitation, precarious according not only to the desires of the villa's inhabitants but also to the urgencies of architectural design and decay, incessantly fall into greater abstractions, hybrid and twisting, signalled by the performance of nationality and citizenship in the narrative' (218, 219). Simpson's allusion to performed nationality and citizenship refers primarily to the English patient, who claims to have forgotten his identity. But despite Hana's insistence that it does not matter who the patient is, it *does* matter who Hana, Caravaggio, and Kip are: while they inhabit the villa, their nations – Canada and India – justify their presence.

Because Canadian citizenship did not exist as such until 1947, officially, Hana and Caravaggio are British subjects. But their involvement in the war effort constitutes an expression of citizenship, for 'one of the central obligations of citizenship ... has been to fight for one's country against the citizens of other countries' (Carter 7). The novel's Second World War setting is particularly significant to Canada's developing sense of nationhood and citizenship. In the First World War, Canada's status as 'a self-governing colony with virtually no control over its foreign affairs' meant that Canada's involvement was tied to Britain's; but by the time of the Second World War, Canada wielded its own authority in matters of foreign affairs and made its own decision to declare war on Germany (Bercuson 5). Ongoing ties to Britain were nevertheless relevant to Canada's involvement in the war, the so-called mother country of Anglo-Canadians providing a 'sentimental link' that drove the nation to participate in the Second World War 'for much the same reason as in 1914' (Morton 104).

Kip's position is more complicated or, rather, more overtly colonial, contrasting Canada's settler-invader colony with India's colony of occupation. Like Hana and Caravaggio, Kip is a British subject, but India's relationship to the Second World War differed from Canada's insofar as 'war was declared on India's behalf by the Viceroy' (J. Brown 290) without consultation with Indian politicians. There was some support for the war in India, comprising both a reluctance among some Congressmen to appear to support fascism and the fact that the Indian Army was composed of volunteer soldiers (Jeffrey 94, 13), but given that Britain decided India was at war, Kip's expression of citizenship through the military is also a subjecthood, more explicitly so than Hana's and Caravaggio's.

Ultimately, as members of Allied nations, Hana, Caravaggio, and Kip are legitimately present at the villa (Hana's desertion notwithstanding) according to dominant politics. Their militarily endorsed presence marks the villa as territory through international conflict and colonial legacy, throwing into relief categories of citizenship and belonging. Apart from a few scenes between Kip and Italian civilians when he is stationed elsewhere, the novel represents no significant interactions between the villa inhabitants and Italians. The villa's relationship to its geography is compromised, the space made international by the people who inhabit it.

Citizenship duties have also been compromised. As a nurse, Hana initially fulfils a female citizen's role during the war, offering 'essential support systems on which men and warriors rely' (Carter 221), but she eventually transgresses her stipulated functions as a female citizen. Not only does Hana abandon her duty to her nation when she remains at the villa with the patient, but she also rejects the role of female citizen when she has an abortion. If 'women's ultimate political duty is motherhood, to give birth for the state, ... creating new life, new citizens' (Pateman 24), Hana refuses this contribution to her country's welfare: 'I lost the child. I mean, I had to lose it. The father was already dead. There was a war' (82). Caravaggio has fulfilled a citizenship duty by joining the Canadian war effort, but he too undermines that duty when he objects to the colonial implications of Canada's and India's involvement. Declaring, 'The trouble with all of us is we are where we shouldn't be' (122), he protests the official legitimacy of their presence in Italy. In particular, Caravaggio identifies Kip's displacement as the most contentious. Although Caravaggio questions Allied presence 'in Africa, in Italy,' he emphasizes India's position, asking, 'What is [Kip] doing fighting English wars?' (122).

Caravaggio 'want[s] to take [Hana] home' (121), where she ostensibly belongs. Desiring her safety, Caravaggio advocates a conventional trajectory for her relationship with Kip, 'want[ing] these two married' (268): 'The correct move is to get on a train, go and have babies together' (122). This proposed resolution prescribes a 'correct' role for Hana as a female citizen, but Caravaggio's suggestion of interracial marriage and mixed-race children is also transgressive, and perhaps easiest to imagine within the international space of the villa, protected for most of the novel from the actual implications of international conflict.

For the protagonist of *Anil's Ghost*, 'going home' to a country at war demands a renegotiation of her relationship to her nation after decades of habitation in the West. The beginning of Anil's narrative of return to Sri Lanka establishes her belonging and *un*belonging:

'How long has it been? You were born here, no?'
    'Fifteen years.'
    'You still speak Sinhala?'
    'A little. Look, do you mind if I don't talk in the car on the way into Colombo – I'm jet-lagged. I just want to look. Maybe drink some toddy before it gets too late . . .'
    'Toddy!' He laughed . . . 'First thing after fifteen years. The return of the prodigal.'
    'I'm not a prodigal.' (9, 10)

This exchange, the first between Anil and a Sri Lankan in the text, simultaneously reinforces and undermines her claims to belonging. Significantly, her fifteen-year absence has encompassed the civil war, which began in 1983. Because her return home depends upon her human rights investigation, the timing of her absence is crucial to how her views of the conflict have been shaped by her Western habitation. Thus, the question, 'You were born here, no?' both supports her claim to Sri Lanka and emphasizes her migration. The fact that Anil only speaks 'a little' Sinhala accentuates the tension inherent in her position as the returned migrant, as the accusation (as Anil interprets it) of 'the prodigal' implies.

This reference to the returning prodigal explicitly aligns Anil's position with Ondaatje's in *Running in the Family:* Ondaatje, travelling in Sri
Lanka, declares himself to be both 'the foreigner' and 'the prodigal who
hates the foreigner' (65). Both Ondaatje and Anil return to Sri Lanka
after an extended absence that has compromised their knowledge of
and affiliation with the country. Significantly, however, Ondaatje identifies *himself* as the prodigal, whereas Anil's response to being so named
is an immediate denial. As a returned migrant, Anil ostensibly cannot
judge her own belonging adequately, as other Sri Lankan characters
seem to indicate, for 'Anil's citizenship is examined in ways in which it
is coveted and relinquished, conferred and revoked' (Sanghera 83–4).
Whereas Ondaatje identifies his own prodigality in a pre–civil war context, Anil's identification as such takes place after her absence has coin-
cided with violence in her nation of origin, making claims to know and
to belong in the country more politically charged.

Citizenship itself, in the context of civil war, must necessarily alter,
as citizens are not unified through antagonism towards another nation-
state, but divided in their antagonism towards each other. *Anil's
Ghost* frequently refers to Sri Lanka's citizens, emphasizing the relation between individuals, as 'legal personalit[ies]' with 'rights and
obligations' (B.S. Turner, 'Liberal' 23), and their state in the midst of
civil war. A stark contradiction emerges between theories of citizenship and its·practice in the Sri Lankan context, for 'citizenship presupposes a functioning state, the rule of law and basic human rights
guarantees' (Castles and Davidson xii). Ondaatje makes reference to
citizens early in the novel as he describes daily life continuing: 'The
streets were still streets, the citizens remained citizens. They shopped,
changed jobs, laughed. Yet the darkest Greek tragedies were innocent compared with what was happening here' (11). This passage
aligns citizenship with an identifiable normalcy, comprising both
public engagement and private response, suggesting that some things
have remained intact; but human rights cannot be guaranteed for Sri
Lanka's citizens, thereby throwing their citizenship into question in
the first place.

Ondaatje also uses the language of citizenship to realign Anil's claim
to belonging. She has distanced herself from her past Sri Lankan life,
viewing her home country 'with a long-distance gaze' (11), which leads
her colleague Sarath to compare her to Western journalists (27, 44). But
her work with Sarath and Ananda at the *walawwa* leads to a renewed
affiliation through community, as she is 'citizened by their friendship'

(200). Later, when Sarath listens to Anil giving her report at the auditorium, he reassesses her legitimacy:

> It was a lawyer's argument and, more important, a citizen's evidence; she was no longer just a foreign authority. Then he heard her say, 'I think you murdered hundreds of us.' *Hundreds of us.* Sarath thought to himself. Fifteen years away and she is finally *us.* (271–2)

By naming Anil a citizen through witnessing her performative belonging, Sarath bestows upon her the status of host, undoing her prior labelling as a prodigal. It is a temporary belonging, however, as the state's retribution will force her to flee the country: the moment of her renewed belonging also makes it impossible for her to live out both her rights and her duties as a citizen.

Cosmopolitanisms

The complexities of belonging compromised by displacement that underpin both *The English Patient* and *Anil's Ghost* lead these novels to consider competing forms of cosmopolitanism. In *The English Patient*, the patient himself embodies a romanticized form of cosmopolitanism, which Ondaatje juxtaposes to the critical cosmopolitan perspective that Kip articulates at the end of the novel, while in *Anil's Ghost*, Anil herself encompasses both critical and uncritical forms of cosmopolitanism, the novel ultimately advocating a cosmopolitanism from below.

In *The English Patient*, the villa echoes the patient's memories of his desert community. The novel most explicitly engages with cosmopolitanism through the figure of the patient himself, who exhibits 'a receptiveness to art and literature from other places, and a wider interest in lives elsewhere' (Appiah 4). Despite the development of ideas about cosmopolitanism since the Cynics and Stoics through to the modern age's permutations from the Renaissance to the Enlightenment to the nineteenth and twentieth centuries, the patient's views most resemble Enlightenment thinking. He celebrates his community of explorers, seemingly untainted by nation-state or economic interest: 'We were a small clutch of a nation between the wars, mapping and re-exploring' (136), who 'wished to remove the clothing of our countries' (139). Like the *philosophes* of the eighteenth century, the patient and his fellow explorers claim 'membership of a privileged elite that happens to cross national boundaries' (Carter 8). Despite the patient's celebration of transcending the limitations of nation-state boundaries, this community has other categories of limitation. Although Bruce Robbins claims that 'the pleasures of dislocation and mobility that Count Almasy [sic] enjoys are less tied to his rank than to his expertise' ('Village' 24), rank is a prerequisite, as the explorers' 'aristrocratic, cosmopolitan world' grants them 'the ability and privilege to move itself beyond nationality and identification' (Novak 218). The group is also exclusively male prior to the arrival of Katharine; even she is only present as Geoffrey Clifton's wife. If wealthy, powerful men comprise this community, the patient nevertheless insists that it is untainted by power interests: 'Outside of this there was just trade and power, money and war. Financial and military despots shaped the world' (250).

Considering himself a good desert guest, the patient claims that he seeks 'to erase [his] name and the place [he] [has] come from,' in contrast to those who 'wanted their mark there,' naming geographical features after themselves in acts of colonial reinscription (139). He emphasizes the explorers' 'cosmopolitan fellowship and sensibility' (Lemos Horta 67), but does not foreground their 'hosts,' the desert inhabitants. The explorations between 1932 and 1934 consist of 'not seeing each other for months. Just the Bedouin and us, crisscrossing the Forty Days Road. There were rivers of desert tribes, the most beautiful humans I've met in my life. We were German, English, Hungarian, African – all of us insignificant to them' (138). As Shannon Smyrl argues, the patient 'blur[s] the "rivers of desert tribes" with the landscape itself,' thereby removing the tribes 'from the spaces of political and cultural power' (11) and naturalizing his own presence. The hospitality of the 'desert tribes' is passive, perhaps simply a toleration; or the land itself is figured as the host, suggesting a problematic parity between the legitimacy of Bedouins and Europeans there.

The patient declares, 'The desert could not be claimed or owned – it was a piece of cloth carried by winds, never held down by stones, and given a hundred shifting names long before Canterbury existed, long before battles and treaties quilted Europe and the East. Its caravans, those strange rambling feasts and cultures, left nothing behind, not an ember' (138–9). Conceptualizing the desert as 'a place in which time and space are liberated from their inherited historical meanings' (Spinks 193), somehow exempt from territorial claims, the patient elides the implications of the explorers' cartography, complicit with 'defin[ing] boundaries and lines of ownership' (Emery 211). Although the patient romanticizes the desert for its apparent hospitality, its lack of *overt* territorial boundaries accommodates the explorers, allowing them to navigate and map the terrain with apparent ease and legitimacy. The development of a theatre of war ultimately contradicts the patient's claims about the desert resisting ownership or appropriation, revealing the patient's version of cosmopolitanism to be either naïve or wilfully blind. Once 'all of Europe [are] fighting their wars in North Africa' (19), the ideals of desert neutrality and pure community have clearly shattered.

When the patient announces that he and Kip 'are both international bastards – born in one place and choosing to live elsewhere. Fighting to get back to or get away from our homelands all our lives. Though Kip doesn't recognize that yet' (176–7), he suggests this international bastardy as a kind of luxury, a cosmopolitan, voluntary rootlessness, ignoring the colonial and military bases of Kip's displacement. As Marlene Goldman notes, '. . . this statement is not of [Kip's] choosing. Although both men experience invisibility, the text clarifies that invisibility means different things, depending on one's position' ('War' 187–8). Initially, Kip is an ambivalent figure in relation to the West, 'a man from Asia who has in these last years of war assumed English fathers, following their codes like a dutiful son' (217), and, like *In the Skin of a Lion's* Nicholas Temelcoff, sings Western songs while he works. Kip appears to have crossed a threshold, having 'stepped into a family, after a year abroad, as if he were the prodigal returned, offered a chair at the table, embraced with conversations' (189). This language not only undoes the patient's invocation of 'bastard' through an affiliative suggestion of family, but it also demonstrates a shift from guest to host, a recognition that he belongs as 'one of them.'

But this status does not extend beyond his personal relationships with Lord Suffolk, Miss Morden, and Mr Harts, as his experiences with other members of the English cultural host indicate: '. . . he was ignored in various barracks, and he came to prefer that. The self-sufficiency and privacy Hana saw in him later were caused not just by his being a sapper in the Italian campaign. It was as much a result of being the anonymous member of another race, a part of the invisible world' (196). While enjoying private relationships with English individuals whom he trusts, Kip is nevertheless aware of the colonial context in which he operates: he 'remain[s] the foreigner, the Sikh' (105). The villa inhabitants present substitutes for the dead Suffolk, Morden, and Harts: Kip finds himself in the company of two men and one woman from different racial and national backgrounds than he, and racial difference seems irrelevant. In the villa, where each of them is a foreigner, everyone appears to be as legitimate as each other. But Kip's 'guest' position in relation to the villa accrues racial implications after the atomic bombings of Hiroshima and Nagasaki and Kip's rejection of the West.

Kip enters the villa without invitation after hearing about the atomic bombs dropped on Hiroshima and Nagasaki. Having learned from Lord Suffolk that 'people think a bomb is a mechanical object, a mechanical enemy. But you have to consider that somebody made it' (192), Kip targets the English patient as a representative individual on the other side of the bomb. When Caravaggio tries to tell Kip that the 'English' patient 'isn't an Englishman' (285), Kip steps away from specific nationalities to condemn Western power and its white supremacist implications: 'American, French, I don't care. When you start bombing the brown races of the world, you're an Englishman. You had King Leopold of Belgium and now you have fucking Harry Truman of the USA. You all learned it from the English' (286). Caravaggio explicitly agrees with the sapper: 'He knows the young soldier is right. They would never have dropped such a bomb on a white nation' (286). Tellingly, the patient asks of Kip's outburst, 'What was going on outside?' (283), suggesting not simply the space outside the villa, but outside the West, far from the concerns of the villa inhabitants. Only Kip has acknowledged the war beyond their immediate geography, stating prior to the bombings, 'When the war with Japan is over, everyone will finally go home' (268), a declaration that implicitly acknowledges the territorial threat to Kip's own country through the war with Japan. Kip does not kill the patient, but leaves 'the three of them to their world, is no longer their sentinel' (286). His departure from the villa community has a practical impact upon them, for without Kip, they are at greater risk from the latent violence of the land mines. Necessary and useful to the host without being the host himself, Kip symbolizes the role of the Indian Army in the war: protecting British interests in South Asia against Japanese invasion, acting as sentinel for the empire.

Simpson argues that Kip's response to the bombings suggests 'an Asian solidarity set against Western aggression' which 'threatens to fix that continent monolithically in place' (232). But when reminded by his brother that 'Asia is still not a free continent,' Kip replies, 'Japan is a part of Asia, . . . and the Sikhs have been brutalized by the Japanese in Malay' (217). While Kip's solidarity overrides previously acknowledged inter-Asian power dynamics, the novel presents a *realignment* of solidarity when 'the intrusion of racism requires an abrupt change of perspective' (Irvine 143). Kip's rejection of the villa community, his role in the war, and his European location lead him to return to India, where he is at home, as a host: 'At this table all of their hands are brown' (301). By this point in history, India has become independent, and Kirpal lives out his private life within a new political context, working as a doctor for the benefit of Indian citizens. Although Hana laments that '*the personal will forever be at war with the public*' (292), to ignore the political implications of the atomic bombings would have been a luxury for the ex-centric Kirpal, and the seemingly apolitical and cosmopolitan space of the villa was ultimately untenable.

If '*The English Patient* does not tell the story of a war won' (Pesch 120), neither does it include reasons for involvement in the Second World War. The narrative of *In the Skin of a Lion* ends in 1938; *The English Patient* begins its present-day narration in 1945: the dates bracket the Second World War almost perfectly, leaving any political decisions regarding the war by Patrick, Caravaggio, and Hana unarticulated. Involvement in the war might indicate a cosmopolitanism on the part of these characters, if motivated by lending support to nations invaded by aggressors. But Ondaatje's desire for *The English Patient* to become 'an anti-war book' (Dorminey C4) suggests that gestures towards global citizenship in this novel are not to be found in the war effort, echoing the rejection of war that has been part of conceptions of world citizenship from the Early Modern period until the present (Carter 17). Similarly, Hana's refusal to sustain her part in the war and her desire to continue caring for the patient suggest a global citizenship. Her medical care transcends national and political ties, operating in the interests of 'an overriding humanity' (Carter 36), a notion of world citizenship that harks back to the eighteenth century with which the patient's perspectives have strong affinities. Caravaggio's adoption of Hana's private view of the patient – 'He's fine. We can let him be' (265) – also implies a rejection of national distinctions in favour of a more humanist approach.

But Kip's position and his reaction to the atomic bombings diverge from the cosmopolitan arguments suggested by the other characters, as his abrupt departure indicates. The patient's, and even Hana's and Caravaggio's, versions of cosmopolitanism are ultimately too implicated in an idea of 'overriding humanity' that ignores imbalances of power between its members. If 'cosmopolitanism is about intelligence and curiosity as well as engagement' (Appiah 168), the patient's intelligence and curiosity have not been accompanied with any political engagement, marking a clear distinction between the two 'international bastards.'

Through Kip, Ondaatje's version of global citizenship acknowledges the intersection of race and global power, demonstrating that some 'international bastards' are more powerful, more internationally welcome, and more protected than others. Kip embodies a critical cosmopolitanism that, according to Walter D. Mignolo, 'reconceiv[es] cosmopolitanism from the perspective of coloniality' and contests the injustices of 'global designs' (723), for 'there are ... local histories that plan and project global designs and others that have to live with them' (721). Kip's rejection of the West following the atomic bombings invokes the global design of the British Empire, as he traces his experiences of racism and the privileging of other histories over his own local history: 'I grew up with traditions from my country, but later, more often, from *your* country. Your fragile white island that with customs and manners and books and prefects and reason somehow converted the rest of the world ... Was it just ships that gave you such power?' (283). Kip recalls his brother's warning, 'Never turn your back on Europe. The deal makers. The contract makers. The map drawers' (284), those who manage global designs, rather than suffer their consequences. For Kip, the nuclear bombings represent just another manifestation of a (neo)imperial power seeking to define the globe in its own image, and only a critical cosmopolitanism is viable; an apolitical, uncommitted celebration of crossing national borders neglects hierarchies of power that organize nation-states according to wealth and race.

Like *The English Patient*, *Anil's Ghost* also works towards espousing a critical cosmopolitanism. Anil is immediately identifiable as a cosmopolitan through her status as a migrant, her crossing of borders as enabled by her profession, and her involvement in international human rights investigations. The international human rights commission and Anil's association with the United Nations invoke 'an order based on relations between states ... giving way to an order based at least partly on universal laws and institutions' (Carter 2). Her Western education and habitation have led to her being located elsewhere, both physically and officially, for 'she now travel[s] with a British passport' (16) with a 'light-blue UN bar' (9), facilitating her transcendence of nation-state borders and her work in such locations as the United States, Guatemala, and the Congo, and bestowing upon her a 'nomadic identity' (Härting 44). But the extent to which the UN is regarded as a 'universal' authority comes under scrutiny, as Sri Lankan characters regard Anil as a representative of the West, not only comparing her to Western journalists, but also naming her 'the woman from Geneva' (71) and noting her Western clothing (26). Anil partly encourages this Western view of herself, having 'courted foreignness' (54) while living outside her nation of origin. In some sense, her border-crossing, vocation-driven mobility somewhat resembles the English patient's cosmopolitanism, yet she does not completely share the patient's lack of political commitment. Her cosmopolitanism includes elements of professional concerns, habitation, and the adoption of an international political responsibility, incorporated into her work. Anil is therefore both 'a cosmopolitan traveller' (Härting 46) and a global citizen, a critical *and* uncritical cosmopolitan, for much of the text.

When she later stakes a claim to Sri Lanka and, to a certain extent, unravels the foreignness she has courted, Anil seems to reject her earlier uncritical cosmopolitanism. Although her perspective has shifted, and she has relearned the country and reasserted her sense of belonging, the rupture of hospitality necessitates her return to the West, raising questions about the text's arguments about cosmopolitanism and global political responsibility. Despite Anil's efforts to uncover the 'truth,' the novel repeatedly invokes cynicism about the effectiveness of international investigations. We are told that 'nobody at the Centre for Human Rights was very hopeful about' Anil's project (16). Although the investigation seems necessary to process 'everything ... grabbed and collected as evidence, everything that could be held on to in the windstorm of news ... copied and sent abroad to strangers in Geneva' (42), Sarath confirms the suspicions of the Centre for Human Rights: 'International investigations don't mean a lot' (45). Anil has previously had to abandon an investigation in the Congo once the 'Human Rights group [goes] too far': 'So much for the international authority of Geneva ... If and when you were asked by a government to leave, you left. You took nothing with you' (28–9). In both the Congo and Sri Lanka, the fraught relationship of hospitality ruptures, overwhelmed by hostility when international interests conflict with the state in question, and the state asserts its sovereignty over the interests of cosmopolitanism and international law.

Anil has been somewhat successful in Sri Lanka: she and Sarath have identified the skeleton 'Sailor,' and because of Sarath's sacrifice she is able to make her report before fleeing the country. But the investigation produces no sense of political resolution. Heike Härting contends that Anil 'embodies ... a critique of the failure of global justice' (43); however, *Anil's Ghost*'s representation of international human rights commissions does not simply critique 'the inefficiency of non-governmental human rights organizations' (56). Rather, the novel asks whether it is possible to hold sovereign nation-states accountable to global governance, given that 'in order to be effective at the level of political institutions or the popular masses, transnational networks have to work with and through the nation-state in order to transform it' (Cheah 312). The text's debate about the effectiveness of NGOs includes both the lack of genuine hospitality from a state under investigation and the imposition of Western perspectives on non-Western locations. As the Asian Human Rights Commission argues, 'The Western organisations have been more keen to tell the local people how to solve the problem than to listen to the local groups and even the victims' (Fernando n.p.). If Western NGOs fail to provide an arena 'in which everyone participates instead of "being participated"' (Mignolo 744), the agency is stripped from those whose concerns are supposed to be addressed.

Anil's Ghost invokes the limits of Western cosmopolitanism and its potential to perpetuate 'a form of cultural imperialism' (Carter 9) and endorses the attempt to make the nation in question accountable while stressing the importance of *who* holds that nation accountable. After Anil's departure, it becomes clear that the novel is not about Anil, but about Sri Lanka. The restoration narrative that focuses on Ananda's work on the broken Buddha statue privileges the local, for although

> it was assumed that Ananda would be working under the authority and guidance of foreign specialists, ... in the end these celebrities never came. There was too much political turmoil, and it was unsafe. They were finding dead bodies daily, not even buried, in the adjoining fields ... Ananda appeared to stare past it all. He gave two of the men on his team the job of dealing with the bodies – tagging them, contacting civil rights authorities. (301)

This passage removes the lens of the long-distance gaze, allowing the local to speak for itself, as far as is possible when written by a writer living in the West. Although some narrative consonance initially aligns the passage with a Western perspective ('There was too much political turmoil, and it was unsafe'), the focus shifts to Ananda's work. Whether the civil rights authorities are part of a national or international organization, they are invoked here without being present. Ananda protects local people by bringing 'in some of the villagers to work ... It [is] safer to be seen working for a project like this, otherwise you could be pulled into the army or you might be rounded up as a suspect' (301–2).

The '"neutral" and "innocent" fields around the statue and the rock carvings' are possibly 'places of torture and burials' (300), but 'by the time the monsoon [comes] the murders [have] subsided, or at least this area [is] no longer being used as a killing field or a burial ground' (301). Regeneration becomes the primary narrative focus. Although the majority of Sri Lankan Buddhists are Sinhalese, the dominant group in power, Ondaatje does not present the statue in a politically exclusive manner; rather, 'Buddhism and its values [have] met the harsh political events of the twentieth century' (300), and the statue has 'seen the wars and offered peace or irony to those dying under it' (304), implying a neutrality.

This representation of neutrality and reconstruction resonates with the role that doctors and hospitals play throughout *Anil's Ghost*, embodying Ondaatje's notion of 'furious heroic pacifism' ('Remarks' 2), by offering sites of healing and hospitality in the midst of armed conflict. The novel repeatedly presents scenes of doctors and nurses providing care to patients regardless of their ethnicity or political affiliation. To a certain extent it seems that Tamils might be excluded from hospitality, as suggested by the Buddhas in hospitals and the Kynsey Road Hospital sign 'printed in Latin, Sinhala and English' (66), Tamil noticeably excluded here from the linguistic and ethnic host position. But as Ondaatje describes Gamini's time working in the hospitals in the northeast, 'The doctors were coping with injuries from all political sides and there was just one operating table' (243). In this civil war context, one might expect the hospital's power to be linked to the state, with 'techniques for assessing and determining health (techniques of separation, but also of circulation, surveillance, classification, and so forth)' (Wallenstein 33) potentially accruing particular significance in the midst of ethnic conflict. But the novel imagines the hospital differently, as it figures as a politically neutral space (particularly the operating table), and the medical staff as agents of reconstruction and healing.

The primacy of hospitality in the ethos of the hospital becomes especially apparent in a scene where insurgents infiltrate Colombo's Ward Place Hospital:

> They had come looking for one patient. 'Where is so and so?' they had asked. 'I don't know.' There was bedlam. After finding the patient, they pulled out long knives and cut him to pieces. Then they threatened the nurses and demanded they not come to work anymore. The next day the nurses returned, not in uniforms but in frocks and slippers. There were

gunmen on the roof of the hospital. There were informers everywhere.
But the Ward Place Hospital remained open. (127)

This confrontation echoes a scenario described by Derrida with reference to Kant's arguments about the limits of hospitality. Discussing Kant's question 'Should I lie to murderers who come to ask me if the one they want to assassinate is in my house?' Derrida notes that 'Kant's response ... is [that] one should speak the truth, ... and thus risk delivering the guest to death ... It is better to break with the duty of hospitality rather than break with the absolute duty of veracity' (*Of Hospitality* 71). In Ondaatje's passage, however, the absolute duty is hospitality to and protection of the guests (patients), privileging healing rather than veracity as 'fundamental to humanity' (*Of Hospitality* 71).

At the site of the Buddha reconstruction, although Ondaatje initially emphasizes that the statue is 'broken stone. It [is] not a human life' (300), he then describes it precisely as a body in need of healing: '... once the stones were identified as to what likely part of the body they came from, by someone at the head of the triage, as it were, these were placed in the appropriate section' (301). Further, Ananda 'overs[ees] the work in the mud trench, which resemble[s] a hundred-foot-long coffin' (301). The imagery of war, burial, and hospitals, the acquired neutrality and safety of the field, recall the text's earlier representations of hospitality and healing, suggesting that the field synecdochically represents an operating theatre of potential reconstruction and healing for the nation. Ananda's efforts do not claim some kind of 'wholeness' or 'unity' (Goldman, 'Representations' 36), for the Buddha's scars remain visible: 'Up close the face looked quilted' (*Anil's* 302), underscoring both the wounds and the act of healing. Significantly, this healing is effected not by Anil, the returned and once more departed migrant, but in local Sri Lankan terms instead, the Buddha reconstruction depending upon local participation, as opposed to 'being participated' in the activities of Western groups.

Circuits and Celebrations

Ondaatje has expressed concern that because he is 'well known in the west, and not many Sri Lankan novelists are,' *Anil's Ghost* 'would get taken as representative' (Jaggi Interview 6). The novel acknowledges the cultural marketplace in which books circulate through Gamini's castigation of Western individuals who dabble in developing world crises and report back to their audiences at home:

> American movies, English books – remember how they all end? . . . The American or the Englishman gets on a plane and leaves. That's it. The camera leaves with him. He looks out of the window at Mombasa or Vietnam or Jakarta, someplace now he can look through the clouds . . . That's enough reality for the West. It's probably the history of the last two hundred years of Western political writing. Go home. Write a book. Hit the circuit. (285–6)

Ondaatje challenges himself to avoid replicating this all-too-predictable pattern of representation. But he also foregrounds the 'circuit' of publishing, reception, and celebration that has featured prominently throughout his career, particularly in relation to the novels in discussion here.

By the time of *In the Skin of a Lion*'s publication, Ondaatje, having already won two Governor General's Awards, was no stranger to state celebration. But *In the Skin of a Lion* was his first text to deal extensively with Canada as its subject, and, given its critique of the nation-state, the novel's various awards invite questions about the ideological implications of celebration. *In the Skin of a Lion* won the City of Toronto Book Award and the Trillium Prize, was nominated for the Governor General's Award for English-language fiction, and preceded Ondaatje's entry into the Order of Canada. Whereas the City of Toronto Book Award was established 'to honour authors of books of literary and artistic merit that are evocative of Toronto' ('Toronto' n.p.), the Trillium Prize, of which *In the Skin of a Lion* was the first winning text, aims to 'recognise excellence, support marketing and to foster increased public awareness of the quality and diversity of Ontario writers and writing' ('Trillium' n.p.), and is funded by the Ontario government's Ministry of Culture. The Trillium is open to 'Ontario writers who have lived in Ontario for at least three out of the past five years and who have been published anywhere in the world' ('Trillium' n.p.), and, unlike the City of Toronto Book Award, does not prescribe setting or content, focusing instead on Ontarian citizenship.

Ondaatje's municipal and provincial celebrations for *In the Skin of a Lion* were not duplicated at the national level, as this novel lost the Governor General's Award to M.T. Kelly's *A Dream like Mine*. But Ondaatje was honoured in a different manner by the federal government when he received the Order of Canada in 1988. The Governor General's office describes the Order of Canada as 'recogniz[ing] people who have made a difference to our country. From local citizens to national and international personalities, all Canadians are eligible for the Order of Canada – our country's highest honour for lifetime achievement' ('Order' n.p.). In the absence of the Governor General's Award, then, Ondaatje was nevertheless granted the state's 'highest honour.' Having 'made a difference' to Canada, it is clear that from the state's perspective, Ondaatje plays an integral role in Canadian culture, as indicated by his entry in the Order of Canada files: 'One of Canada's most successful experimental writers, [whose] work blends the factual and the imaginary in poetry and prose and is extraordinarily visual, which accounts for his interest in film as a complement to literature. But he is first and foremost a poet whose talent is recognized throughout the English-speaking world' ('Michael Ondaatje' n.p.). Ondaatje received the Order of Canada because of his *success* as a writer, and not only his national but also his international recognition. Part of his role as a Canadian cultural figure depends upon this external validation, his representative status for Canadian culture within an international circulation.

On the heels of *In the Skin of a Lion*, this 'representation' served a dual purpose: both Ondaatje's own international reception as it contributes to the recognition of Canadian culture generally, and the representation of Canada within his novel. In contrast, Ondaatje's Governor General's Award for *The Collected Works of Billy the Kid* in 1970 attracted some controversy precisely because of a perceived failure by Ondaatje to represent Canada. Following the prize announcement, former prime minister John Diefenbaker not only condemned 'the language of the book' as 'atrocious' but also objected to Ondaatje's subject matter: 'He complained about the inappropriateness of giving a Canadian prize – the Governor General's Award – to a writer who dealt with an American subject' (Jewinski 83). Although Diefenbaker was neither part of the judging process nor running the country at this point, his objections invoke an anxiety about representations of Canada. Thus, with *In the Skin of a Lion* seventeen years later, Ondaatje's representativeness of Toronto, Ontario, and Canada was underscored by the celebrations this novel attracted, the Order of Canada honouring Ondaatje after the publication of his only work set exclusively in Canada. Having become a Canadian citizen in 1965, Ondaatje's 'legitimate' claim to being Canadian, 'one of us,' was already established from a legal perspective. But whereas *In the Skin of a Lion*'s characters claim their belonging in different ways, Ondaatje is claimed by external factors that reinforce his belonging and host position, as defined by various levels of the state.

That the City of Toronto Book Award, the Trillium Prize, the Governor General's Award, and the Order of Canada should all be administered by various levels of government displays a degree of contradiction between the novel's critique of power and its cultural celebration. Granted, critical debates about the novel's politics suggest that it is not immediately recognizable as posing a threat to the dominant order (see Beddoes; Davey, *Post-national;* Dobson), and what some critics read as an uncertain political position perhaps renders the novel more 'celebrateable' by Canadian state-sponsored prizes. But *In the Skin of a Lion's* historical setting is a key factor in assessing the implications of celebration: if the novel indicts power relations in the first four decades of the twentieth century, the federal, provincial, and municipal governments at the time of the novel's publication perhaps appear exempt from Ondaatje's critique.

Significantly, however, *In the Skin of a Lion* gestures towards its moment of production, implicitly extending its critique of the nation-state's power. As Winfried Siemerling notes, *In the Skin of a Lion* redresses gaps in official history, presenting 'another world that silently coexists within Toronto's written history and its present-day surface reality' (154). That surface reality includes both the water-filtration plant and the Bloor Street Viaduct to this day. Harris justifies the excesses of the waterworks' lavish interior, claiming, 'You watch, in *fifty years* they're going to come here and gape' (*Skin* 236, my emphasis). He is correct, as indicated by guided tours that have been run of the waterworks at the east end of Queen Street. Patrick tries to destroy the plant on 7 July 1938 (229); *In the Skin of a Lion* was published in 1987, *forty-nine years* after the fictional version of Harris (a 'real,' 'historical' person, commemorated on a plaque at the waterworks) insists that visitors will gape at the plant's interior. Just as visitors have been able to witness the results of Harris's lavish tastes, so the definition of Canadianness has remained a site of contestation.

Ondaatje's invocation of Canadian citizenship in a novel set prior to the Canadian Citizenship Act suggests we should read his treatment of Canadianness in dialogue with the time in which *In the Skin of a Lion* was written, as the novel offers 'an implicit critique of the ongoing racial stratification of contemporary Canadian society' (Lundgren 17). The fracture between citizenship and national belonging is crucial, for it distinguishes between who is legally Canadian and who is perceived to belong in Canada. Despite Canada's official multicultural policy, as Frank Cunningham notes, 'in English-speaking Canada proclamations of commitment to multiculturalism, especially outside a few large urban centers, do not go much beyond toleration for occasional folk festivals and mask a fair measure of continuing Anglo – indeed, Anglo-Protestant – chauvinism' (45).

The novel's publication the year before the Canadian Multiculturalism Act (1988) attests to the cultural climate of the nation 'during a peak period of immigration' (Lundgren 16), and to debates about the ways in which the state encourages the nation to view and represent itself. The act asserts that

> the Government of Canada recognizes the diversity of Canadians as regards race, national or ethnic origin, colour and religion as a fundamental characteristic of Canadian society and is committed to a policy of multiculturalism designed to preserve and enhance the multicultural heritage of Canadians while working to achieve the equality of all Canadians in the economic, social, cultural and political life of Canada. (*Canadian Multiculturalism Act* n.p.)

The state claims both to recognize and encourage a Canadian host position forged out of multiplicity and to take responsibility for the ethnic and economic concerns outlined in *In the Skin of a Lion*, in contrast to the state as represented in the novel through figures like Police Chief Draper. The act presents responsibilities on the part of the Canadian government to Canadian citizens with reference to affiliations operating alongside nation-state citizenship, but it leaves the dominant construction of the host position intact. As Smaro Kamboureli argues, it 'recognizes the cultural diversity that constitutes Canada, but it does so by practising a sedative politics, a politics that attempts to recognize ethnic differences, but only in a contained fashion, in order to manage them' (*Scandalous* 82). The state's sedation of difference emerges through its 'pay[ing] tribute to diversity and suggest[ing] ways of celebrating it, thus responding to the clarion call of ethnic communities for recognition. Yet it does so without disturbing the conventional articulation of the Canadian dominant society' (82). The dominant Canadian host position remains unquestioned, merely supplemented by token recognitions. If Canada's 1982 Constitution 'entrenched [a] commitment to multiculturalism' (Cunningham 45), the 1988 act itself entrenches the status of the 'founding' groups of Canada.

Fifteen years after its initial publication, *In the Skin of a Lion* was granted an afterlife through the inaugural Canada Reads competition, run by the CBC, a recognition that inserted the text into precisely the 'sedative' multiculturalism that Kamboureli diagnoses. *In the Skin of a Lion*, selected as the winning text over Margaret Atwood's *The Handmaid's Tale*, George Elliott Clarke's *Whylah Falls*, Margaret Laurence's *The Stone Angel*, and Rohinton Mistry's *A Fine Balance*, was the best-selling paperback in Canada in 2002 (see 'Bestsellers' D13), with booksellers claiming that more copies were sold in the first two weeks after its Canada Reads win than had been sold in the previous year (see MacDonald R3), indicating that Canada Reads' suggestion of the novel as worthy of consumption by Canadians was successful. The CBC ran a parallel 'People's Choice' competition, in which *A Fine Balance* was selected as the winner, with *In the Skin of a Lion* placing fourth behind *The Stone Angel* and Alistair MacLeod's *No Great Mischief*. If *In the Skin of a Lion* was not the 'winning' text for the Canadian reading public, hostility towards Ondaatje's novel in the Canadian press (see chapter 1) suggests a more aggressive rejection of *In the Skin of a Lion* than the 'People's Choice' poll and the book's rejuvenated sales imply.

Like national literary prize-winners, any text that wins such a competition occupies the position of uniting Canadians by virtue of their, and the text's, Canadianness, of linking the national population to the national culture, and forging community out of the consumption of national cultural products. In its framing of *In the Skin of a Lion* as a book 'all Canadians should read,' Canada Reads duplicated the novel's back cover blurb description of the text, defusing the novel's politics. The text is characterized for the purposes of marketing, both by its publisher and by Canada Reads, as 'a love story and an irresistible mystery set in the turbulent, muscular new world of Toronto in the '20s and '30s' that 'entwines adventure, romance and history, real and invented, enmeshing us in the lives of ... the politically powerful, the anarchists, bridge builders and tunnellers, a vanished millionaire and his mistress, a rescued nun and a thief who leads a charmed life'; the description finally characterizes the novel as 'a haunting tale of passion, privilege and biting physical labour, of men and women moved by compassion and driven by the power of dreams – sometimes even to murder' ('Canada Reads Champion' n.p.). This synopsis attempts to popularize the text, focusing on romance and mystery in a way that the novel's detractors do not: 'Plot? Yeah, right. We're talking about Ondaatje here' (MacGowan C12). Granted, the Canada Reads and publisher's description tries to entice potential readers, but it highlights elements easily identified with popular, 'marketable' narratives. As Laura Moss argues of the panel's debates about the text, the 'depoliticized discussions' of the Canada Reads judges ultimately 'divert readers, critics, and writers from the political dimensions of literature' ('Canada' 8). For *In the Skin of a Lion*, in particular, the Canada Reads apparatus sidesteps the novel's position of critique, emphasizing the historical setting in a way that contains the text's politics. Further, as Moss notes, Canada Reads interpolated the novel into the discourse of 'the growth of Canada as a multicultural nation' in a way that both congratulates Canada for being a 'truly multicultural place' (9) and is inattentive to persistent social injustices. As Danielle Fuller reminds us, however, despite the methods used by Canada Reads to promote and celebrate Canadian literature, the project itself does not dictate the kinds of meanings to be gleaned by the readers themselves (see chapter 1). Ultimately, the Canada Reads framing circulates in contradiction to the novel's own critique of Anglo, capitalist power in Canada, presenting a disjunction between the text itself and the extratextual apparatuses that increase its further circulation.

Following the original publication of *In the Skin of a Lion*, Ondaatje stated, 'Canada has always been a very racist society, and it's getting more so' (quoted in B. Turner 21). The Canadian Multiculturalism Act has failed to legislate an anti-racist nation into being. Not everything in *In the Skin of a Lion* can be contained by its temporal setting: English is still the language of power in Toronto, in Ontario, in Canada, and official multiculturalism and bilingualism have not refashioned the Canadian cultural host. The right-wing Reform Party of Canada was established in 1987, the year of the novel's publication. The party and its later incarnation, the Canadian Alliance, have been associated with hostility towards multiculturalism – not because it fails to make Canada more just, but because they believed it threatened Anglo dominance in Canada – as well as bilingualism and immigration; further, the current Conservative Party of Canada includes many Reform Party figures. These political developments in the last two decades testify to the persistence of many of the issues outlined by *In the Skin of a Lion*. For Ondaatje to criticize power structures at municipal, provincial, and national levels, only to be awarded at each of these levels, suggests that the licensing, or sedating, of his transgressions operates in tension with *In the Skin of a Lion*'s underlining of the continuing distinction between citizenship and national belonging, and its protesting of the Canadian cultural host's exclusiveness.

Although Ondaatje's subsequent novel, *The English Patient*, also met with national celebration in Canada through the Governor General's Award for English-language fiction, this recognition was eclipsed by Ondaatje's sharing the Booker Prize with Barry Unsworth's *Sacred Hunger*. The transnational prize ensured both that this novel would become Ondaatje's most internally recognized work and that Ondaatje himself was granted an augmented international status that secured his significance to contemporary Canadian literature, for no Canadian had ever won the Booker Prize. Derek Finkle writes that prior to his Booker win, Ondaatje, 'in Canada, had not yet approached the status or popularity of the past Booker finalists Margaret Atwood, Robertson Davies, and Mordecai Richler'; following the win, however, he 'suddenly vaulted onto the same podium' (92). Conversely, Daniel Johnson of the *Times* declared that Ondaatje was 'widely recognized as the leading Canadian novelist' (1), implying a discrepancy between Ondaatje's reputation within Canada and outside the country.

That the convergence of Ondaatje's status within and without Canada was effected by the Booker Prize is telling. Eleanor Wachtel effuses, 'I found it particularly gratifying when Michael Ondaatje became the first Canadian to win Britain's leading fiction award, the Booker Prize – or rather to share it with the English writer Barry Unsworth – because Michael Ondaatje is a writer of such grace and accomplishment that he does us proud in the world' (quoted in Interview 250). Wachtel here underscores the enormity of Ondaatje's victory for Canadian literature, the association of the Booker with British literary culture, and the prize's reinforcement of Ondaatje's status as a cultural ambassador for Canada. With regards to national literature, Ondaatje's win 'provided a sense of vindication for Canadian literature generally – even if the prize was shared' (Aspinall 13). Ondaatje's nomination alongside writers from other countries, and sharing the prize with an English writer, placed him in the context of international writing; this context implies a transcendence of Canadian literature that paradoxically validates that same literature, suggesting a parity of circulation of national literatures in an international literary community and marketplace.

The Booker Prize's celebration of literature through a Commonwealth-based catchment area while maintaining the status of a British prize raises questions about its celebration of *The English Patient*. Carla Comellini writes of the novel's conclusion, 'Kip will finally become Kirpal Singh again and a doctor in a clinic when he returns home to an India which is no longer part of the British Empire. There, the only link left [with Hana in Canada] is the Commonwealth' (168). Given that the Commonwealth is a legacy of the British Empire, the celebration of *The English Patient* through the Booker Prize appears to replicate the celebration of the transgressive *In the Skin of a Lion* in Canada: 'Asked if the English weren't masochists to give him the prize, Ondaatje laughed and said, "I didn't think it'd be a book the English would like"' (Heward, 'Canadian' A2). Significantly, however, the Booker is not a state-sponsored prize. The novel's Commonwealth Writers' Prize for the Canada and the Caribbean region, in contrast, represents a part–publicly funded prize, and possibly another licensed transgression. However, this prize's more centrifugally structured administration demonstrates that it is more concerned with celebrating multiple national cultures than simply with Commonwealth texts that have found publication in Britain.

The Booker Prize constructs an international literary community, of which Ondaatje is a celebrated, welcome member. In this sense, the Booker projects a hospitable cosmopolitanism wrought from the legacy of colonialism. Although not administered by the British government, the Booker Prize is nonetheless part of British literary culture. As such, British literary culture is contributed to, and partly sustained by, cultural products written outside the former imperial centre. 'British' literary culture is therefore both British and not, comprised of both host and guest cultural products, but this guest status is tempered, mediated by former colonial relations: it is because of Canada's (and Sri Lanka's) Commonwealth status that Ondaatje is *entitled* to contribute to British literary culture through Booker eligibility.

Although the Booker Prize enhanced Ondaatje's status as an international representative of Canadian literature, journalism about Ondaatje around the time of the Booker nominations and award announcement contested his nationality. Kenneth Oppel noted in *Quill & Quire* that 'some British reviewers [have] seemed uncomfortable classifying Ondaatje as a Canadian' (13). Responding to the *Financial Times'* characterization of Ondaatje as 'a Sri Lankan poet, domiciled in Canada' (J.D.F. Jones XI), Oppel argued that it 'appeared as if Canada were simply an accidental, and probably temporary, resting place on a longer voyage' (13). Oppel betrays an anxiety about maintaining Canada's claims to Ondaatje in the face of his possible transcendence of the nation and its culture. Ondaatje affirmed his self-identification as Canadian when he 'addressed this issue explicitly in *The Guardian*,' the effect of which was the conclusion of the British reporter that 'now it seems that it is possible to be a Canadian writer even if the person has not been born in Canada. There is an acceptance of the foreign born' (13). This comment might apply to the constitution of the Canadian host culture, wherein 'the foreign born' can become a host. Ondaatje's celebration within Canada, which began early in his career, suggests that this acceptance where Ondaatje is concerned is not exactly new. However, Ondaatje's position as a celebrated hyphenate Canadian is not indicative of hospitality towards immigrants in Canada generally. Ondaatje's contribution to the dynamics of reshaping national identity, through his work and through the Canadian recognition of his work, is significant in terms of the constitution of the Canadian host position, but he has been designated a legitimate contributor to Canadian culture.

The English Patient's success outside Canada was mirrored within the country through Ondaatje's second Trillium Prize and third Governor General's Award. George Woodcock, echoing A.J.M. Smith's privileging of 'cosmopolitan' over 'native' writing, claims that *The English Patient*'s setting outside Canada represented a new maturity in Canadian writing, one which depends upon transcending the nation, allowing literature to 'cu[t] away from national self-consciousness and begi[n] to look outside once again, for forms and inspirations' (22). But this achievement of Ondaatje's for Canadian culture is problematic (especially considering Ondaatje's earliest prose works were also set outside Canada), for it depends upon an absence of *overt* 'Canadianness' in the assessment of literary maturity. Although *The English Patient* may not address Canada as explicitly as *In the Skin of a Lion*, it grapples with questions of nation, identity, and citizenship in such a way that contests any sense of Ondaatje's 'outgrowing' Canadian concerns. The novel's arguments about larger political responsibilities than those to the nation-state, the implications of taking on such responsibilities, and the kinds of communities that might be viably created from difference contribute to discussions of both Canadian identity and Canada's international status. To a certain extent, the villa community reads as an allegory of Canada in its postcolonial context: the meeting of different identities, with the performance of Englishness at its centre and ethnic minorities at the margin. Ondaatje has said that he wrote about Kip partly in response to 'the basic racism' (quoted in Heward, 'Canadian' A2) of the Baltej Dhillon case in Canada, which contested the right of Sikh RCMP officers to wear turbans on duty. Further, the novel's ending reminds us that to be a citizen of the Canadian nation-state is also to be implicated in violence on a global scale, timely for a novel written in part during the Gulf War. Thus, the celebration of Ondaatje's fiction through the state-sponsored Governor General's Award presents some political contradictions, although as with *In the Skin of a Lion*, the displacement of issues onto the past suggests a safe distance that may facilitate such celebration.

Adapting Cosmopolitanism

Although *The English Patient* received considerable attention within and outside Canada as a Booker Prize–winning novel, Anthony Minghella's 1996 film adaptation truly cemented the commodification of the novel and its author, to a certain extent altering readings of the original text. Minghella's film, celebrated by critical responses 'rang[ing] from the reverent to the positively ecstatic' (B. Thomas 197) and by nine Academy Awards (for Best Film, Director, Supporting Actress, Cinematography, Art Direction, Costume Design, Sound, Editing, and Dramatic Score), was immersed in cosmopolitan discourse. The film's producer, Saul Zaentz, frequently referred to *The English Patient* as 'an international film' (Halliburton and Guttridge 8), given the numerous nationalities represented by the director, producer, cast, crew, and production locations (e.g., Italy, Tunisia). Zaentz's description of the film's internationalism fits neatly into an Enlightenment version of cosmopolitanism based upon individuals of different nations brought together by common interests and profession.

Emphasis on *The English Patient*'s internationalism displaces it from Hollywood cinema, but alterations made from novel to film suggest what is typically considered a Hollywood adaptation, particularly in Minghella's privileging of Almásy and his affair with Katharine. Because the film dwells on the pre-war, desert narrative at the expense of Hana's, Caravaggio's, and especially Kip's stories, its arguments about nation and citizenship diverge from the novel's. As Raymond Aaron Younis argues, Katharine, at the centre of the film, speaks many 'poetic and memorable lines' (3) not attributed to her in the novel. For example, in the film she writes in Almásy's copy of Herodotus, 'We're the real countries, not the boundaries drawn on maps,' a line not found in Ondaatje's text that nevertheless reflects the patient's views. Thus, the film *The English Patient* 'shunts aside the narrative rejection of the English patient's vision' (Smyrl 36), and the patient's version of cosmopolitanism ends up speaking for the film both within and without the cinematic text. Although Minghella has said that the novel *The English*

Patient 'resonated with one of his own favourite themes, the "hinge between the private world and the public one"' (Lacey C2), the adaptation, in 'substituting passion for history' (Hawkins and Danielson 139), proves more hospitable to the private than to the public. The erasure of the atomic bombings and Kip's rejection of the imperialist West ensures that no sense of global responsibility or awareness of power imbalances between nations clutters what is primarily a romantic film. Unsurprisingly, the novel's indictment of American militarism did not make the cut in what was ultimately welcomed and celebrated by Hollywood as a multiple Oscar-winning film.

As an adaptation of a Canadian text, *The English Patient* occupies a peculiar relationship to Canadian culture. Although Canada does not form the setting of Ondaatje's novel, there are several references to Caravaggio's, and especially Hana's, pasts there. These characters' experiences of war depend upon their removal from Canada, the fracturing of habitation and nation: 'Where was and what was Toronto anymore in her mind?' (50). In the film, any invocation of Toronto is absent. As the *Globe and Mail*'s Liam Lacey writes, 'The first thing you notice about the new adaptation of Michael Ondaatje's Booker Prize–winning novel, *The English Patient* ... is that Hana, the young nurse from Toronto ... has a French accent' (C2). Lacey explains that the casting of Juliette Binoche as Hana necessitated a shift in 'the character's home town ... to Montreal'; likewise, Caravaggio, who in Minghella's version is not a 'family friend' but a stranger, is also from Montreal (C2). Ondaatje has said that he was 'rather startled that the Canadianness survived to some extent, and ... he was always glad that that was there' (quoted in B.D. Johnson 43). But this Canadianness is qualified by the fact that Willem Dafoe's accent is clearly not a Canadian one, and Binoche's is French, not French-Canadian. Curiously, despite the film's problematic representation of Canadianness, Canadian actors appear in various minor roles in the war hospital scenes, which feature Matthew Ferguson, Torri Higginson, Geordie Johnson, and Liisa Repo-Martell. Because no part of the film was shot in Canada, the decision to use Canadian actors is something of an in-joke for Canadian film audiences, or, rather, for audiences of Canadian films. As Charles Acland notes, although 'Canadian audiences are not absent from theatres ... , audiences for Canadian films are typically sparse' (283). Minghella's adaptation thus offers unconvincing portraits of Canadianness in the lead characters, but also a reward for viewers of Canadian cinema who can spot the 'real' Canadians in *The English Patient*.

To a certain extent, the film's prizes have been translated into rewards for Canadian culture, despite the adaptation's problematic nature. Ondaatje's frequently invoked participation in the filmmaking process apparently subdued reviewers of the film: 'If fans of the novel despair of the film, they'll have an argument with *The English Patient*'s author, Michael Ondaatje, who has enthusiastically supported and even participated in making the changes needed to create the movie' (Lacey C2). Ondaatje's friendship with Minghella and Zaentz, acknowledged in the filmmakers' numerous acceptance speeches at awards ceremonies, subsumed Ondaatje into the cosmopolitan discourse of the film and its production. If Brian D. Johnson assures Canadians in *Maclean's* that 'we can ... take some modest pride' (42) in the film, Glen Lowry argues that this appropriation strategically testifies to the vitality of Canadian culture: not only has the film 'further facilitated Ondaatje's entrance into the fold of Canadian arts and culture,' but it has also 'brought CanLit into the realm of global culture, and, perhaps because it raises the stakes considerably, few seem to be willing to quibble with its success' (Lowry 220). Perceptions of Minghella's film as beneficial to Canadian culture, treated hospitably in the global cultural marketplace through its incarnation in the adaptation, help explain why the film's depoliticized narrative has been so under-acknowledged and under-criticized. The film leaves us with 'an empty cosmopolitanism' rather than 'the historical specificity of Canada' (220), but this empty cosmopolitanism has allowed Canadian culture to circulate globally.

The film's circulation translated the viewer back into the reader, as the novel's enormous jump in sales after the film's release indicates (Whittell and Alberge 2). But the novel's commodification, largely effected by the award-winning film, appears to have influenced how the book is read, not only through the standard repackaging of the novel with a film still on the cover (Ralph Fiennes as Almásy and Kristin Scott Thomas as Katharine embracing in bed) but also through explicit rereadings of Ondaatje's text. Tellingly, John Bemrose, who reviewed *The English Patient* in *Maclean's* following the novel's publication, later altered his reading of the novel to suit the film. Whereas the initial review ('Casualties' 71) invoked the novel's major elements and characters, and accordingly did not dwell on Katharine (whose actual presence in the novel is less significant than the quartet of protagonists'), Bemrose's brief description in 2000 for a list of Canada's best twentieth-century fiction declared *The English Patient* 'the best romantic novel by a Canadian,' a '1992 tale [which] unearths the secrets of an illicit love affair in the North African desert' ('Best' 241).

Celebration in the Aftermath

As Ondaatje's first novel after *The English Patient*, *Anil's Ghost* emerged in the aftermath of the earlier novel's celebration, popularization, commodification, and repackaging. In describing the intervening period between the two novels' publications, Silvia Albertazzi invokes a conversion of symbolic and economic capital, effected by both the Booker and the Oscars, when she states that 'Ondaatje ... turned from a cult writer appreciated mainly by sophisticated readers of Canadian literature to an author of best-sellers, translated into dozens of languages and acclaimed throughout the world' (Review 74). *Anil's Ghost* continued *The English Patient*'s international recognition for Ondaatje, as he won prizes outside of Canada, not only sharing the Kiryama Prize, awarded to books 'that encourage greater mutual understanding of and among' countries of the Pacific Rim and South Asia (Pacific Rim Voices n.p.), but also winning the Irish Times Literary Prize for International Fiction and the Prix Médici (Étranger) in France. Whereas the Kiryama asserted Ondaatje's (and his novel's) South Asian context, and the Irish Times and Médici prizes embraced Ondaatje as a welcome guest in Irish and French culture, in Canada, *Anil's Ghost* was the first book to win both the Governor General's Award for English-language fiction and the Giller Prize, awards that highlighted anxieties about Canadianness and celebration.

After being a welcome guest in international circulation and literary cosmopolitanism, Ondaatje's status in Canada apparently required redefinition or explanation: did he now have a renewed 'guest' status in Canada, following his international reception? As Lorraine York notes, Ondaatje's Booker- and Oscar-generated fame has meant that 'the claims of international and national fame are met; Ondaatje is both ours and the world's' (138). But whereas York reads Ondaatje's identity, as it is negotiated within Canada, as being attached to exoticism and eroticism (167), I see instead an anxiety about his Canadianness that was prompted by his international celebration. With reference to *Anil's Ghost*, the *National Post*'s Noah Richler asked Ondaatje, 'Canada doesn't make it in ... Too cold?' ('Ondaatje' B5). Albertazzi goes so far as to declare in *Wasafiri*, '*Anil's Ghost* is not a Canadian book' (74). The Sri Lankan setting of *Anil's Ghost* acts as a reminder of the other half of Ondaatje's hyphenate identity, the Sri Lankanness that precedes his Canadianness. Richler, writing for a Canadian newspaper, displays an expectation of Canada's presence in the novel, an expectation that is neither shared by Albertazzi, writing for a British journal, nor met by the text of *Anil's Ghost*. Yet the Governor General's Award and Giller Prize for *Anil's Ghost* subsume the novel and its Sri Lankan setting within Canadian literary culture. The content of *Anil's Ghost* presents some analogies to Ondaatje's celebrated position within Canadian literature after *The English Patient*'s success. The reference to Anil's homecoming in Sri Lanka as 'the return of the prodigal,' echoing Ondaatje's self-positioning in *Running in the Family*, resonates further: the celebration of *Anil's Ghost* within Canada suggests another 'return of the prodigal,' the internationally famous and popularized Ondaatje, seemingly returning, or made to return, to his former Canadian literary self.

If the Governor General's Award has been generally considered more unconventional in its winning texts, in contrast to the Scotiabank Giller's reputation for conservative selections (see chapter 1), the 2000 Governor General's Award for English-language fiction shortlist was considered by some to have taken 'a sharp turn towards the Establishment' (Gessell, 'Year' C21). Ondaatje's acceptance speech at the Governor General's Awards referred to his first Governor General's Award, for *The Collected Works of Billy the Kid* in 1970, when 'being a poet [felt] "inappropriate"' ('Remarks' n.p.), perhaps because he was denounced by Diefenbaker. Ondaatje's statement that 'Canadian writing today evolves from a dedicated nurturing by the Canada Council and CBC Radio that has to continue with today's young and inappropriate writers' ('Remarks' n.p.) suggests an awareness that he is no longer 'inappropriate,' much closer now to the 'Establishment' of Canadian literature.

But the fact that *Anil's Ghost* won both the Governor General's Award and the Giller Prize raises questions about these awards, and about how the novel fits into their respective frameworks. Does *Anil's Ghost* reflect both the Governor General's Award's 'bold but flaky selections' (Ross, 'Heads-up' D10) and the Giller Prize's 'industry prize' (quoted in Renzetti C1) for household names of Canadian literature? Certainly, Ondaatje's star status is not in question; and *Anil's Ghost* was his first work eligible for the Giller Prize since the foundation of the award. That Ondaatje won the Governor General's Award for 'a more linear work' (Ondaatje and Egoyan D6) than his previous novels suggests that *Anil's Ghost* was not necessarily a bold choice in stylistic terms; however, the novel's constant attention to questioning Western perspectives implies a bold political choice. Ultimately, *Anil's Ghost*'s two Canadian literary prizes do work to reassert the novel's Canadianness. The Governor General's Award's and Giller Prize's upholding of *Anil's Ghost* as worthy Canadian writing for the Canadian reading public operates as another negotiation of Ondaatje's identity, post–*English Patient*, bringing Ondaatje back home to the Canadian nation-state in the aftermath of his international circulation and celebration, and bestowing upon him a hospitality-at-home.

Given Ondaatje's popularization prior to *Anil's Ghost*'s publication, it is unlikely the novel needed these prizes to augment its public access. Ondaatje and his accompanying international status confer recognition on the prizes, speaking for the Giller and Governor General's Award, instead of the reverse. But in *Anil's Ghost*'s two Canadian literary prizes, national, popular, cultural, and commercial interests converge: Ondaatje is beneficial to the nation because of his contribution to high-culture literature; to the publishing industry, because his books will sell; to Canadian culture because he has become recognized within and without the nation, and therefore has increased the value of Canadian cultural currency as it circulates nationally and internationally. As Ondaatje acknowledged at the 2000 Governor General's Awards, where he championed the cause of independent bookstores, 'Let's admit it – we never could get into the big bookstores until we were useful to them' ('Remarks' n.p.). National celebration reinforces Ondaatje's contribution to contemporary Canadian literature by asserting Ondaatje's own Canadianness in the first place, and asserting his usefulness to Canadianness as a whole. This Canadian celebration of Ondaatje, in the face of international hospitality and reception, bestows upon him the status of one who is no longer a guest, but rather an integral part of the host's culture in Canada. Ondaatje's undermining of Westernized positions, as presented in *Anil's Ghost*, is thereby reinscribed extratextually by the interests of his Western nation of habitation, which claims Ondaatje as belonging.

By the time Ondaatje won his fifth Governor General's Award for *Divisadero*, his usefulness to big bookstores, through both symbolic and economic capital, was more than assured, given his Canada Reads success with *In the Skin of a Lion* in between *Anil's Ghost* and the publication of his 2007 novel. Whereas Canadian prizes for *Anil's Ghost* and its Sri Lankan setting might be understood to privilege Canada's multicultural projection of itself, allowing Ondaatje to focus on his nation of origin because he had earlier paid his dues to representing Canada in *In the Skin of a Lion*, *Divisadero*'s setting in California, Nevada, and France does not represent either pole of Ondaatje's identity. However, Ondaatje's fifth Governor General's Award saw him tie with Hugh MacLennan, a fact included in many Canadian newspaper headlines, and which underscored Ondaatje's Canadianness and his location within Canadian literary history. If Sam Solecki, in 1985, declared that Ondaatje occupied an 'anomalous status' (7) in the Canadian literary tradition, Ondaatje's matching of MacLennan's total in 2007 asserts both his position within the tradition and the ways in which his celebrated contributions to it have altered its shape. Journalists' keen quotation of Ondaatje stating he was 'pleased to hear his name connected with that of Hugh MacLennan,' a writer who, Ondaatje claimed, is 'still with [him]' (Donnelly D1), suggests a continuing need for Canada both to have the nation and its culture infused, and reinfused, with capital, and to have its anxieties soothed when it comes to its celebrated, exportable writers.

3 The 'American-Not-American': Carol Shields's Border Crossings and Gendered Citizenships

Just as Michael Ondaatje has come to be primarily associated with *The English Patient*, so Carol Shields is first and foremost remembered as the author of *The Stone Diaries*, winner of the Governor General's Award and the Pulitzer Prize, and shortlisted for the Booker Prize. This constellation of honours should be impossible according to the awards' national eligibility criteria, testifying to the borders Shields crossed in her life, her work, and its celebration. If Ondaatje has been credited with helping Canadian culture resist the threat of Americanization, Shields presents a peculiar challenge to the opposition of Canadian and U.S. culture, as *The Stone Diaries'* celebration suggests in its anointing as a text representative of both Canadian and American literature.

For much of Shields's career, there was little debate about her Canadianness, for despite her birth as Carol Warner in Oak Park, Illinois, in 1935, she emigrated to Canada in 1957 after marrying Don Shields, a Canadian engineer. Shields did not begin publishing books until much later, after the birth of her five children. Thus, her development as a writer occurred entirely within Canada, the site of production of her texts, and she received assistance from the Canada Council, inserting her into state-supported national culture. That she credited her Council grants with alleviating her domestic work – 'she used the money to pay for babysitters and to send her husband's shirts to the dry cleaners' ('Farewell' A22) – in order to enable her writing illustrates Lorraine York's claim that portraits of motherhood and domesticity have dominated Shields's representation in the media (151). These extratextual discussions of Shields's domesticity intersect with her textual interests in addressing gendered claims to cultural and economic power. In fact, much of the scholarship on Shields has focused primarily on her interest in gender, not on her representations of nation. But the competing national claims to Shields through the celebration of *The Stone Diaries* foregrounded her dual citizenship, making her status as a Canadian writer a site of negotiation, and, to a certain extent, highlighted the role of nation within her writing.

If reception and celebration of Shields's work ultimately underscored her mobile national identity, it has also demonstrated the slipperiness of aesthetic categorization. Shields's varied career, encompassing poetry, short fiction, plays, essays, criticism, biography, and novels, has been identified as having a turning point in *Swann* (1987) and its formal play. Having already published four novels previously – *Small Ceremonies* (1976), *The Box Garden* (1977), *Happenstance* (1980), and *A Fairly Conventional Woman* (1982) – as well as two poetry collections and a collection of short fiction, Shields had been considered 'easy to dismiss' (Hancock C9). *Swann*, a 'transitional tex[t] in Shields's corpus' (Ramon 58), departs from the earlier works in its formal experimentation through invocation and subversion of the mystery genre, four distinct narrative voices through its main characters, and the screenplay form of its final chapter. Shields's publications after *Swann* include two short fiction collections and a collection of poetry, as well as the innovations of a collaborative novel (with Blanche Howard), *A Celibate Season* (1991); *The Republic of Love* (1992), which seeks to rewrite the romance genre; *The Stone Diaries* (1993), a fictional auto/biography with a postmodern narration and construction of subjectivity; *Larry's Party* (1997), a playful fictional biography that privileges 'a spatial figuring of Larry's life' (Howells, 'Larry's' 16) over a temporal one; and *Unless* (2002), a metafictional exploration of the middlebrow woman writer that uses (unsent) letters to protest persistent gendered imbalances in public power. Shields's work has been variously located in middlebrow and highbrow contexts, an indication not only that such judgments are largely dependent upon the reader rather than intrinsic elements of the work itself, but also that Shields's writing, particularly her later works, has managed to satisfy both middlebrow and highbrow categories, appealing to popular readership while engaging in formal experimentation.

Shields's work was celebrated through literary prizes, first at the national and then international levels, in the second phase of her career, initiated by the publication and reception of *Swann*, which began to align Shields with celebrated national culture in Canada. Even more successful, her later novels *The Stone Diaries* and *Larry's*

Party increased Canada's investment in Shields just as her American citizenship came into the foreground through her American celebration. All three of these novels engage with issues of hospitality, border crossing, citizenship, habitation and nation, and cosmopolitanism, as they grapple with constructions of the Canadian host position and the often hostile negotiation of internal difference. They also frequently examine the relationship between Canada and the United States, chiefly through the representation of border crossings. Although these representations invoke 'sameness,' they also undercut it. Shields's texts demonstrate how being a Canadian citizen includes an awareness of the more powerful neighbour to the south, with whom 'neighbourliness' is a relationship of hostipitality in which Canada struggles to assert economic and cultural power. Just as Shields exposes the power imbalance between these two countries, so too she probes the distinctions between gendered citizenship roles, and how access to power is regulated through these roles. These manifestations of and struggles for power that occur both within and across nation-states are paramount in Shields's works, as they focus on claims of legitimacy and entitlement.

Border Crossings: Sameness and Difference

Swann, The Stone Diaries, and *Larry's Party* all examine the Canada-U.S. border as a site of negotiating identity and the relationship between nation and habitation. In *Swann,* Canada-U.S. border crossing pertains chiefly to Mary Swann biographer Morton Jimroy, a Canadian temporarily resident in the United States. In *The Stone Diaries* and *Larry's Party,* protagonists Daisy and Larry relocate for lengthy periods that suggest the possibility of habitation writing over nation altogether, facilitated by the slippage between sameness and difference that the Canada-U.S. border presents. The adoption of roles of host and guest unfolds within a troubled hospitality between the two countries.

In *Swann,* Jimroy's temporary habitation in California as 'Distinguished Visitor' to Stanford University offers a juxtaposition of nationality across the Canada-U.S. border, and an assertion of Jimroy's Canadian citizenship and his perception of its attendant rights. From Jimroy's perspective, Americanness presents difference, as he assesses 'the calm way Sarah Maloney writes *honor* and *center* – these words, with their plain American spellings' (119). Whereas Sarah does not articulate a sense of national difference when in Canada, Jimroy begins to perceive himself as different in the United States, 'hear[ing] his own voice, priggish and full of Canadian vowel sounds' (83), becoming strange to himself in unfamiliar surroundings. Further, Jimroy posits others' perceptions of him as different, reading his Californian hosts as 'cheerful, intelligent friends who regard him, he knows, as a minion from the North, a role he fancies' (116). Outside the territory that delineates his citizenship, Jimroy imagines his nationality speaking for him.

On his re-entry into Canada, Jimroy explicitly refers to his citizenship during his exchange with the immigration officer in the film script:

IMMIGRATION OFFICER (bored): How long do you intend to be in Canada, Mr. Jimroy?

JIMROY (testily): Four days. And I happen to be a Canadian citizen, and I am not obliged to stand –

IMMIGRATION OFFICER (mechanically): Business or pleasure, Mr. Jimroy?

JIMROY (annoyed; he is a man who takes all questions seriously): Business. Pleasure. Both (He pauses; the immigration officer eyes him sharply.) A meeting. A symposium, to be precise. I will be attending a –

IMMIGRATION OFFICER: Nature of meeting? (He holds a rubber stamp in his hand.)

JIMROY: I resent this interrogation. As a Canadian citizen I am not required –

IMMIGRATION OFFICER: Meeting you say? Nature of which is? (302)

The immigration officer's first question implies that he mistakes Jimroy for a non-Canadian (most likely U.S.) citizen, given that he asks how long Jimroy will be in Canada, rather than how long he has been away. But Jimroy's assertion, 'I am not obliged to stand,' indicates that he has been waiting for some time to be processed through immigration, and that he is not legally required to so. Yet because all travellers, regardless of citizenship, must be processed through immigration, Jimroy posits rights that he does not actually possess, implying that his host (the immigration officer) is acting badly by acting as a host to Jimroy in the first place. When the immigration officer 'stamps the paper and hands it to Jimroy' (302), Jimroy is presumably entitled to enter Canada. But Jimroy wants to be welcomed home as a host who is not required to wait for a welcome, but to enter of his own volition. Jimroy's 'home' is unavoidably circumscribed by its political boundaries, the point of border crossing regulating host and guest status before permitting entry.

Jimroy's narrative presents a literal difficulty of crossing the world's longest undefended border, though, in part, he makes this experience difficult himself by failing to submit to the border guard's authority to assess host and guest status. To a certain extent, Jimroy's self-inflicted border-crossing trouble bears out Russell Brown's assertion that in Canadian novels, crossing the border is 'literally, as well as psychologically, difficult' (10). In contrast, Daisy's and Larry's narratives efface actual border crossings. Writing of *The Stone Diaries*, Gordon E. Slethaug emphasizes 'the various dislocations [Daisy] endured in moving from place to place in Canada and the United States' (72–3), but, in fact, the experience of dislocation goes unrepresented. Just as Daisy and her father are poised to cross the border, leaving Winnipeg following Cuyler's job offer from the Indiana Limestone Company, the narrative jumps ahead eleven years to the chapter 'Marriage, 1927.' The narrative ellipsis comprises the rest of Daisy's childhood, her adolescence, and her college education. Daisy's impending marriage to Harold Hoad appears to the reader through newspaper clippings that identify her as 'Miss Daisy Goodwill of Bloomington' (79), suggesting a realignment of her origins.

Although this realignment initially suggests that 'the border doesn't mean much' (Howells, *Contemporary* 81) to Shields's border-crossing protagonists, the representation of apparently easy transitions from Canada to the United States unravels on further investigation. Shields subtly but consistently exposes the circulation of cultural power within representations of Canada from an American perspective. In *The Stone Diaries*, the narrative voice undercuts the amnesia implied by the Americanized view of Daisy and her father: 'You should know that when Cuyler Goodwill speaks ... about "living in a progressive country" or "being a citizen of a proud, free nation," he is referring to the United States of America and not to the Dominion of Canada, where he was born and where he grew to manhood' (93). This description of Cuyler's new national affiliation elides both the psychological experience of migration and the legal process of becoming an American citizen. Cuyler has adopted a stereotypical – and stereotypically American – view of his nation of origin. The text's earlier, precise descriptions of Canadian locations, such as Winnipeg's 'wide, new boulevards' and 'an immense new legislative building in the neo-classical style' (68), give way to 'forests and lakes and large airy spaces ... [lying] now on the other side of the moon' (93) once Cuyler identifies himself as an American citizen.

The narrative voice fluctuates between aligning itself with these generalized images and puncturing them, sometimes through corrections consonant with Cuyler's perspective:

> There are educated Bloomingtonians – he meets them every day – who have never heard of the province of Manitoba, or if they have, they're unable to spell it correctly or locate it on a map. They think Ottawa is a town in south-central Illinois, and that Toronto lies somewhere in the northern counties of Ohio. It's as though a huge eraser has come down from the heavens and wiped out the top of the continent. (93)

The gap between Canadians' and Americans' knowledge about each others' countries has implications for relations of hospitality and hostility, relations which inform Shields's representation of both Canada for its own sake and an American version of Canada. Marshall McLuhan claims that 'the majority of Canadians are very grateful for the free use of American news and entertainment on the air and for the princely hospitality and neighbourly dialogue on the ground' (247). But although the acceptance of U.S. culture might be considered hospitable on the part of Canadian culture, this hospitality is twinned with hostility, as the economic advantage of American cultural endeavours often overwhelms Canadian cultural production, and American cultural presence in Canada is not reciprocated. Shields's image of an erased country questions national hospitality: can one nation be hospitable to another nation's culture if it does not acknowledge its presence, or indeed, its difference?

Cuyler's image of the top of the continent having been wiped out invokes the diverging conventions in Canadian and American newspaper weather maps. Eve Kosofsky Sedgwick employs the image of a weather map – minus the top of North America – to illustrate how the United States does not define itself in relation to Canada, whereas Canada includes the United States in its self-location. Comparing American newspaper weather maps to their Canadian counterparts, Sedgwick points out that 'the "same" experience at the Toronto airport turns out to be completely different' (149) from the American experience: whereas American 'weather maps ... bounded by the precise, familiar outlines of the forty-eight contiguous United States,' appear to 'naturaliz[e] the exclusion of Canada' and suggest 'that the North American continent drops off into the sea across the top of the United States,' in contrast, 'every ... Canadian newspaper [Sedgwick] has seen ... runs a weather map that extends southward at least as far as the Mason-Dixon line in the United States' (149), acknowledging the geographical and meteorological integrity of the two countries.

The idea of 'sameness' turning out to be 'different' underpins the cultural function of the Canada-U.S. border. As Lorraine Code explains, a Canadian can 'pass, almost always as a native speaker' (82) in the United States, her Canadianness indistinguishable from Americanness – 'as long,' Code admits, 'as [she doesn't] say "out" or "about"' (82). Her difference marked here by one vowel sound, Code acknowledges that distinctions between Canada and the United States range from 'mere variations in cultural *timbre,* inflection, intonation' to evidence of 'deep divisions in the histories that have made each of these two nations what they are, both locally and globally' (82). Erasure of difference implies no *need* for hospitality, that the Canada-U.S. border is 'both arbitrary and nondifferentiating' (Staines 2).

The question of what differences are noted, and by whom, configures cultural power and hospitality. Cuyler has adopted the United States as his nation, not just his site of habitation; no longer a guest, he has conformed to the cultural and national identity of the American host. Reintroducing Canada, the narrative voice states that Cuyler 'has not spent one minute grieving for his lost country,' then qualifies this assertion:

> That country, of course, is not lost at all, though news of the realm only occasionally reaches the Chicago and Indianapolis dailies. The newspaper-reading public of America, so preoccupied with its own vital and combustible ethos, can scarcely be expected to take an interest in the snail-like growth of its polite northerly neighbor, however immense, with its crotchety old king ... and the relatively low-temperature of its melting pot. Canada is a country where nothing seems ever to happen. A country always dressed in its Sunday go-to-meeting clothes. A country you wouldn't ask to dance a second waltz. (93)

Chicago's and Indianapolis's 'occasional' Canadian news contrasts sharply with McLuhan's characterization of Canadians' gratitude for 'the free use of American news and entertainment.' If 'nothing seems ever to happen' in Canada, is this inactivity mere perception? The feminizing image of Canada being asked to dance, waiting for another's invitation, echoes Margaret Atwood's assessment of Canada's having 'to play the female lead' (*Second* 389) in its relationship with the

United States. This description replicates stereotypical associations of Canada with dullness and passivity, combining them with exotic references: 'realm' makes the nation sound fantastical, scarcely imaginable – perhaps because it has been erased from the continent.

The novel's setting returns to Canada after Daisy's brief, disastrous first marriage. Daisy does not intend a permanent return to Canada; rather, she has simply been 'thinking of going on a trip' (131). She is tentative about her claim to Canada: '"I feel as though I'm on my way home," she wrote in her travel diary, then stroked the sentiment out, substituting: "I feel something might happen to me in Canada"' (132). Anticipating her visit, Barker Flett 'can picture Daisy darting about Bloomington, well dressed, nicely shod, prettily gloved, a healthy, hearty American girl' (154). Daisy herself has adopted some generalizations about Canada: 'A cool clean place, is how she thinks of it, with a king and queen and Mounties wearing red jackets and people drinking tea and speaking to one another in polite tones, never mind that these images do not accord in any way with her real memories of the hurly-burly of the Winnipeg schoolyard and the dust and horse turds of Simcoe Street' (133). Daisy's acquired stereotypes position her as an outsider, and she plans her 'modest, touristy' itinerary with the help of 'a pile of train schedules and travel booklets' (132). Daisy occupies the role of guest in her native country, her expectations shaped by promotional brochures: at Niagara Falls, 'she [is] not "seized with rapture" as the travel booklet ha[s] promised' (133).

Despite Daisy's renunciation of her claim to Canada as home, the narrative events lead to her renewed Canadian residence, as the chapter concludes with the rushed wedding of Daisy and Barker. Daisy's status as a tourist, an unmarried (or widowed) woman, an 'American,' and even her name change from one chapter to the next: after an eleven-year narrative ellipsis, Daisy appears now as 'Mrs. Flett,' at home *in* her home in Ottawa. The narrator announces, 'People the wide world over like to think of Canada as a land of ice and snow. That's the image they prefer to hang on to, even when they know better. But the fact is, Ottawa in the month of July can be hot as Hades' (157). Daisy might have formerly been included among those who imagine Canada to exist in perpetual winter, 'even when they know better.' At this point, however, as Mrs Flett, she has apparently shifted her nation and habitation once again.

Larry's Party articulates national difference, from a Canadian perspective, as a kind of afterthought. The Chicago maze commission prompts a change in both Larry's profession – he 'quit[s] his job as manager of a Flowercity outlet' (124) to become a full-time maze designer – and his national location. When Larry's mother identifies Chicago as 'a long, long way from home, and it's another country even' (125), distance supersedes national difference, but nation adds to the perception of distance: although Chicago is 'a thousand miles away [from] Winnipeg' (188), Larry might have moved such a distance within Canada. Similarly, when Larry characterizes himself as having 'lived in two cities, Winnipeg and Chicago. Make that two countries' (169), national difference occurs to him belatedly.

Once Larry has settled in Chicago, however, national difference is attributed to him, a Jimroy-like 'minion from the North':

> His voice . . . radiates an impression of calm, seasoned good will. Low tones predominate and respectful pauses, and these are generally, and generously, attributed to Larry's Canadian Background, since it's well known among his and Beth's good friends that he was born and brought up in the Canadian city of Winnipeg. Just where this city is located is less well known: somewhere *up there*, somewhere northerly, a representative piece of that polite, white, silent kingdom with its aging, jowly Queen and snowy mountain ranges and people sugaring off and drinking tea and casting for trout and nodding amicably – much as Larry nods at his neighbor across a backyard patio in Oak Park and sips his glass of California Chablis, and casts his glance fixedly up at the arch of maple boughs when asked for his views about the intentions of George Bush or about the exorbitant cost of National Public Radio. As for the politics of a universal health care plan, Larry is noticeably silent. (206)

Using strategies similar to those in *The Stone Diaries*, this passage invokes the different political histories of Canada and the United States, emphasizing Canada's place within the Commonwealth through reference to the queen and presenting this position as an exotic but outdated affiliation, as the fairytale connotation of 'kingdom' suggests. 'Snowy mountain ranges' provide generalizations about Canada through expansive natural features while the vagueness of 'somewhere *up there*' betrays an ignorance about Canadian geography. Associating Larry's silence on political matters with maple boughs might allude to his Canadian origins, but perhaps this link questions the simplistic perception of Larry's American friends, who mark him as different.

Larry's sense of affiliation with the United States develops gradually. Shortly after his cross-border move, 'Winnipeg [is] still his here and now ... even though he now [stands] in a living room in suburban Chicago' (154). Such references as 'Larry was back in Winnipeg just a month ago' (159) emphasize Larry's emigration from Canada, implying a return to a point of origin, both geographical and temporal. Later, Larry is described as 'formerly of Winnipeg, Canada' (210), the larger national, rather than provincial, context invoking an American perspective. The statement of Larry's having 'a twelve-year-old son up in Canada' (164) both erases Larry's emigration, positioning him as an American, and indicates only the vast country north of the United States.

Gendered Citizenship

Of Jimroy, Daisy, and Larry, only Jimroy explicitly articulates his citizenship; whether Daisy and Larry are single or dual citizens goes unreported. However, it is significant that many of Daisy's border crossings occur in the context of her relationship to a man: first, as Cuyler's daughter, moving to the United States; then, as part of her honeymoon with Harold; and although she visits Canada on her own terms after Harold's death, she moves back to Canada after marrying Barker. As Daisy's border crossings differ greatly from the professional opportunities that characterize the crossings of Jimroy, Cuyler, and Larry, Shields invites us to interrogate the distinctions between male and female citizenship duties.

The Stone Diaries, in particular, engages with gendered citizenship roles. As Caroline Andrew states, 'The basis of women's citizenship in Canada has been historically linked to their role as mothers, a fact that, at least in part, can be seen as an effort to exclude them from the public sector and confine them to the private realm' (323). Daisy fulfils her duty to the Canadian nation-state by giving birth to three children. Whereas women are seen to fulfil their citizenship duty through motherhood, men fulfil theirs as 'workers and soldiers' (Pateman 19); women risk their lives for their country through childbirth, men through combat. The Stone Diaries' narrative encompasses most of the twentieth century and refers to both world wars, in which none of the male characters participates. In Winnipeg, 'back in the bad old days of the Great War,' Clarentine profits when 'her wholesale flower enterprise unexpectedly prosper[s]' (127), implying that she both contributes to morale and profits from community grief through flowers for the war dead. Significantly, the text foregrounds Clarentine's success in 1916, the year Manitoban women won the right to vote: she therefore extends her fulfilment of the female citizen role by her business's role in the community.

In contrast, inactivity and lack of engagement characterize Barker's relationship to the war:

> The men of Wesley College, all except for Edward Wood, an epileptic, and tiny misshapen Clarence Redfield – forty-eight inches high with one foot bent out sideways – have put on the uniform of the Dominion and gone to war. Why is it that Professor Flett is not himself away fighting at the Front?
>
> Rumours abound. It is hinted that he is perhaps a pacifist, but one who has yet to declare himself. Or that he has a weakened heart . . . Or else his eyesight can scarcely be expected to confront the Kaiser. (42–3)

The possibilities that 'his ongoing work on new strains of wheat has been deemed crucial to the war effort,' or that he has been 'ruled ineligible' because of his 'support of his elderly mother and a young niece,' are also acknowledged, the latter version both 'favored' and 'true, or almost true' (43). Explanations of Barker's absence from the front are first invoked through potential physical ailments. Pacifism arises as a sickness or disturbing choice, regarding which Barker may not have 'outed' himself. The possibility of his research being 'crucial to the war effort' suggests essential service to the nation-state; however, his family provides the 'almost true' explanation, feminizing Barker from a larger social perspective, as this familial role keeps him from fulfilling the role of the male citizen. Moreover, Clarentine's business success undermines Barker's role of family support, indicating he is somewhat irrelevant.

During the Second World War, Barker is married to Daisy rather than trying to raise her, and is too old to fight, 'a man who's lived through two world wars and served in neither' (163–4). In fact, the novel most closely associates a female character with the military through Barker's niece, Beverly, who serves with the WRENS. Having 'just come back from England where she'd been "right in the thick of things,"' Beverly supplies the Flett children with war stories, 'telling them about the soldiers on D-day, flying missions in the darkness, dropping bombs on the enemy' (176). She becomes the example of military service to the nation-state and adopts the role of the male citizen. But as mother to

Victoria, Beverly also fulfils the traditional role of female citizenship. Indeed, the text provides far more examples of women fulfilling traditional citizenship through giving birth than of men fulfilling their citizenship duties through combat. Not only are several of the female characters mothers (e.g., Clarentine, Mercy, Daisy, Beverly, Alice, Joan), and have thereby risked their lives for the nation-state in the creation of new citizens, but Mercy, Daisy's mother, citizen of a nation-state decades away from introducing universal health care, also realizes this risk by dying in childbirth. Mercy's death highlights both the risks the other women run and the fact that none of the male characters fulfils the ultimate male citizenship duty.

If male citizenship also depends upon labour, Shields implicitly interrogates the lack of defining female citizenship along these lines through her representation of women's work. After Barker's death, Daisy takes up his gardening column for the *Ottawa Recorder*, renaming herself 'Mrs. Green Thumb' after Barker's 'Mr. Green Thumb' pseudonym. The column would not likely be considered crucial to the nation-state, unlike Barker's earlier work with the Dominion cerealist, with its implied national importance; as a civil servant, Barker presumably labours in the interests of public good. But the positioning of 'Work, 1955–1965,' in which Daisy appears as 'Mrs. Green Thumb,' directly after 'Motherhood, 1947,' suggests a pairing of public acknowledgments of Daisy's roles, one not present in such headings as 'Childhood,' 'Love,' 'Sorrow,' etc.

The 'Work' chapter, comprised of letters written to Daisy, entirely excludes her voice, relying on the perspectives of almost everyone else in the text. Naming becomes especially important here, for none of the letters is addressed to 'Daisy': although she is called a litany of different names ('Mrs. Flett,' 'Auntie,' 'Daze,' 'Mother,' 'D.'), most often Daisy is addressed as 'Mrs. Green Thumb,' a persona arguably more constructed than Daisy's other roles, but nonetheless vital to her. Alice states, 'Work and self cannot be separated' (242); Daisy's public self, 'Mrs. Green Thumb,' cannot exist without her work. Alice credits Daisy's gardening column with making her 'a different person, a person who worked. Who worked "outside the home," as people said in those quaint days, though, in fact, she did her writing under our own roof' (237). Although Daisy does not work in a public space, she reaches a public audience, which grants her a public identity. The fragility of this public status becomes clear when Daisy loses her job to a competing male journalist, after which she is 'back to being Mrs. Flett again'

(240); the depression that follows constitutes a mourning period, grieving the loss of her 'Mrs. Green Thumb' identity.

Daisy's loss of her column apparently damages her personal happiness, but there is no mention of how it affects her financially. Her
son, Warren, identifies Daisy as 'a middle-aged woman, a middle-class
woman, a woman of moderate intelligence and medium-sized ego
and average good luck' (252). Daisy's hardship has only been relative,
but despite her privilege, her possibilities have been limited because
of her gender: 'She is powerless, anchorless, soft-tissued – a woman.
Perhaps that is the whole of it, that she is a woman. Yes, of course'
(150). Shortly after she has 'this flash of insight' (151), Daisy arrives
in Ottawa and will marry Barker. She lives out her social limitations,
marrying because marriage is available to her, becoming a mother and
thereby fulfilling her role as female citizen. Only Barker, working with
the Dominion cerealist, and Cuyler, through his involvement in constructing various public buildings and monuments in the United States,
enjoy explicit links between their work and civic acknowledgment. The
labour of these male characters is considered significant to their respective nation-states, while the female characters, as florists, columnists,
gallery managers (Fraidy), or domestic workers (Cora-Mae Milltown),
and even Alice as an academic, are not socially acknowledged as such,
not the privileged citizens of the liberal democratic nation-state.

Canadian In/hospitality

If Daisy's gender qualifies her citizenship, she nevertheless enjoys economic privilege and belongs to the dominant definition of Canadianness through her ethnic-majority identity. *Swann*, *The Stone Diaries*, and
Larry's Party all undermine the notion of Canadian hospitality through
narratives focusing on immigrant experiences that are not contained by
Canada-U.S. border crossing, where difference is readily perceived *as*
difference and therefore excluded from the host position.

In *Swann*, Frederic Cruzzi is described as an 'intellectual nomad':
'Retired newspaper editor Frederic Cruzzi of Grenoble, Casablanca,
Manchester, and Kingston, Ontario, aged eighty, is such a [nomad] –
equally at home grafting an apple tree or poaching a salmon or reading
a page of Urdu poetry or writing one of his newspaper columns on the
diabolism of modern technology' (219). Cruzzi's multiple locations of
origin indicate a cosmopolitan status, as he has been a welcome guest
the world over, successfully negotiating strangeness: '... he spent a

number of years travelling and testing the shock of strangeness in such places as Morocco (a second home to him), Turkey, India, Japan, and the United States (the world being in those days, before the invention of work visas and inflation, more accessible, more welcoming)' (228). The reference to work visas highlights the limited hospitality of nation-states seeking to protect their economy and regulate access to their territory.

Cruzzi's relationship to Canadianness, as defined by the Kingston community, exemplifies hostipitality. When Cruzzi and Hildë emigrate to Canada, 'where they naively believed they might keep a foothold on the French language' (229), they are presumably welcomed within the boundaries of the nation-state. But their cosmopolitan position, coupled with their tastes, compromises their claims to Canadianness in the eyes of Cruzzi's newspaper readers, demonstrating the fracture between national belonging and legal citizenship. The overtly xenophobic out-cry over Cruzzi's cancellation of 'The Poet's Corner' seeks to Other Cruzzi in order to undermine his judgment: 'He was labelled a philis-tine and a brute journalist of the modern school. The word foreigner was invoked: Frenchy, Limey, Wog – there was understandable confu-sion here' (252). Although the 'understandable confusion' stems from Cruzzi's multiple habitations, the range of epithets indicates that *any* assignation of difference will do to undermine Cruzzi 'with his heavy tweed suits and strangely unbarbered hair, his queer way of talking, his manners and pronouncements' (252). After reinstating 'The Poet's Corner,' Cruzzi becomes integrated into the community; in particular, 'he and Hildë befrien[d] and gr[o]w fond of the local poets' (253). But the earlier reaction of the community, and the exclusive, national terms used, indicates a precarious hospitality. The Cruzzis become more welcome, more legitimated as hosts, because they involve themselves in the production of Canadian culture when they establish Peregrine Press. When 'their second poet . . . the elegant Glen Forrestal of Ottawa, later [wins] a Governor General's Award' (255), the press is located within state-supported national celebration. Such an external recogni-tion and location of the press within a national framework combines with increasing affiliation: Hildë announces, '"Whatever we decide to publish must have a new sound." She said this in a voice that contained more and more of the sonorous Canadian inflection' (255).

In *The Stone Diaries*, Abram Skutari, the figure of difference to whom the community responds with hostility, is not an intellectual nomad, but a religious Other. Skutari enters the narrative through a larger dominant social perspective, and through Clarentine Flett's point of view, as 'the old Jew' (22): 'His arrival is everywhere dreaded, for almost invariably he asks for the refreshment of coffee or a swallow of cold water, and then there are the cups and glassware to be scalded after him' (20). The expectation of or request for hospitality appears monstrous – 'You hear that knock and you know who it is' (21) – eliciting hostility and a suggestion of violence needed to erase evidence of hospitality.

Initially, Clarentine's perspective seems aligned with this larger social response. She 'pull[s] herself away from him, feeling faint with disgust,' but then 'unaccountably longs to reach out and touch' the sore on his lip (21). Through Clarentine's attempts to fill in Skutari's context, the text begins to explore his position in Canada:

> She wonders ... if the old Jew might possibly have relations somewhere in the neighborhood, a roof, a warm stove, a bed of his own to return to. If so, he might also have a woman's body next to his under the bedclothes, and a sack of loose blue flesh between his legs like every other man. These thoughts are repellent, she must shift her gaze to what is wholesome and good. And a name, of course, he must have a name, you can't enter this country and become a citizen without a name. Two or three names perhaps. Unpronounceable. Unspellable. (22)

Unlike Derrida's assertion that absolute hospitality occurs 'before any *identification*' (*Of Hospitality* 77), the nation-state demands a name for entry and citizenship. But Clarentine also betrays her construction of Skutari's Otherness: she must *imagine* his foreignness, as the speculations surrounding his name indicate; 'repellent' thoughts are the responsibility of Clarentine, who thinks them, rather than Skutari, their object. After the reader learns of attempts to exclude Skutari from the community, Clarentine accommodates his position in the nation, or at least acknowledges it by her assumption that he is a 'citizen.' He has entered the country, and therefore, at least legally, been offered hospitality, though not welcomed by the local community.

Later, we learn 'the old Jew's' name, Abram Gozhdë Skutari, his age (thirty-four), and his origin ('born in the Albanian village of Prizren'), as well as a condensed narrative of his ancestry 'back to the fifteenth century' (37). Whether Clarentine also ultimately discovers these details goes unreported, but her identification of Skutari as a citizen is significant nonetheless. Given that Canadian citizenship did not exist until 1947, it does not operate at the time of Daisy's birth (1905), when

Clarentine considers Skutari's position; but the term clearly indicates legally legitimated belonging. Throughout the text, Shields uses 'citizen' most often in reference to immigrants: Cuyler considers himself an American citizen; Clarentine positions Skutari as a citizen in Canada; and the narrative voice describes 'seven hundred settlers, representing nearly every European nationality, [who] reached Montreal last week, arriving abroad four rather motley steamers: the *Letitia*, the *Athiaunia*, the *Pennland*, the *Bergenfjord*. But what difference, you say, can a mere seven hundred citizens make in all that vastness? A grain of sand added to a desert. A teaspoon of water dribbled into the ocean' (93–94). The word 'difference' both emphasizes the contrast between the vastness of the land mass and its sparse population, and functions as a reminder of cultural difference, of the degrees to which these immigrants will be perceived to belong.

But although the reference to citizenship insists upon the immigrants' right to habitation, 'what difference' can be made to how the nation constructs itself? Like *In the Skin of a Lion*, *The Stone Diaries* repeatedly uses the word 'Dominion' to refer to Canada. We are told, for example, that 'the Dominion is growing' (93). In his discussion of post-war constructions of Canadian identity, Philip Resnick includes 'the waning use of the term "Dominion" by Canadian governments' in the second half of the twentieth century amongst the examples of Canada's loosening its ties to Britain (288). During the earlier part of *The Stone Diaries'* narrative, however, this cultural shift has yet to take place, and the use of 'Dominion' indicates that Canada's self-construction operates largely through British cultural referents. Thus, the influx of immigration, 'representing nearly every European nationality,' has not yet 'made a difference' to official constructions of Canadian nationhood, although the fact that these new citizens are of varying national origins undermines these official constructions.

Larry's Party offers a British immigration narrative, one that both troubles the equation between Englishness and English-Canadianness and confirms Anglo-chauvinism in Canada. In this novel, hospitality negotiates difference from both outside and within the country. The text identifies Canada's dominant cultural constructions through the translation of Larry's parents, immigrants from England, from guest to host status. The dramatic emigration narrative follows Dot Weller's accidental fatal poisoning of her mother-in-law at a family dinner: 'Murder was the word Dad Weller used. Even, *deliberate* murder' (51). Her father-in-law's 'finger of blame' (51) drives Dot and her family to emigrate: '. . . for

Larry, who was born just two months after his parents settled in Winnipeg, the flight from the home country has the flavor of Old Testament exodus' (52). The 'home country,' the family's origin, is no longer 'home,' and Dot can no longer fill a 'host' status in England, both in superficial terms (through the disastrous dinner) and in the more profound sense of being unwelcome in her own country.

The Wellers, although foreign-born, are not too foreign to be assimilated, for the most part, into dominant constructions of the Canadian host. But they occasionally mark their difference in their use of language:

> ... after all this time they still say railway, for example, instead of railroad. Larry's mother calls her kitchen stove a cooker, and Larry's dad says petrol instead of gasoline. Larry wouldn't dream of saying railway or cooker or petrol himself, but the words coming out of his parents' mouths ... give his heart, every time he hears them, a twist of happiness, as though his fumbling, stumbling mother and father have, if nothing else, improvised for themselves a crude shelter in an alien land. They can hide there. Be themselves, whatever that means. (89)

Larry's parents' guest status continues in this sense, their use of language signalling their immigration and incomplete assimilation. The 'crude shelter in an alien land' emphasizes the relationship between language and hospitality while underscoring the fact that his parents *are* alien, that their 'being themselves' differs from the way in which individuals more 'recognizable' as Canadian would be themselves.

The emphasis on the Wellers' difference also strategically undermines Larry's father's assessments of difference within Canada. Not only does Stu Weller tell offensive jokes about 'Newfies' and 'Frenchies' (58), but he also assumes a position of judging foreignness:

> When Larry was a kid his mother was forever listening to the radio ... and sometimes, out of curiosity, she stopped the dial at a place where foreign languages came curling out of the radio's plastic grillwork: Italian or Portuguese or Polish, they were all the same to Larry, full of squawks and spit and kicking sounds.
>
> 'Jibber jabber,' Larry's father called this talk, shaking his head, apparently convinced, despite all reason, that these 'noises' meant nothing, that they were no more than a form of elaborate nonsense ... These foreigners were just pretending to talk, trying to fool everyone.

Larry knows better. Everyone in the world walks around with a supply
of meaningful words inside their heads. (88)

Stu, whose English origins correspond to dominant definitions of Canadianness, adopts a host position in his relegation of Italian-, Portuguese-,
and Polish-Canadians to the status of unwelcome guests. His anxiety
about foreignness emerges in his suspicion that those who do not speak
English are 'trying to fool everyone,' their difference unreadable to him.
The description of Larry's parents' own linguistic differences, which
follows Stu's dismissal of other languages as 'jibber jabber,' undercuts
Stu's exclusive assertion of the host position, serving as a reminder that
he too has had to negotiate his way out of a guest position in Canada,
that his own identity is hyphenate.

Trading in North America/nness

Although these novels negotiate Canadian identity through internal difference, they also do so through posited sameness in relation to North
America. Stephen Henighan characterizes *The Stone Diaries* as 'the flag-
ship novel of Free Trade Fiction,' accusing the novel of 'preach[ing] an
untroubled, ahistorical North Americanism in which Canadians plac-
idly assimilate into continental (i.e., U.S.) norms,' and asserting that 'it
can hardly be a coincidence that this book was one of the most popular works of fiction in both Canada and the U.S. . . . during the months
in which NAFTA was implemented' (184). Although I disagree with
Henighan's reading of North Americanness in *The Stone Diaries*, the
framing of Shields's work in relation to continental economics offers
other, more productive, critical possibilities. *Swann* and *Larry's Party*, in
particular, respond to the complications of a North American identity
and its attendant anxieties. Along with *The Stone Diaries*, these two novels
thematize, rather than advocate, Canadian assimilation into the continent, as attested to by the complexities of Shields's border-crossing narratives and her representation of how Canadianness is constructed from
a U.S. perspective that strips Canadianness of its cultural power. *Swann*
and *Larry's Party* especially illustrate the pitfalls of 'post-nationalism,'
the earlier text echoing concerns about the future of Canadian culture
post-FTA and *Larry's Party* returning its protagonist home to Canada in
a reinsertion of the nation between the local and the global.

Swann was published the year the Free Trade Agreement between
Canada and the United States was signed. On the one hand, cross-border
trade might indicate hospitality, an invitation to border crossing. As

Georg Cavallar writes, 'Commerce, often also called "merchandise," has a narrow meaning, where it is identical with trade and business. Its broader meaning encompasses any form of interaction, communication, and interchange among humans, for instance of ideas' (71); indeed, Kant looked to commercial trade to bring about a 'form of sociability' (Cheah 290). On the other hand, however, even if the logic of Kant's arguments suggests that 'commercial relationships cross the world, just as nature intended' and that 'the guarantee of perpetual peace is therefore actually commercial globalization' (Foucault, *Biopolitics* 58), Kant did acknowledge that states engage in trade through 'their mutual self-interest,' rather than from 'motives of "morality"' (*Perpetual* 114) or ideals of hospitality. In particular, trade agreements between Canada and the United States, and the fraught discussion surrounding them, undermine and interrogate a sense of trade shaped by hospitality. That these agreements do not equally benefit the nation-states involved and 'appea[r] to have increased the power asymmetry between the hegemon ... and its neighbours' (Clarkson 42) compromises the notion of hospitality and partnership through trade.

Although all of *Swann*'s four main characters – Jimroy, Sarah, Rose, and Cruzzi – are complicit in various ways in obscuring or destroying the truth about Mary Swann, regardless of their national identities, the process of the attempted canonization that unfolds effaces the nation. Ultimately, the symposium results in the eradication of Swann's text. Some critics of Shields's novel have argued that the academics attempt to secure Swann's position within a Canadian canon. Brian Johnson contends that one of Sarah's and Jimroy's motives is 'to insert her into the canon of Canadian Literature by proving that she is not the *poète naïf* contemporary criticism makes her' (64). Faye Hammill extends this argument, reading the novel as a critique of national literatures that 'exposes the meaningless way in which national labels are tacked on to writing, thus effectively delimiting its capacity to signify outside fixed patterns of interpretation' (89). Certainly, as Hammill argues, Kurt Wiesmann's difficulty in finding a publisher – which ultimately results in the Cruzzis founding their own press – suggests the potential rigidity of national criteria: '... publishers in Canada found Wiesmann's poems "too European"; American publishers thought them "too Canadian," and a British publisher sensed "an American influence that might be troubling" to his readers' (*Swann* 254). These publishers fail either to encourage or to perceive a hospitality of reading, deeming national literature an exclusive category, not on the basis of the poet's actual nationality, but rather on the basis of how the work appears to fall into another nation's seemingly monolithic aesthetic. However, Wiesmann is ultimately hailed as 'a fresh new Canadian voice' (255) in a Toronto newspaper: after publication, Wiesmann's reviewers take his nationality for granted, rather than judge him against a prescriptive national standard.

Swann's work, too, is largely read by the academic characters in a manner that either takes her nationality for granted or ignores it. Whereas Hammill contends that the novel's academics 'insist on forcing her work to fit established but uncongenial patterns of "Canadian literature"' (87), I would argue that the reading trends of the academics detract from the context of Canadian literature. Although Sarah reads Swann 'in terms of the dominant theme of survival' (Hammill 89), implying an Atwood-based Canadian context, Sarah's use of survival diverges from Atwood's: in contrast to Atwood's diagnosis of Canadian literature's fixation with victimhood and survival, Sarah is concerned with the positions of survivor and victim for women in no particular national context. Sarah identifies Swann as a survivor (curious in itself, given Swann's brutal murder by her husband) because she is 'a woman . . . , self-created' (32).

Sarah occasionally invokes Canadian literary critical discourse, referring briefly to 'the garrison mentality' (18), Northrop Frye's diagnosis of the Canadian condition in the *Literary History of Canada;* however, Sarah uses the term to describe not Canadian literature but the 'pretensions' of scholarship (18). She exhibits no knowledge of Canada, much less its literature. Her discovery of Swann's poems in Wisconsin betrays geographical and cultural generalizations about Canada: 'How Mary Swann's book found its way down from Canada to a cottage on a lonely Wisconsin lake was a mystery, *is* a mystery. A case of obscurity seeking obscurity' (13–14). Swann's location in rural Ontario perhaps suggests a degree of obscurity, but Sarah refers to Canada as a whole, in contrast with her own more precise location of a Wisconsin lake. More importantly for a discussion of national literature, Sarah, unlike readers of Shields's novel (see Addison 159; Atwood, 'To the Light House,' 28) who link the biographical details of Pat Lowther and Mary Swann, mentions no other Canadian poets.

Similarly, the symposium itself, despite being 'organized to canonize the poetry of Mary Swann' (Godard, 'Sleuthing' 61), does not address the Canadian canon; in fact, gestures towards Swann's Canadianness are often undermined. Willard Lang's introduction to Jimroy's paper does label Swann an 'obscure Canadian poet' (325), but this national location of Swann contrasts with that of Jimroy's previous subjects, American poets Ezra Pound and John Starman. Lang refers to Pound and Starman as 'giants of our literature' (325), the possessive 'our' presumably not an indication of nationality, unless Lang writes over his own nationality, and the nationality of all non-Americans in the audience, with Americanness. Lang appears either to attempt to elevate Swann to the status of a North American or international literary figure, or to efface her Canadianness, as well as the Canadianness of any Canadians in the audience.

Jimroy further undercuts the identification of Swann with Canadian literature by declaring that Swann is 'always referred to as "a Canadian poet," but I suggest the time has come to leave off this modifier and to spring her free of the bolted confines of regionalism. Hers is an international voice' (327). Whereas Rose reads Swann's work in local terms – for instance, linking one of Swann's water poems to the fact 'that there's no well out there on the Swann property' (183) – Jimroy asserts Swann's transcendence of national (which he conflates with regional) significance. Jimroy suggests that a national reading limits Swann's significance, but no national reading of her work has been presented in the first place. Thus, although Shields has demonstrated the hostilities of national aesthetics, as perceived by the publishers who reject Wiesmann, she also presents hostilities of reading that exclude the national in order to read for one's own gain. The characters (including the Cruzzis, who have recreated the manuscript after its accidental deterioration) make Swann in the image of their own reading practices, and preclude her from being what serves them no purpose. Jimroy's declaration of Swann as international rather than Canadian puts her on the same footing as Pound and Starman, likely increasing his readership.

The symposium is hosted in Canada, but its hotel location suggests a neutral, non-national space, where all those present are guests. To a certain extent, the hosts are those who have organized the symposium proceedings, but the fact that they all stay in the hotel puts everyone on a more or less equal (paying) guest footing, the space and staff of the hotel acting as hosts in the 'commercial logic that governs hotels,' where this kind of hospitality 'imitates the signs of generosity' for commercial gain (Rosello 34). Frank Davey notes that 'voyages, air flights, and international hotels' (*Post-national* 259) characterize 'post-national' anglophone-Canadian literature. In *Swann*, the non-national space of the hotel, which acts as host to a symposium largely seeking to write Swann out of her Canadianness, functions as a cautionary tale, particularly if we consider the novel's publication the year that FTA was signed. The symposium represents the ultimate commercial gain alongside the ultimate destruction of culture when Brownie manages to steal all remaining copies of *Swann's Songs*. As Sarah acknowledges, '... there's no Swann industry if there are no texts' (381). Similarly, opponents of FTA worried that there can be no national literature if Canada's cultural industries are left vulnerable to free trade agreements with the United States. While some have since argued that 'the cultural threat' of U.S. economic power 'has receded' (Cavell 29), others note that 'increasingly, international trade regimes place substantial limits on the ability of the Canadian state to influence the production and diffusion of culture within its borders' (Godard, 'Notes' 226).

Whereas *Swann* implicitly represents North Americanness, *Larry's Party* explicitly frames Canada within the continent. Shields frequently invokes North America, but, crucially, she does so largely with reference to Canadian settings and characters. Winnipeg, where Larry's father works 'for a custom coach company ... , the largest of its kind in North America' (53), is described as 'the windiest city in the country, in North America' (13), suggesting the city is equally North American and Canadian. These insertions of Canadian locations and characters into a continental framework imply that Canada's self-perception includes and inserts itself within an idea of North America, and that Canada cannot forget continental relations and their imbalances of power.

Larry's Party takes place during negotiations of the Canada–U.S. Free Trade Agreement, NAFTA (1994), and the (ultimately unsuccessful) Free Trade Area of the Americas (FTAA). The novel repeatedly invokes shifting economies and locates Larry within a global economic framework. Larry has been working 'at Flowerfolks for twelve years' when 'all twelve Flowerfolks stores [are] swallowed up by Flowercity, the California-based multinational' (61). This takeover occurs in 1981, eight years before the ratification of FTA, but the American origin of the multinational, coupled with the apparent powerlessness of the chain being 'swallowed up,' suggests Canadian fears of U.S. economic invasion. Flowercity is not the chain's last incarnation: five years later, it is 'taken over by Flower Village, a Japanese conglomerate' (126). This shift increases the scale of international economics and invokes the discourse of globalization through the name 'Flower Village,' gesturing towards McLuhan's global village. The 'city' of Flowercity ostensibly becomes more intimate, as 'village' implies, yet the global economics that have effected the change in name compromise this suggestion.

Larry's florist work highlights the relationship between production and consumption, foregrounding a global circulation of goods through 'the gingers [that] get shipped to Manitoba from South Africa, freesia from Holland, and carnations from California' (74). The tracing of these flowers back to their origins demonstrates a globalized network of trade within which Larry locates himself and his access to the rest of the world: 'He's part of the action, part of the world's work' (77). As the description of the alstroemeria's growth suggests, this consciousness of 'the world's work' arises largely through awareness of Canada's hemispheric location (itself owing significantly to the development of NAFTA and negotiations of the FTAA):

> This flower, an herb really, started out as a seed way down in South America in Colombia. Some Spanish-speaking guy, as Larry imagines him, harvested the seeds of this flower and someone else put it back into the earth, carefully, using his hands probably, to push the soil in place. They earned their daily bread doing that, fed their families, kept themselves alert. It's South American rain that drenches the Colombian earth and foreign sunshine that falls on the first green shoots, and it all happens, it all works. (76)

This passage uses Shields's technique of locating Canada in vague, generalized terms to indicate U.S. ignorance. Here, however, a Canadian struggles with details about Colombia: whereas Canada is 'up there' in relation to the United States, South America, for Larry, is 'way down' from Canada.

Larry expands the alstroemeria narrative, supplementing his initial, romanticized image of a Spanish-speaking man and acknowledging his own ignorance, thus bearing out Carlos Fuentes's claim that 'every North American, before this century is over, will find that he or she has a personal frontier with Latin America' (8). Although this frontier 'can be starved by suspicion, ghost stories, arrogance, ignorance, scorn and violence' (8), Larry attempts to imagine beyond his ignorance and reflects on his relationship to the 'Spanish-speaking laborers equipped with hoes arriv[ing] to beat back the weeds, but are they men or women who do this work? Maybe both, and maybe children, too, in that part of the world' (76). Larry recognizes the disjunction between the locations of production and consumption, wondering whether the Colombian labourers,

> when they perform this tedious and backbreaking work ... have any idea ... that [the flowers] will be transported across international frontiers, sorted, sold, inspected, sold again, and that ... they will come to rest in the hands of a young Canadian male in an ordinary mid-continental florist establishment, bringing with them a spot of organic color in a white and frozen country. (76)

Despite its vague assumptions, Larry's alstroemeria narrative strives towards some specificity and the recognition of the implications of global capitalism as it tears open the false seamlessness of capitalist production and consumption; that Larry wonders at all about production breaks the illusion of absent labour. Further, it demonstrates Canada's relationship not only with the United States, but also with South American countries, more easily marked as 'different' from Canada in climate, language, and economic privilege. As the global economy largely regards the South as a 'low-wage, low-skilled labor market' (Deibert 147), 'global interconnectedness' does not counteract 'the persistence of North-South divisions' and 'the asymmetry of power relations' (Slater 194). Whereas Gloria Anzaldúa describes the U.S.-Mexico border as a location 'where the Third World grates against the first and bleeds' (25), Shields depicts Canada as another such location, not at a physical border but within Larry's consciousness.

If 'North America' signifies differently in Canada than in the United States, the novel also problematizes dominant Canadian conceptions of this continent that includes Mexico. The alstroemeria narrative posits an opposition between North and South America, based on Larry's imagining linguistic and economic differences that displace 'Spanish-speaking labourers' out of North America. Larry's consideration of the alstroemeria, coupled with the novel's concern with global economics, punctures the exclusive view of North America while including Canada within a larger context of the Americas. The novel thereby invokes exclusive constructions of North America and subtly argues in favour of 'making' the continent three countries, not two.

Despite its representation of an increasingly globalizing economy, and the concomitant implications for the nation-state's authority, *Larry's Party* both explores the networks of a globalizing planet and reasserts the nation-state's presence. On the one hand, this text resonates with many of

Davey's contentions in *Post-national Arguments*, sharing with the novels studied the 'various discourses of intimacy, home, and neighbourhood, together with others of global distance and multinational community' (258). The reintroductions of Larry at the beginning of each chapter foreground his local communities, particularly Winnipeg. Gradual addition of detail fills in the particulars of his house, friends, family, and neighbourhood even as his florist work exposes him to globalization. Further, Larry's mobility, afforded him by the Guggenheim fellowship (allowing him to travel to Ireland, Britain, continental Europe, Japan, and Australia) and his transatlantic marriage to Beth, invokes those 'voyages, air flights, and international hotels' associated with post-national literature. On the other hand, whereas Davey finds the 'post-national' novels lacking in 'constructions of region, province, and nation' and 'any social geography that can be called "Canada"' (*Post-national* 259), *Larry's Party* reinserts the nation between the local and the global. Larry's work both depends upon local specificity – the McCord maze in Toronto, for instance, requires 'five-leaf aralia (tolerates polluted air well)' and 'ninebark, which bears up against wind and cold' (289) – and can transcend the local in terms of his administrative base: 'He could do his maze design work and consulting from any major city in North America' (259). But if Larry can live anywhere on the continent, 'he finally chooses to settle in Toronto and be a Canadian' (Colvile 90). Although Davey observes that in 'the Prairie pattern of meaning ... Toronto signifies exploitive business practices' (21), *Larry's Party* does not present Toronto as contentious for its Winnipeg-born and bred protagonist. National identification overrides regional rivalry: 'This is Canada, that cold crested country with its changeable weather and staunch heart' (290).

The novel consolidates the reinscription of nation through Larry's hospitalization during his coma, when his renewed host status in Canada, his 'at-home-ness,' carries practical implications. Where *Swann* uses the hotel as a space devoid of national meaning and culture, one of costly, empty hospitality, *Larry's Party* privileges the hospital, both as a marker of distinction between Canada and the country that shares its border and as a site that merges hospitality with healing. *Larry's Party* implicitly reintroduces the nationally circumscribed debate about medicare, to which Larry does not contribute in Chicago, by making him the recipient of medicare delivered in Toronto. Although Shields provides minute details of Larry's hospital stay – 'Hundreds of hands had touched him during the twenty-two-day period of his unconsciousness' (283) – she tellingly stays silent about the cost of this 'meticulous care and almost constant surveillance' (282); 'the TV that Midge had rented' (272) constitutes the only aspect of Larry's hospitalization with a cost at the point of delivery. In contrast, *The Stone Diaries* declares of Daisy's Florida hospitalization for an emergency double bypass and a cancerous kidney removal that 'Blue Cross covers almost everything' (316).

Given *hospitality*'s etymological connections to *hospital*, Larry's host status upon his move to Toronto fittingly effects his reinitiation into Canada's universal medicare. Larry's recovery both rests on and reinforces his interpellation as a Canadian, as indicated by the televised coverage of the 1996 Olympic Games in Atlanta, which he watches from his hospital bed. Although Larry has woken from his coma and is 'seduced ... back to life' (273) by his hospital meals, he does not fully rejoin the world until 'the Olympic Games, finally, beamed from Atlanta, Georgia ... sav[e] him' (273). A 'carnival of muscle and precision' brings Larry 'back to his own body,' but 'watching Donovan Bailey run the hundred meter dash and take the gold medal' (274) particularly effects Larry's recovery, as indicated by his celebration with his friend Bill:

> ... they filled the room with little yips of joy. Bill whipped off his T-shirt, waving it like a flag over his head, and performed a mad hopping dance at the foot of the bed, two hundred pounds of gesticulating male flesh, and Larry, still connected to his tubes and wires, felt the bright juice of euphoria surge through his deadened tissues. Breath, beginnings. He was on the mend ... He was alive again in the housing of his skin and blood, and for the moment that was enough. (274)

Whereas Larry's hospitalization emphasizes the state's role, implicitly arguing both that 'states still perform essential functions' (Deibert 213) and that health-care delivery remains an essential function despite 'the attack by market-identified forces on the social protective power of the nation-state' (Angus 20), Bailey's victory arouses Larry's national affiliation, appealing to and reinforcing his emotional attachment to Canada. Shields never mentions Bailey's Canadianness, but she does not need to for Canadian readers, who surely supply the national implications of Larry and Bill's celebration and read national significance into the simile of the flag.

Reception and Categorizations

Larry's celebration of Bailey's victory enacts a national positioning of himself, an assertion of his location following his series of cross-border migrations. Similarly, Shields's work has been consistently positioned and repositioned, in relation to both national and aesthetic classifications, a process that has been echoed in both the kinds of celebrations her work has attracted and in responses to those celebrations. If *Swann* implicitly introduces a debate about national literature within its narrative, then outside the text, this novel was also Shields's first to be inserted into the context of national literary celebration. For some critics, *Swann* represented an aesthetic departure from Shields's earlier novels. Geoff Hancock, for instance, characterizes her previous books as 'well written, and certainly intelligent, but they flirted with the very tedium of ordinary life she tried to describe' (C9).

This 'ordinariness' may be partly responsible for the ongoing association of Shields with the middlebrow, although this association is by no means unanimous amongst critics. Although the term 'middlebrow' functions 'less as a static categorization than as a dynamic fluctuating between competing forces of cultural respect and economic success' (York 22), I am also interested here in the spectrum of categorizations that have been attached to Shields, even to the same texts. When *The Stone Diaries* was nominated for the Booker Prize, responses ranged from the assertion that she had not 'received anywhere near the recognition she deserves' (Yanofsky, 'From the Authentic' J15) to the claim that Shields, 'a middle-brow sort of writer,' constituted a 'puzzling' (Wordsworth S8) presence on the Booker shortlist. With respect to *The Stone Diaries*, not all critics agreed that 'Shields is an artist of the highest degree' (A. Craig 30), suggesting not only an interrogation of awards juries' taste, but also a slipperiness of taste: there is no clear consensus as to whether Shields fits into the middlebrow category in the first place. The fact that 'Shields's fiction has focused on the common, almost banal events of middle-class, middle-age [*sic*] characters' ('Carol Shields 1935–' 394) suggests a relation between subject matter and the classification, by some, of Shields as middlebrow, as 'Shields's diligent and often comic anatomization of the mundane, homely world has prompted both amusement and irritation from critics' (Dvořák and Jones 4). Araminta Wordsworth, who concurs with Shields's middlebrow classification, declares her 'an endangered species in Canada, where the difficult etc. vogue is full cry [*sic*] and to be accessible is not necessarily an asset. She produces sensitive, thoughtful novels about ordinary people, done with a great deal of craft' (S8). Wordsworth implies an association of the middlebrow with audience and accessibility, and, indeed, Bourdieu identifies accessibility as one of the middlebrow's characterizing features, as it comprises 'accessible versions' (*Distinction* 323) of aesthetic experimentation.

But reviews of *Larry's Party*, generally positive but almost unanimously positioning this novel as a lesser work in relation to *The Stone Diaries*, retroactively bestowed a highbrow status upon the earlier novel. Writing for the *Dallas Morning News*, Jerome Weeks declares that 'one of the achievements' of *The Stone Diaries* 'is its ability to entrance highbrows and average readers' (43A), implying that the high-culture status of *The Stone Diaries* does not compromise its accessibility, or vice versa. Mark Schechner in the *Jerusalem Post* claims that *Larry's Party* 'lacks the former book's comprehensive vision of life ... But one finds bursts of sunstruck clarity here and a steady, confident humanity, and even a book off the back burner – Shields lite – has pleasures to offer' (21). Schechner articulates his praise for *Larry's Party* in negative terms, by what the novel is *not*: not *The Stone Diaries*; lacking, 'weak'; 'a book off the back burner.' Nonetheless, the book 'has pleasures to offer,' perhaps too much pleasure and not enough difficulty. Michael Dirda of the *Washington Post* also focuses on 'the great deal of pleasure' presented by *Larry's Party*, while acknowledging that 'to say that a novel is extremely enjoyable may seem like faint praise,' but that *Larry's Party* 'is, before anything else, just that' (1). Assessments of *Larry's Party* as a 'feel-good novel' (Stoffman, 'Life' D1) and of Shields's writing style as 'so charming, so readable' (Walter 14) imply a relegation of the material to the middlebrow after the highbrow success of *The Stone Diaries*. Evaluations of the pleasure and enjoyment offered by *Larry's Party* imply that this novel is easier, more accessible, less demanding than a novel such as *The Stone Diaries*. 'Shields lite' invokes the language of diet, a 'low-fat' alternative to the weightier work of the earlier novel. Bourdieu's discussion of taste in terms of 'sick-making' (*Distinction* 56) resonates with responses to *Larry's Party*, as in Michèle Roberts's complaint that Shields 'ends up dishing out spoonfuls of Saccharine gloop' (34), which invokes 'the register of oral satisfactions' (*Distinction* 486) and indicates an unacceptable taste that is both gastronomic and literary.

Shields's work is indeed 'accessible,' but her play with form, particularly in these later novels, adds a layer of complexity that aligns her with Canadian literature that meets with celebration, certainly within Canada itself. Indeed, some critical response to *Swann* elevated Shields's writing by claiming it had now become more sophisticated: Raymond E. Jones asserts that *Swann* presents Shields's 'most complex treatment' of concerns developed in earlier texts, namely, the representation of 'ordinary identity' and 'the ways in which honest attempts to transcribe it fail to tell the whole truth' (114); and Catherine Addison highlights Shields's formal innovations, declaring *Swann* 'a much more ambitious and self-reflexive text than any of her previous work in [the novel] genre' (158). Nevertheless, the awards that *Swann* won and was nominated for mimic the more general critical disjunction between Shields's accessibility and her highbrow achievements worthy of the national literature. *Swann* was nominated for the Governor General's Award for English-language fiction, and although it did not win, the nomination conferred upon Shields the status of state-supported celebration, an official recognition of having contributed to the Canadian national literature. This text depicting the attempts to canonize the work of a poet was therefore accorded its own 'pre-canonical' status, effected by national literary celebration.

Just as 'taste classifies' (Bourdieu, *Distinction* 6), so literary prizes classify the works they honour according to their mandates of celebration. In addition to its Governor General's Award nomination, *Swann* won the Arthur Ellis Award for Crime Writing, which inserted the text into the category of genre fiction. To a certain extent, the subtitle with which the novel was originally published – *Swann: A Mystery* – contributed to this classification; the original publisher, Stoddart, made this decision, presumably for the purposes of marketing, without consulting Shields herself (interview). In more recent Canadian editions of the novel, the title is simply *Swann*, but the cover announces the relationship between the text and crime writing by foregrounding the Arthur Ellis Award. This prize has been given since 1984 by the Crime Writers of Canada, whose mandate is 'to promote Canadian crime writing and to raise the profile of Canadian crime writers from coast to coast' ('About the CWC' n.p.). Like the Governor General's Awards, the Arthur Ellis Award functions to recognize Canadian writing within Canada; however, the crime writing prize, through its generic focus, celebrates work unlikely to be included on a Governor General's Award shortlist.

The 'mystery' of *Swann*'s original subtitle invites consideration of its relationship to genre fiction. As Raymond E. Jones argues, '... the word *mystery* forms a motif as the various characters attempt to understand their own lives, the creative life and brutal death of Mary Swann, and their connections to the growing academic industry that feeds upon Swann's life and work' (115). Certainly, the last section of the novel, in which the main characters attempt to determine who has been stealing the Swann documents, and for what purpose, positions them as detectives of a sort. As Barbara Godard declares in her analysis of *Swann*'s invocation of the detective genre,

> There is a murder, there are thefts, but no criminals are detected, indeed none is explicitly pursued ... *Swann* subverts the genre of the detective novel by 'developing' its generic norms in such a way as to disappoint them. So it enters into the dialectical contradiction of the work and the genre as 'literature,' not as detective fiction ... Shields' novel ultimately subverts the genre by becoming unique and 'literature,' that is, productive of its own reality. ('Sleuthing' 58)

This assessment offers an explanation for the text's celebration within the diverging frameworks of crime writing and high-culture national literary celebrations. Shields's novel contains enough elements of the detective novel to qualify as crime writing, while 'almost entirely eliminat[ing] the narrative of suspense' (58), and therefore disappointing readers enough in terms of the conventions of its invoked genre in order to facilitate its status as 'literature.'

Thus, the reception and celebration of *Swann* through both a generic (albeit national) prize and a state-sponsored literary award mirrors the novel's content through the different readings and reading values it presents, the categories they belong to, and the interests and preferences they uphold. *Swann*'s cultural valuing as both a contribution to the national literature, echoing the attempts to canonize Mary Swann, and as crime fiction, which fits the reading preferences and practices of Rose (herself valued in *Swann* for her competence in reading this genre), exemplifies Shields's insertion into different pockets of culture by critics uncertain about how to classify her work.

Swann's afterlife also included national celebration through the film adaptation of the novel by British director Anna Benson Gyles (1996) and its nominations for Genie Awards in the categories of Music / Original Score, Lead Actress, Lead Actor, Art Direction / Production Design, and Costume Design. Shields's involvement in the adaptation 'was limited to selling the rights' (Rosborough, 'Time' C1). Although she praised the film as 'subtle and intelligent' (C1), she was not involved in the adaptation process in the way that Ondaatje was in the film version of *The English Patient*. Key differences between *Swann* the novel and *Swann* the movie include the fact that in the film, Rose, not the Cruzzis, is responsible for reconstructing Swann's manuscript, and Brownie, the thief, shreds all copies of *Swann's Songs* out of revenge for Sarah's having ended their relationship. Sarah's relationship with Brownie in the film is more volatile, and the film itself, as Shields acknowledged, focuses more on violence against women (Horton E8). Despite the absence of Mary Swann from the present-day narrative of the film, she is present through flashbacks. Rose becomes a surrogate for Swann, both through her reconstruction of the manuscript and through references to the body. The scene between Sarah and Rose at the Swann farm is cross-cut with shots of the murder sequence, including Mary's bloody handprint on the silo door. Rose points to her own arms to describe the 'deep cuts' where Angus stabbed his wife. Rose also becomes a more authoritative character in the adaptation: whereas the novel's screenplay ending presents a communal reconstruction, in the adaptation Rose recites 'Lost Things' from memory.

Reviews of the film were uneven, ranging from criticism of a 'disastrous screenplay and weak direction' (Gerstel C3) to characterizations of the adaptation as 'a film whose every element down to the smallest detail feels perfectly right' (Kemp 63). Canadian critics assessed the film as a Canadian film, claiming its Canadian identity within the framework of the film's hyphenate status as a Canadian-British co-production. The film received funding from numerous sources, including Telefilm Canada, the CBC, the Ontario Film Development Corporation, and CityTV in Canada, and BBC Films in the U.K. Noel Taylor acknowledges the film's Canadian-British co-production status but declares that it 'looks and feels much more Canadian than British' (F3), perhaps due to the film's setting and shooting in Ontario. John Griffin also alludes to the co-production status but weighs the film's aesthetic successes and failures against assumptions about Canadian cinema, arguing that scenes including Rose 'glow like the best of Canadian film,' while Sarah's Chicago scenes presents 'a joke – Canuck film at its corniest' (D4).

Griffin's juxtaposition of 'the best' with 'a joke' illustrates diverging but competing popular assumptions about Canadian film, both of which factor in explanations of low audience numbers for Canadian films and the construction of a national taste. Much Canadian film criticism since the 1990s has noted 'the improved quality of Canadian films' (D. Weaver C1). This 'improvement' has been perceived in relation to the 'tax shelter' filmmaking of the late 1970s and early 1980s, which produced many 'horrible films with second-rate American stars and disguised locales,' largely responsible for the assumption that 'if it's Canadian it can't be good' (MacInnis H8). But now, Canadian films, having had success 'at international film festivals and in international markets' (Acland 288), are as likely to be associated with art-house cinema, like the national cinemas of European countries that have functioned 'both to counter American domination of their indigenous markets in film and also to foster a film industry and a film culture of their own' (Neale 11). Canadian films encounter difficulties with distribution, due to 'the U.S. control of Canadian movie theatres' (Acland 282); as a result, Canadian films often reach very few Canadian cinemas, particularly outside major metropolitan centres. But the current art-house trend of Canadian film also has implications for audience numbers: although Canadian films may be more concerned with Canadian locations, narratives, and concerns, they also exhibit an 'affinity with an international art cinema' that renders them 'foreign,' 'at a distance from popular taste' (284).

Like national literary awards, celebration of Canadian cinema concerns itself with developing a national taste. In fact, the Canadian Film Awards (renamed the Genie Awards in 1980), established in 1949, were modelled on literary celebration in the 'hop[e] that these new awards would be comparable in stature with the Governor General's Awards for literature' (Topalovich 1). Like Canada's national literary prizes, the Genie Awards attempt to marry the Canadian audience to Canadian culture and 'to situate a set of dispositions as central to a national character' (Acland 292) where all Canadians should presumably feel at home, within a national habitus. But the difficulties of Canadian film distribution frustrate the project of celebration, for films celebrated by the Genie Awards are often completely unknown to the national audience. *Swann*'s Genie nominations affirmed its status as a Canadian film (since only Canadian films are eligible for the awards), but it also indicated what kind of audience the film was likely to attract. In 1997, for example, Atom Egoyan's *The Sweet Hereafter* (a multiple Genie Award–winner and double Oscar nominee) was declared 'the first English-language film supported by Telefilm Canada to make money in 12 years' (Everett-Green C2). Genie Awards ceremonies frequently attract less than one million viewers, and in some years have not been televised by live broadcast (see G. Roberts 333).

As such, the celebration of Canadian cinema, intended to promote Canadian films, often needs promotion itself. In this respect, it differs from both the celebration afforded by the Academy Awards and the celebration represented by the Governor General's Awards. The film *Swann* did not increase the circulation of the novel in any detectable way, in contrast to the renewed attention to *The English Patient* in the wake of its adaptation. Further, *Swann* and its adaptation illustrate the difference in viability of Canadian literature versus Canadian cinema. There is a perceived hostility towards Canadian films by Canadian audiences, given that attendance numbers in Canadian cinemas are so low; the hosts go largely unexposed to Canadian national cinema, conferring a guest status on their country's own films (as indicated by the classic example of 'finding a Canadian film in the 'Foreign' section of the video rental store' [Acland 283]). In contrast to Shields's Governor General's Award nomination beginning the process of her national celebration, *Swann*'s Genie nominations invoked a national celebration largely invisible to the nation's public.

Celebration and Identification across Borders

Just as the discrepancy between the effect of *Swann*'s Genie nominations and *The English Patient*'s Oscar victories on the (re)circulation of the novels indicates, in part, the extent to which American culture presides as an authority over Canadian culture, so too *The Stone Diaries*' Pulitzer Prize win in 1995 provides another testament to the unsettled relationship between Canada and the United States and their respective cultures. Like Carol Shields, *The Stone Diaries* has dual citizenship as its Pulitzer Prize, Governor General's Award, and Booker nomination indicate. Through these prizes, *The Stone Diaries* was made representative of American, Canadian, and Commonwealth literature. Media discussion of Shields receiving these honours reveals a negotiation of her national identity as well as the relationship of hostipitality between Canada and the United States that shapes this negotiation.

In fact, *The Stone Diaries*' publication in Britain and Canada one year prior to its publication in the United States delayed the unsettling of Shields's nationality. In an *Independent* discussion of the 1993 Booker shortlist, Robert Winder describes the list as 'cosmopolitan' and declares that it endorses 'the growing view that the best novelists in the Booker's bizarre cachment [*sic*] area – Britain, Ireland, South Africa and the Commonwealth, but not the US – are not English. Ignatieff and Shields are Canadian, Malouf is Australian, Doyle is Irish, Fischer is Hungarian-born and Philips [*sic*] West Indian-born' (3). Winder emphasizes the absence of the United States from inclusion within the Booker's 'bizarre' geographical boundaries; however, he effaces Shields's own Americanness, writing it over with a seemingly unproblematic Canadianness in order to explain her inclusion on the Booker shortlist. Any debate about Shields's national identity takes place off the page, if at all.

Ultimately, celebration of *The Stone Diaries* complicated the apparently easy equation of Shields with Canadian identity when she won the National Book Critics Circle Award and, more visibly, the Pulitzer Prize in the United States. Because Americans are excluded from Booker Prize eligibility, and non-Americans excluded from the American awards' eligibility, Shields's 'hyphenate' (Gussow C13) status moved into the foreground. Although nominated for the Booker Prize, *The Stone Diaries* did not receive that award; its Pulitzer win, however, generated much media attention and claim to Shields in Canada. Negotiation of Shields's nationality occurred on both sides of the border. For example, although Mel Gussow in the *New York Times* explains that Shields 'was born in Oak Park, Ill., and is a naturalized Canadian with dual citizenship,' he uses textual evidence to support this dual claim, noting that her novels 'take place in the United States as well as Canada' (C18). Shields's national representations apparently furthered her claim to Americanness, for she had not abandoned the United States in her fiction despite her own move to Canada several decades beforehand. Shields was not nearly as well known in the United States as in Canada at the time of *The Stone Diaries'* publication, as book sales suggest: at the time of Shields's National Book Critics Circle Award, *The Stone Diaries* had 'sold 14,000 hardcover copies in the United States since its 1994 release,' compared to 'the blockbuster success of her book in Canada, where combined hardcover and paperback sales total[led] well over 100,000' (Rosborough, 'Award' D8). Thus, Gussow positioned himself as introducing her to the American reading public. Shields's National Book Critics Circle Award preceded her Pulitzer Prize, but her Pulitzer received more attention, on both sides of the border.

In Canada, the Pulitzer functioned both to validate the worth of Canadian literature and to cause some anxiety about Shields's Canadianness. Roch Carrier, then director of the Canada Council, commented, '... sometimes Canadians need to be told by someone else they have some value' (quoted in Prokosh and Rosborough C8). Carrier positions Canadians in opposition to Americans, who are the 'someone else'; the Canadians to which Carrier refers might be Canadian readers, or writers, or all Canadians, but perhaps not Shields herself, who was at least American 'enough' to have qualified for the Pulitzer in the first place. Shields's Pulitzer prompted her then-local newspaper, the *Winnipeg Free Press*, to declare, 'She's one of ours' (Rosborough, 'She's

One' D8). As York argues, this article illustrates 'the celebrity tug-of-war between the local and the international,' which 'tends to appear at these moments of special consecration such as the winning of prizes beyond the national borders' (149). Here, the *Free Press* demonstrates both pride and perhaps a need to reassert Shields's claim to Canada, or Canada's – as well as Winnipeg's – claim to Shields. Following the Booker nomination, claims made of Shields were not simply national or local but also provincial and regional: the nomination constituted a recognition for 'Manitoba authors,' considered 'overdue' both nationally and internationally (Lyons A1). The *Calgary Herald* reprinted a *Vancouver Sun* article that lauded Shields as 'the first Western Canadian writer to be nominated for a Booker Prize' (Andrews, 'Writer' A19), the interests of Alberta and British Columbia uniting in their investment in Shields as a Western Canadian. The national media also highlighted Shields's regional affiliation, with *Maclean's* entitling its article on Shields's prize 'A Prairie Pulitzer' (Turbide 299), privileging Shields's Prairie identity over her Canadian one.

The fact that *The Stone Diaries'* Pulitzer generated more excitement than its Governor General's Award the previous year upholds Carrier's claim that Canadians look outside their borders for validation. Martin Levin describes *The Stone Diaries* as 'the convention-shattering novel about the life of a Manitoba woman that won Shields the 1995 Pulitzer Prize for fiction, among other awards' (12), rendering the Governor General's Award apparently incidental or unworthy of mention. Further, the taste of the Canadian nation as represented by the Governor General's Award was sanctioned by an American taste-making body, namely, the Pulitzer jury, regardless of the legacy of dubious judgments over the history of the Fulitzer Prize for fiction. Shields was thereby reappropriated by Canadian culture even as she was being celebrated, through the Pulitzer, for *The Stone Diaries'* contribution to American literature.

What, then, do we make of the celebrations on either side of the border for this border-crossing text *about* border crossings? How do we read *The Stone Diaries'* multiple celebrations in the context of what York refers to as Shields's 'national graft' (160), the fact that she is 'a transplanted American citizen whose success has been measured in terms of both her Canadian and her American citizenships' (161)? What do these differently located measurements of Shields's success imply about the novel itself? With respect to the Governor General's Award and the text's representation of Canada, this prize might sedate Shields's illustration of the Canadian cultural host's inhospitality, particularly in Skutari's narrative, considering its expression by an immigrant writer who has become part of the cultural host. The depiction of the Canada-U.S. relationship suggests that the novel addresses Canadian and non-Canadian readers differently, that Canadians are meant to 'recognize' the stereotypes about their country *as* stereotypes delivered from an American perspective. Thus, the Governor General's Award might indicate a further recognition of this cultural relationship of hostipitality and a celebration of Shields's diagnosis of it. In contrast, the American celebration of the text suggests that *The Stone Diaries'* critique of Canada-U.S. hostipitality wrought by power imbalance is tempered, absorbed within American culture. Significantly, Seymour Topping, administrator of the Pulitzer Prize, raised the issue of stereotypical American perspectives of Canada: 'Despite what Canadians may think, the board recognizes that Canada and the United States are both part of the same North American continent' (quoted in Prokosh and Rosborough C8). Topping's comment makes little sense in the context of the Pulitzer Prize, however, which is not a prize for North American fiction – 'the author must be American to be considered' (C8) – and therefore functions at the exclusion of Canadian writers. But his statement suggests a peculiar reading of Shields and her text. Is Shields a Canadian who thinks American institutions are ignorant of Canada's place within North America, as *The Stone Diaries'* image of the top of the continent having gone missing suggests? Or, in the context of the Pulitzer, is Shields an American who portrays Canadian views on such matters? If Marshall McLuhan's 'insights into the American culture machine' are due to his status 'as a Canadian who was on the outside looking in, ... a viewpoint unavailable to the insider' (Cavell 41), Shields's doubled insider/outsider status on either side of the border produces insights into both Canada and the United States.

The Stone Diaries' Pulitzer initiated a recasting of Shields's national identity, particularly outside North America. The Booker nomination had cemented Shields's Canadianness in the U.K.; when *Swann* was published in Britain as *Mary Swann*, Shields's first British publication, reviewers varied in their attributions of her nationality, ranging from references to Shields's reputation in 'her native Canada' (Sackville-West 42, Perrick 6, 6), to others, recognizing that Shields was not native to Canada, positioning her as 'an American now resident in Canada' (Cockburn 19) or 'an American writer who has lived in Canada for more than 30 years' (Coe 26). Despite recurring debates about whether the Booker should include American writers within its catchment area, references to *The Stone Diaries'* nomination only referred to Shields as Canadian. However, the novel's Pulitzer Prize altered this national equation, as British media responses to *Larry's Party* indicate. The *Scotsman* described Shields as 'an American writer originally brought up in the suburbs of Chicago, who has lived for all her writing years in small-city Canada' (A. Smith 10), and the *Guardian* declared her 'an American, settled in Ontario' (Brownrigg 10), thereby mistaking Winnipeg's provincial location, despite the novel's persistent contextualizing of Winnipeg in Manitoba. Identifications of Shields as an American living in Canada divorced Shields's nation from her habitation, privileging nation of origin over habitation. The *Boston Globe* and the *Los Angeles Times* offered similar versions of Shields's identity: the former referred to Canada as 'where Shields lives' (G. Caldwell F15); and the latter announced the American awards garnered by *The Stone Diaries* before adding 'and, because Shields lives in Canada, Canada's Governor General's Award' (Hall 10). Indeed, the British emphasis on Shields's American national identity would continue in the debates surrounding the 2002 Man Booker Prize shortlist, in which Shields's *Unless* appeared alongside Rohinton Mistry's *Family Matters* and Yann Martel's *Life of Pi*, with the fact that all three writers were born outside Canada generating debate between the British and Canadian media as to whether these writers were 'really' Canadian.

In Canada, *Larry's Party* was not nominated for the Governor General's Award, disqualified from consideration 'because Shields [had], until recently, served on the board of directors of the Canada Council, which administers the awards' (Marchand, 'Ladies' J6). Shields had therefore been deemed too integral a part of the structure of Canadian cultural production and celebration to compete for an award administered by that same structure, though Philip Marchand asked in the *Toronto Star*, 'Does anybody really think jury members would have been swayed by the fact that Shields was a member of the Canada Council's board of directors?' (J6). *Larry's Party* was nominated for the Giller Prize, but lost to Mordecai Richler's *Barney's Version*. But as with Ondaatje following the publication of *In the Skin of a Lion* and its failure to win a national prize, Shields was recognized by the state through the Order of Canada, to which she was appointed on 6 May 1998. Shields's entry in the Order of Canada files diverges significantly from Ondaatje's, particularly in its emphasis on her popular readership. Although Shields is 'ranked among the best English writers today,' ostensibly for 'her prize-winning novels,' the entry underscores Shields's novels' 'enjoy[ment] by people around the world and, as evidence of their popularity, [their] translat[ion] into twenty-four languages' ('Carol Shields, C.C.' n.p.). While Ondaatje's entry focuses on his international circulation as well, the fact that he is described as 'first and foremost a poet whose talent is recognized throughout the English-speaking world' ('Michael Ondaatje' n.p.) sidesteps the issue of popularity and enjoyment, articulating the difference in cultural categorizations for these two authors.

Soon after Shields's Order of Canada, *Larry's Party* won the Orange Prize, an award outside the boundaries of Canadian national celebration. Established in 1996 for fiction written in English by women, the Orange Prize has no restrictions pertaining to the author's nationality, but, as with the Booker Prize, the work must be published in the U.K. The Orange Prize was developed in response to the 1991 Booker shortlist, which 'didn't have a single woman on it, in a year when writers like Angela Carter, Margaret Atwood and Michèle Roberts had novels eligible' (McLean 3), and therefore sought to redress a gender imbalance in literary celebration. The prize has attracted controversy for its gender restrictions, and such authors as A.S. Byatt, Anita Brookner, and Nadine Gordimer have spoken out against the award, claiming it 'ghettoizes women' and constitutes a celebration 'judged by gender' (Moseley 297). For her part, Shields, upon receiving the Orange Prize in 1998 for *Larry's Party*, declared that she was '100 per cent behind this prize. It's important that men should read women's work' (quoted in Longrigg 3), indicating that she assumed the awards process guides readers to texts deemed worthy of attention. As Merritt Moseley notes, however, 'Whether the prize with its separate female sphere has done anything to interest male readers in women's fiction is unproven' (301).

Although the Orange Prize does not use national identity as a category of eligibility, discussions of nation have nevertheless emerged with respect to this award. Within Britain itself, discussions of nationhood reveal that despite the award's internationalism, there is some anxiety about British authors *not* winning the prize. Orange judges such as Lisa Jardine and Lola Young have criticized British writing: Jardine characterizing British novels as 'smug and parochial'; and Young 'describing too many of the current British women's novels as "piddling"' as compared to American novels (Moseley 300). On the one hand, Clare Longrigg declared that 'Shields lift[ed] [the] Orange Prize out of [the] ghetto' (3), implying that Shields's status conferred a credibility upon the award itself. On the other hand, Shields's win prompted Sylvia Brownrigg to ask, 'Is English women's writing really so thin ... ?' (10). The British association of Shields with the United States was particularly strong in the context of the Orange Prize, with both the *Times* (Whitworth 6) and the *Daily Telegraph* ('American' 2) describing Shields as an American author. Brownrigg also identified Shields as 'an American,' which preceded her reference to 'the outcry: only one English finalist!' (10). The identification of Shields as American rather than Canadian appears to amplify an anxiety about British writing and international cultural competition (as though Shields presents a 'troubling' Americanness akin to her character Kurt Wiesmann's, as described in the British publisher's rejection) and a fear of cultural domination that is not present in the fact of one Canadian author winning the Orange Prize the year after another Canadian (Anne Michaels for *Fugitive Pieces*).

While Shields's winning the Orange Prize for *Larry's Party* underscored gender as a primary category of identity (one which the prize founders and Shields agree is in need of further celebration), it was also recruited into discussions of national literatures. The Orange Prize, despite its gender criterion, is more hospitable than many literary awards in that it has no limitations on the author's nationality. However, this international hospitality gives rise to anxiety about cultural competition, reflecting differently on the nationality of the author where different national interests emerge. This aspect of international competition resonates with *Larry's Party*'s depiction of the 1996 Olympics, whose link between health and national victory is suggestive for literary prizes, particularly international literary prizes' conferring or indicating a vitality of national literatures. Further, the site of hospitality becomes an issue in international competition. That Donovan Bailey, a Canadian runner, should take the title of fastest man in the world in an American location, resolves the Canada-U.S. hostipitality in an unexpected way: the Canadian guest bests the American host (and, indeed, all the other guests). Thus, questions of 'turf' become important, both within and without the text, as the British media coverage of Shields suggests. In keeping with the novel's depiction of identity, British coverage of Shields might have accorded her a North American status and included both halves of her hyphenate nationality; the writing of Shields's identity as specifically American demonstrated a cultural hostipitality that presumably does not function in the same way between Britain and Canada, the former colony that ostensibly retains cultural ties (through such entities as the Booker Prize) to belonging in, and to, Britain. If, as an American recipient of a Britain-based prize, Shields presented a more threatening guest than she would as a Canadian, in the United States,

Shields's Orange Prize win seems to have had little or no presence in the news media. But the Canadian media applauded Shields in national terms, as the headline 'Canadian Wins U.K. Book Prize' ('Canadian' D1) attests, underscoring Shields's Canadian host status and acclaiming her representation of Canada in international competition. Thus, Shields's hyphenate identity that had come into the foreground with *The Stone Diaries'* Pulitzer Prize and Governor General's Award was suppressed, both by the British media who strategically privileged the first half of this hyphenate identity, and by the Canadian media who privileged the latter half. The Canadian celebration of Shields's win indicated a different anxiety than that of British literary culture, namely an anxiety about her having transcended Canadian culture through her international circulation that exposed her to other definitions of her nationality. The Orange Prize's gendered competition was recruited for the interests of celebrating Canada itself, reclaiming Shields and her success for the nation.

As we have seen, Ondaatje's Canadianness has also been a source of anxiety for the Canadian media, discussed and reaffirmed in the wake of his international exposure. But the process of negotiating Shields's identity differs from Ondaatje's, primarily because the United States constitutes her nation of origin. The troubling of sameness and difference between Canada and the United States not only features as an integral part of of Shields's fiction, but it also extends outside the text to perceived cultural relations between the two countries and to the configuration of Shields's identity. Political theorist Melissa S. Williams describes the conceptual confusion of combining Canadian and American identities:

> If to be Canadian means to be 'not American,' as we so often hear in laments over the lack of a distinctive Canadian identity, then what is it to be an American immigrant to Canada? One must be an oxymoron, a hyphenated 'American-not-American.' Perhaps the cognitive dissonance intrinsic in such an identity partially explains why the naturalization rates for immigrants to Canada from the United States are among the lowest for all immigration groups, and why US immigrants to Canada take longer than any other group to adopt Canadian citizenship. (216)

The maintenance of difference between Canada and the United States is seemingly impossible to imagine as bridged by the hyphen in American-Canadian identity, but that difference itself appears necessary to maintaining Canadian identity in the first place. How can the two be separated from each other as well as united? As Code points out, many of the differences are not easily detectable. Such a linking of American and Canadian identity presents a confusion of not quite welcome and not quite unwelcome, not quite at-home and not quite not-at-home.

With respect to Carol Shields and her celebrated, representative status as a Canadian literary figure, Canada-U.S. hostipitality becomes even more complicated, for how can she be representative of Canadian culture when she is also a representative of American culture, against which Canadian culture defines itself? I do not wish to complicate this discussion unnecessarily. Gussow quotes Shields describing herself as having 'a foot on either side of the border' (C13); but she also, when asked whether she considers herself Canadian, responded in the affirmative: 'I feel like I'm a Canadian. Because I was only twenty-two when I emigrated. But I had an American education and an American childhood, so that's with you forever. And then I had a little bit of Canadian education, too ... But I certainly feel more Canadian *now* – I know how everything works in Canada' (interview). Shields should not be considered any 'less' a Canadian writer because she was born and raised in the United States, but because of her American origins and continued citizenship, certain adjustments must be made to the imagining of Canadian identity in order to render her the status of a representative Canadian cultural figure.

In individual terms, these adjustments can be explained by Shields's long habitation in Canada, her Canadian citizenship (which she adopted in 1971, 'partly so that she could vote' in the federal election for the NDP ["Carol Shields" 34], indicating a desire to fulfil both a right and duty of citizenship in Canada), the Canadian setting of much of her work, her predominantly Canadian readership until the publication of *The Stone Diaries*, her involvement in Canadian cultural institutions such as the Canada Council, and the fact that Canada formed the site of production of her work. In more general, cultural terms, Canadian hospitality towards this American-born author might be accounted for by her choice to join the host culture in Canada (and her decision to remain within it), her articulated consideration of herself as part of Canadian culture, and, because of the slippage between Canadian and American sameness and difference, the ease with which she could 'pass' as a Canadian host. Further, her international success confers recognition upon Canada, and it is in the Canadian nation-state's interests to claim her as an integral part of the nation-state and its culture in order to

lay claim to that recognition as well. Her dual citizenship has also facilitated a specifically *American* recognition of Canadian literature, even as
the Pulitzer's recognition of *The Stone Diaries* as the best American novel
of 1994 is ostensibly to claim it as exclusively American. The imbalance
of political, economic, and cultural power between the United States
and Canada no doubt contributes to Canada's wanting to lay claim
to Shields's Pulitzer success, to Shields herself as 'one of ours,' and a
contributor to the increasing exchange rate of our cultural currency in
the wake of Shields's international success. Thus, even as the Pulitzer
reminded Canadians that Shields did not *only* belong to them, it also
allowed them to share in her American recognition, by insisting that she
still *did* belong to them, that she belonged, herself, north of the border.

Although Derrida writes, 'The stranger is, first of all, he who is
born elsewhere. The stranger is defined from birth rather than death'
('Hostipitality' 14), when Shields died on 16 July 2003 in Victoria, BC,
the response in Canada, the United States, and Britain indicated that
her American birth did not make her a 'stranger' in Canada. Rather, her
death in Canada figured as simply one more factor in her Canadianness,
her belonging to and within Canadian culture. Although obituaries in
no way effaced Shields's birth in Oak Park, Illinois, coverage of her
death demonstrated a tacit consensus that this birth did not speak
for her identity. The Americanness conferred upon Shields following
the Pulitzer Prize, strategically asserted by some British newspapers
responding to her Orange Prize win for *Larry's Party,* disappeared in the
announcements of her death and tributes to her life and career. She was
hailed in Britain as 'stand[ing] alongside such international superstars
as Margaret Atwood and Alice Munro' in 'the pantheon of Canadian
writers' (Goring 20), in the United States as 'the Pulitzer Prize–winning
Canadian novelist' (Lehmann-Haupt C11), and in Canada as 'the most
beloved of Canadian writers' (Urquhart A6), 'a national treasure'
('Farewell' A22).

Following her death, Shields's integration into the Canadian cultural
host was emphasized, particularly in Canada, by underscoring her affiliation with Canadianness: '... with each success, this compassionate
feminist from Oak Park, Ill., home of such unabashedly macho artists
as Ernest Hemingway, Tarzan creator Edgar Rice Burroughs and Frank
Lloyd Wright, seemed to become more like "one of us" – or the "us" so-
called ordinary Canadians imagine themselves to be' (J. Adams A1). This
designation of 'one of us' duplicates the language of citizenship, and,
indeed, as York notes (163), Shields was frequently described in terms

of a citizen's contributions to society. The *Ottawa Citizen's* reference to Shields as 'much more than an award-winning writer' through her 'other services to literature and to writers' as a 'valuable mentor,' 'a reviewer,' and a literary prize juror ('Canadian Treasure' A16) portrays Shields as a citizen committed to her local and (Canadian) national communities.

Celebratory statements by both the prime minister and the governor general of Canada recognized Shields as an exemplary Canadian writer: Jean Chrétien praised Shields as 'one of the bright lights of Canadian literature,' whose 'eloquent works are a testament to her compassion, her humour and her lifelong love of the written word'; and Adrienne Clarkson paid tribute to Shields's 'deceptively simple writing style with [its] penetrating observation and a profound compassion for the individual' (quoted in Sokoloff A2). That these state figures should have honoured Shields in this manner corresponds to her promotion within the Order of Canada, to Companion, in October 2002, which bettered her initial appointment as Officer in 1998. Her Companion entry in the Order's files declares her 'one of Canada's most widely acclaimed contemporary authors and well-loved educators,' whose 'works have garnered some of the world's highest literary honours and attracted an enormous readership' ('Carol Shields, C.C.' n.p.). The entry credits both her writing and her 'commitment to our next generation of writers' with Shields having 'deeply influenced Canadian literature' (n.p.).

Shields's promotion within the Order of Canada evinced similar timing to Ondaatje's appointment to the Order in 1988 and Shields's initial appointment in 1998, when these state recognitions emerged after texts by these writers were nominated for, but did not win, national literary prizes: Ondaatje's appointment following *In the Skin of a Lion*, Shields's following *Larry's Party*. Shields's promotion to Companion occurred after the multiple national and transnational award nominations for *Unless* by the Governor General's Award, the Giller Prize, the Orange Prize, and the Man Booker Prize. That the novel did not win any of these prizes, but that its nominations preceded Shields's promotion within the Order, suggests not only a desire for increased state celebration of Shields while there was still an opportunity, but also that these multiple nominations for *Unless* only increased Shields's stature within and importance to Canadian culture. In this sense, the American-not-American was held up, not as a figure against whom Canadian culture can be measured, but rather a figure who speaks for Canadian culture, keeping her, imagining her, and celebrating her on one side of the binary, one side of the border.

4 The 'Bombay-born, Canadian-based Banker': Rohinton Mistry's Hospitality at the Threshold

With a Governor General's Award, a Giller Prize, two overall Commonwealth Writers' Prizes, three Booker nominations, and an Oprah's Book Club selection to his name, Rohinton Mistry is no stranger to either Canadian or international celebration, in both popular and highbrow contexts. Like Carol Shields's work, his writing appears to satisfy the criteria for different aesthetic categories; like Ondaatje, Mistry seems to be, to the world outside Canada, 'invisibly' Canadian, as his Canadianness does not assert itself in his literary output. But for Mistry, even more so than for Ondaatje and Shields, his predominant fictional setting has prompted an equation between his texts and his national identity. The fact that most of Mistry's work takes place in Bombay has influenced the assessment of his Canadianness both outside and within Canada. If Mistry's resounding success and immense readership puts him in the company of Ondaatje and Shields, his representative Canadian status is less assured than that of the other two writers.

Like Ondaatje and Shields, Rohinton Mistry immigrated as an adult to Canada, where he subsequently became a writer. Born in Bombay in 1952, Mistry followed his fiancée, Freny, to Canada when he was twenty-three years old. He worked for CIBC for ten years before quitting to write full-time, enabled by a Canada Council Explorations grant (see Stone C7). Having studied mathematics at the University of Bombay prior to emigration, he began taking English literature at night at the University of Toronto. Prompted to begin writing by the Hart House short-story competition, he won the prize two years in a row.

Mistry's work has always been accompanied by and circulated in various contexts of celebration. His first book, the short-story collection *Tales from Firozsha Baag* (1987), was nominated for the Governor

General's Award for English-language fiction. He won this prize with his first novel, *Such a Long Journey* (1991), which also won both the Canada and the Caribbean regional and the overall Commonwealth Writers' Prize. His subsequent novel, *A Fine Balance* (1995), repeated these Commonwealth awards and also won the Giller Prize; later, it attracted popular celebration through Oprah's Book Club and Canada Reads in 2002. His most recent novel, *Family Matters* (2002), like the two previous, received a Booker Prize nomination. An Indo-Canadian writer who writes largely about Bombay, Mistry, like Ondaatje and Shields, has had his identity configured for him in national and international media in the face of national and international celebration. Mistry's subject matter has played a significant role in this negotiation and has prompted much discussion within Canada about his choice, thus far, to focus primarily on Bombay's Parsi community.

A Parsi himself, Mistry is not only part of the Indian diaspora, as Nilufer E. Bharucha notes, but he was also 'in Diaspora even in India' ('When Old' 57). Comprising .007 per cent of India's population (Gabriel 28), Parsis are the descendants of Zoroastrians who fled Persia following the Arab conquest and settled in Gujarat. Given Parsis' minority status, Mistry's portrayals of this community raise questions about religious and ethnic difference in the make-up of the Indian nation. The perception of Parsis as 'the most staunch and loyal allies of the British and, consequently, if not logically, the most Anglophile and "westernised" community' (Singh 30) has affected their social and economic status in post-independence India, leading many Parsis to emigrate to Western countries (Bharucha, 'When Old' 58). An emigrant Parsi himself, Mistry has written narratives of migration to Canada in *Tales of Firozsha Baag* and *Family Matters*, but has more frequently explored the negotiation of difference within India.

Mistry's work also concerns itself with questions of home on an intimate scale that invoke the micro-politics and -economics of hospitality while suggesting an interconnection between private units and the nation. His fiction constantly returns to domestic spaces to address issues of power and belonging, through the locations of Firozsha Baag in his short stories, the Khodadad Building in *Such a Long Journey*, Dina's flat in *A Fine Balance*, and the Chateau Felicity and Pleasant Villa flats that become domestic battlegrounds in *Family Matters*. Power infuses the relationships between host and guest (as well as various other roles, like the neighbour, the paying guest, the tenant, and the rent-collector) that play out in these spaces; further, Mistry's representations of spatial arrangements often probe and problematize hospitality's links to healing. Questions of accommodation extend beyond the parameters of these spaces to considerations of both local and national community in ways that are not simply specific to their Bombay settings but also engage with, just as they contribute to the shape of, Canadian culture.

Hospitality at Close Quarters

Mistry employs domestic settings not as mere backdrops, but as integral elements that determine characters' relationships to each other and to power. As W.H. New writes of *Tales from Firozsha Baag*, the eponymous 'apartment block is also a metaphor, a kind of walled neighbourhood in which the interplay between insider and outsider spells out what it means to feel "at home," "in one's element," "secure"' (263). These concerns of security and at-home-ness permeate Mistry's entire oeuvre. But although New suggests a sense of belonging generated by the apartment block, perhaps in terms of the community it represents, belonging as ownership is largely absent in Mistry's first three texts. The occupants of Firozsha Baag are tenants, their habitation of this space regulated by the building's trustees, as indicated in 'The Collectors' when the recently widowed Mrs Mody has 'decided to make the flat her permanent home now, and the trustees of the Baag [have] granted her request "in view of the unfortunate circumstances"' (108).

Security presents a vital concern for many of Mistry's characters. Presiding over the space of the flat that she shared with her late husband, Dina of *A Fine Balance* suffers harassment by her landlord's deputy, the rent-collector. Dina, subject to the hostile conditions of her landlord's 'hospitality,' resists his attempts at eviction and denies that she uses her flat 'for commercial purposes' (414); however, the landlord's 'goondas' (hired thugs) violently break in, destroying furniture and tearing the fabric the tailors need to sew the clothes that provide Dina with both her and their livelihoods. As Dina has been told, 'Paying the rent means nothing!' (81). The landlord punishes Dina for her assumption of the host power, her attempt to dictate how the flat's space will be used and who will occupy it. The hierarchy of claim to Dina's flat privileges the landlord, but also includes Dina, through her lengthy occupation of it, preceded by her husband's occupation; Maneck, who takes Dina's bedroom in his role of paying guest; and the tailors, Om and Ishvar, who inhabit the space both as labourers during the day, and ultimately as part of the household, although separate, when they sleep on the veranda.

Both *A Fine Balance* and *Tales from Firozsha Baag* explore the role of the paying guest; indeed, the novel overtly refers to the collection's story 'The Paying Guest' when Dina expresses her reservations in response to her friend's suggestion that she 'take in a boarder': 'You mean, like a paying guest? ... Never. Paying guests are trouble with a capital t. I remember that case in Firozsha Baag. What a horrible time the poor people had' (66). Boman and Kashmira's attempts to supplement their income through a 'temporary' arrangement, 'two years at best, till [Boman] got his raises and they could again afford the full rent' (134), become an intratextual cautionary tale for Dina, underscoring these characters' precarious hold on the host position. Merely tenants, Boman and Kashmira adopt the power of hosts. The 'hospitality' they provide is hardly Derrida's ideal of absolute hospitality, the financial arrangement foreclosing the possibility of unconditional welcome. Boman and Kashmira relinquish some of their adopted host authority by dividing the flat: 'They had given up the kitchen and decided to keep this room with its attached bathroom – the kitchen went with the other to the paying guests' (133). But their attempts to reclaim this space once Khorshedbai and Ardesar's contribution to their finances is no longer necessary prompt Khorshedbai's assertion of equal claim, despite her husband's protestations:

'... you know it is their flat, they have a right to ...'
'A right to what? Put us on the street? Don't we have rights? At last to have a roof, eat a little *daar-roteli,* and finish our days in peace?' (132)

Ardesar posits some ownership through the possessive – 'their flat' – despite Boman and Kashmira's tenant status. Similarly, Maneck in *A Fine Balance*, as Dina's guest who is sleeping in what was once her bedroom, refers to this room as his own, protesting that the homeless tailors 'could have slept in my room' (304). In this case, the paying guest has some power over the tenant-as-host: if Maneck's claim to Dina's bedroom erases her own claim, she cannot afford the room at all if Maneck does not pay for it.

The category of occupants becomes crucial to security, as Dina makes clear in her refusal to take money from the tailors for allowing them to sleep on the veranda: 'I am not renting anything, just keeping you out of those crooked police hands ... If I accept money, it means a tenancy on my verandah' (386), a violation of her *own* tenancy. Spatial occupation, as Boman and Kashmira discover, and Dina fears from the beginning, alters the relationship of power between host and guest. As Dina explains, 'A trunk, a bag, or even a satchel with just two pyjamas and a shirt is the first step into the flat. Personal items stored on the premises – that's the most common way of staking a claim. And the court system takes years to settle the case, years during which the crooks are allowed to stay in the flat' (305). Dina participates here in the criminalization of unwanted occupation, in part because her own claims to her flat are insecure.

If *Tales from Firozsha Baag* and *A Fine Balance* demonstrate the precariousness of hosting without ownership, *Family Matters* illustrates that ownership creates other problems, primarily when it is relinquished, creating a crisis in hospitality. The ownership of the Chateau Felicity flat passes from his parents to Nariman, but having bought the Pleasant Villa flat for his youngest daughter, Roxana, and her husband, Yezad, Nariman hands the ownership of the Chateau Felicity flat to his stepchildren, Coomy and Jal. Although this flat is Nariman's family home, his stepchildren, especially Coomy, wield their power of the host, ultimately making the space a hostile one for Nariman and effectively evicting him from his home. After Nariman breaks his ankle, Coomy resents caring for her stepfather, and conspires to deliver him to Roxana and prevent his return to Chateau Felicity. Yezad encourages Nariman to exercise authority over the Chateau Felicity flat – 'It's your home, after all. You should put your foot down, chief' (110) – but Nariman confesses he no longer owns the flat: 'Suppose I say, This flat is my home, and I put it in your names because I did not differentiate between you and Roxana. Would you now throw me out in my helplessness' (79). In this Lear-like scenario, Nariman, having ceded the power of the host, becomes an unwanted guest in what was his home, only to become an unwanted guest at Pleasant Villa.

Circulations and complications of ownership also infuse the Pleasant Villa flat. Attempting to convince Roxana that she has the authority to welcome Nariman regardless of Yezad's consent, Coomy emphasizes the financial power that underpins ownership: 'This is your house, your father's money paid for it' (95). Yezad echoes this reasoning when he reluctantly welcomes his father-in-law – 'You're welcome to stay, chief – your house, after all' (110) – and thus acts as host in his invitation but insists that Nariman has the host's power to come and go as he pleases. Nariman tries to reject the equation of money and host power, even as he suffers from an absence of legitimate ownership at Chateau Felicity: 'Never say that, please. Notwithstanding my barging in today, this flat is yours and Roxana's. Your wedding gift. It ill behoves anyone to suggest, after fifteen years, that I am attempting to commandeer these premises' (110). He insists he relinquished his financial power through the act of the gift, which he refuses to frame as a gesture demanding reciprocation. Given that 'for there to be a gift, there must be no reciprocity, return, exchange, countergift, or debt. If the other *gives* me *back* or *owes* me or has to give me back what I give him or her, there will not have been a gift' (Derrida, *Given* 12), Yezad undoes the gift by claiming he must return it and positioning Nariman as owner; 'the gift is annulled' (12) as Yezad positions himself as a guest in Nariman's flat, not a host in his own. Nariman wants his son-in-law's hospitality to be a gift in itself, freely and willingly bestowed, unrelated to Nariman's gift of the flat in the first place.

The spatial dynamics of Pleasant Villa alter through Nariman's presence, as the two-room flat must accommodate another occupant. Coomy reminds Roxana that the Chenoys are better off than most families, despite the added strain: 'By Bombay standards it's huge! You know very well that in chawls and colonies, families of eight, nine, ten live in one room' (79). But Nariman's arrival means one of the boys must leave the space of the flat to sleep, as the settee, usually Jehangir's bed, becomes Nariman's bed, Jehangir takes Murad's cot, and Murad sleeps on the balcony under a tent fashioned out of a rexine tablecloth, borrowed from a neighbour. Before Nariman's arrival, the flat's space already functions in multiple ways; this multiplicity increases in Nariman's presence, given his inability to move to the bathroom, his bodily functions having to occur in the sitting room–cum–bedroom.

Spatial boundaries blur throughout Mistry's fiction, beginning with *Tales from Firozsha Baag*'s first story, 'Auspicious Occasion,' when Rustomji's upstairs neighbours' toilet leaks through the ceiling into Rustomji's own bathroom. Not only do one flat's problems leak into another, but they also necessitate further blurring of boundaries: as Rustomji's wife, Mehroo, suggests, he will have to use another neighbour's toilet. Other stories illustrate how neighbouring flats supplement each other, expanding the borders of space and sense of entitlement to space; for instance, Najamai's fridge in 'One Sunday' becomes somewhat communal. Najamai concedes, 'In a way it is good . . . that Tehmina next door and the Boyces downstairs use my fridge as much as they do. Anyone who has evil intentions about my empty flat will think twice when he sees the coming-going of neighbours' (30). Tehmina, however, resents what she perceives as an illegitimate claim by the Boyces: 'Now those Boyces behave as if they have a share in the ownership of the fridge' (31). Najamai's fridge plays a similar role to Miss Kutpitia's telephone in *Such a Long Journey*, the only phone in the building, except that Miss Kutpitia strictly patrols the borders of her flat – 'no one was allowed into the flat beyond the front hallway' (63) – emphasizing the division between herself and the guests she invites in, just past the threshold, away from the inner sanctum of her flat that contains the dusty, cobwebbed shrine to her dead nephew.

The blurring of private spaces underpins Mistry's characterization of the neighbour, a role that carries particular implications for relations of hospitality in his texts. Derrida writes of the 'at home' that

> my 'at home' was also constituted by the field of access via my telephone line (through which I can give my time, my word, my friendship, my love, my help, to whomever I wish, and so invite whomever I wish to come into my home, first in my ear, when I wish, at any time of the day or night, whether the other is my across-the-fence neighbor, a fellow citizen, or any other friend or person I don't know at the other end of the world). (*Of Hospitality* 51)

This 'at home' presupposes habitation in a developed country, but it raises important issues for Mistry's work; in *Such a Long Journey*, only one resident of Khodadad Building can claim the kind of 'at home' that Derrida describes. For Derrida, the neighbour – the proximate, who perhaps shares a common citizenship – must be invited in, and is therefore positioned along a continuum that includes a 'person I don't know at the other end of the world'; in other words, the neighbour is not at home in my home. In contrast, Mistry's fiction offers less opposition between the tenant-host and the neighbour, although Najamai does *invite* her neighbours to make free use of her fridge, and Miss Kutpitia polices her private space.

But private spaces lack privacy in Mistry's texts, particularly through sound's transcendence of physical boundaries: Tehmina hears the Boyces playing 'The Blue Danube' in 'One Sunday' – 'Grudgingly, Tehmina allowed that . . . they had good taste in music' (38) – and Nariman listens to Daisy's violin practice at Pleasant Villa in *Family Matters*. However, Mistry gives several negative examples of this inescapable overhearing, such as the arguments in 'The Collectors' between Dr and Mrs Mody, heard not only by Jehangir Bulsara in the next room, but also by his mother, in another flat altogether: 'Suddenly, she realized that Jehangir was in there. Listening from one's own house was one thing – hearing a quarrel from inside the quarrellers' house was another' (103). In *Such a Long Journey*, Miss Kutpitia easily overhears the sounds of fighting between Sohrab and Gustad. When she shouts at Gustad, his counter-response – 'Come to my door and speak if you have something to say! I am not living free here, I also pay rent!' (51) – demands that she stand on the threshold of the space where he claims the host position, and that the distinction between their presence be emphasized so that he can claim some power of refusal. Oddly, however, Gustad highlights his lack of ownership through his insistence that he pays rent, that his financial claims, even as tenant, mean that Miss Kutpitia trespasses through a relationship of sound.

The figure of the neighbour posits an extension of the threshold outwards from individual dwellings to the community as a whole. A community identifies strangers in relation to the neighbour/hood, as Sara Ahmed argues in her discussion of Neighbourhood Watch programs, through 'the assumption that we can tell the difference between strangers and neighbours' (3) in attempts to police communities. The border between the host and neighbour presupposed in Derrida's conception of the host's 'at home' ultimately blurs, giving way to the distinction between those who legitimately belong to, and physically in, the community and those who do not. Given Mistry's focus, especially pronounced in *Tales from Firozsha Baag*, *Such a Long Journey*, and *Family Matters*, on Bombay's Parsi community, this renegotiation of the neighbour's status in the face of external difference (which actually 'functions to conceal forms of social difference' [Ahmed 3] within communities) extends to concerns about Parsi identity and its collective Self, as it is manifested in localized spaces.

In 'One Sunday,' Najamai's 'temporar[y] reconcil[iation] towards the neighbours whom she otherwise regard[s] as nuisances' (31) stems from her belief that 'the coming-going of neighbours' (30) using her fridge increases her security in relation to unwanted, uninvited strangers. Francis, however, is not a stranger, but someone who does 'odd jobs ... for anyone in Firozsha Baag who require[s] his services,' which constitute 'his sole means of livelihood ever since he had been laid off or dismissed' (32). Familiar to the Firozsha Baag residents, Francis is not a Parsi, and his homelessness prompts a strict policing of his presence, as Tehmina indicates: 'I do not like it, you skulking here in the hallway. When there is work we will call you. Now go away' (32). When Najamai finds Francis in her flat, she and her neighbours assume he has stolen from her. Several neighbours band together in outrage, with Percy and Kersi pursuing Francis into Tar Gully, a poorer, non-Parsi neighbourhood. But Francis's transgression also redraws alliances: 'A crowd was waiting outside C Block. More neighbours had gathered, including the solitary Muslim tenant in Firozsha Baag, from the ground floor of B Block, and his Muslim servant. Both had a long-standing grudge against Francis over some incident with a prostitute, and were pleased at his predicament' (43). Once caught, Francis is then slapped and admonished by one neighbour: 'At the slap, the gathering started to move in for a fresh round of thrashing' (44). Entreating Najamai to protect him from the crowd, Francis kneels, and 'the Muslim servant [sees] his chance and move[s] swiftly. He [swings] his leg and kick[s] Francis powerfully in the ribs before the other [can] pull him away' because, we are told, 'having few friends in this building, [the Muslim neighbour] was endeavouring to ingratiate himself with [Najamai] while she was still vulnerable, and before she recovered from C Block's excommunication' (44). The violence directed at Francis recalibrates the position of 'the Muslim neighbour' (44), whose naming as such signals that he is a stranger whose strangeness dissolves while he is united with the other residents against Francis. The 'neighbour' thereby functions as both a category of sameness and strategic allegiance, expelling Francis and reasserting his unbelonging.

Occupying the Threshold

Francis does not truly belong in Firozsha Baag not only because he is not a Parsi but also because he sleeps outside the furniture store where he once worked: '. . . the store owner did not mind, and it was a convenient location – all that Tehmina or Najamai or any of the other neighbours had to do was lean out of their verandas and wave or clap hands and he would come' (32). If 'the awning of that store' has constituted 'the only roof [Francis] ha[s] ever known' (32), it is certainly not his, neither through ownership nor through claims to occupying a private space, for the Baag residents exploit the fact that they can wave at Francis from their verandas, accessing what passes for 'his' space while enforcing the borders of their own.

The importance of the threshold recurs throughout Mistry's work, the liminal space, across which the positions of host and guest are usually

accorded, accruing greater significance in the context of Bombay's housing crisis. As Mistry has stated, 'In the city everything can become everything else – homes, hostels, workplaces, prisons, doorways, streets,
whatever' (Mclay Interview 203). The threshold figures most prominently in *A Fine Balance* through the recurring narrative of Ishvar and
Om's attempts to find housing in the 'City by the Sea' (13). Upon arrival,
they see that 'the pavements [are] covered with sleeping people' (153).
The tailors will be scarcely more fortunate: anticipating hospitality
from Nawaz, the friend of Ashraf, who trained both Ishvar and Om's
father as tailors, the pair initially receive denials from Nawaz that he is
expecting them before he 'grudgingly agree[s] to let them sleep under
the awning behind the kitchen for a few days, till they f[i]nd accommodation' (154). Nawaz is hardly hospitable, allowing them the liminal space of his awning but going no further, certainly 'not invit[ing]
them to eat' (154). However, within the context of the city's use of space,
Ishvar and Om are comparatively lucky: one pavement-dweller, 'sleeping in someone else's spot,' suffers the violent retribution of the others,
who 'bas[h] his head' (155) with a brick. Not only does the awning keep
Ishvar and Om safe, then, but Nawaz also emphasizes that his 'hospitality' is free, even as he attempts to drive the tailors out: 'The thing is, if
I wanted people living under my back awning, I would rent it for good
money' (158).

Ishvar and Om have ostensibly resolved their housing problems
when they rent the jhopadpatti on the city's outskirts, the 'last stop' (161)
on the bus route. The jhopadpatti has makeshift walls, 'part plywood
and part sheet metal,' and a roof of 'old corrugated iron, waterproofed
in corroded areas with transparent plastic' (161). If the haphazardly
compiled materials constitute a precarious living space, Ishvar and
Om's claims to the space are even more precarious, given that the city
owns the land: the slumlords, Nawaz explains, 'bribe the municipality,
police, water inspector, electricity officer. And they rent to people like
you. No harm in it. Empty land sitting useless – if homeless people can
live there, what's wrong?' (163). But as much as Ishvar and Om consider
the jhopadpatti their home, this home does not exist, according to the
city. When Ishvar applies for a ration card, he provides 'the name of the
road that [leads] to their row of shacks on the north side' and leaves
blank 'the space for building name, flat number, and street number'
(176). The use of space in the city does not correspond to the city's own
regulation of that space. When Ishvar claims that the jhopadpatti is 'a
roof – for the time being,' the Rations Officer insists, 'A jhopadpatti is

not an address. The law says ration cards can only be issued to people with real addresses' (177). The material reality of the house is irrelevant to the city's regulation of space and citizens: those without a legitimate address cannot assume the same rights; the jhopadpatti is considered not a home but '[a] spac[e] where non-subjects live in "informal circumstances"' (George 24).

The city has tolerated without legitimating the jhopadpatti colony, accommodating without overtly endorsing its presence in a kind of passive, but lucrative, hospitality that offers the colony's residents some sense of 'at home.' But the residents ultimately lose the claim altogether through the Emergency's beautification scheme: 'If shacks are illegal, they can remove them. The new law says the city must be made beautiful' (295). As Peter Morey notes, 'the process of slum clearance' in Bombay 'often meant clearing the poor from areas they had improved and made habitable themselves, so that these juicy slices of real estate could be utilised by ... the property developers' (100). In the novel, the slumlord becomes the 'Controller of Slums' (296), the exertion of his power shifting, but the power itself remaining intact. Ishvar and Om have been preparing to act as hosts to Maneck, having invited him to dinner, but as Om recognizes with grim humour, their lost ability to host will have to be explained by 'the unexpected disappearance of their house' (296).

The loss of the jhopadpatti forces Ishvar and Om to seek accommodation in a series of liminal spaces. Finding 'strangers in Nawaz's house' (298), they turn to the railway station, the transience represented by the station itself mimicked by numerous people forced to sleep there. But even this space has become regulated as accommodation. A railway policeman tells Ishvar and Om that 'sleeping on the platform [is] prohibited,' despite the fact that 'other people are sleeping' there. 'They have special permission,' the policeman responds, 'jingl[ing] the coins in his pocket' (300). As a kind of guard, the policeman adopts the position of host, to the consternation of the tailors: 'Pay him for what? It's not his father's platform' (300). The tailors reject the policeman's claim over the space, but the power he exerts indicates that such claim is unnecessary; dumping a bucket of cold water on the tailors, the policeman emphasizes that hospitality has a price. Following this experience, Ishvar and Om look to the city's thresholds, 'pausing to inspect every doorway, awning, and façade that might offer shelter. But wherever shelter was possible, the place was already taken' (306). Some shop owners actively refuse hospitality at night: 'To discourage pavement-dwellers, one shop had laid down in its entrance an iron framework covered with spikes, on hinges that could be unlocked and folded away in the morning'; however, 'an enterprising individual' circumvents this hostility, covering the 'bed of nails' with 'a rectangle of plywood over the spikes, and then his blanket' (306).

These liminal spaces operate in similar ways to the rented flats in Mistry's fiction insofar as the fear of being 'killed for taking someone's spot' (306) highlights that these spaces generate claims of belonging, even if that belonging consists of bribing a policeman or guard. When the tailors convince a chemist's nightwatchman to let them sleep in the doorway, he becomes their 'new landlord' (310). But ultimately, the legitimating powers of the city redefine the space in conventional terms: whereas Om refers to the doorway as their 'new sleeping place' (310), Sergeant Kesar insists, 'Sleeping in any non-sleeping place is illegal. This is an entranceway, not a sleeping place' (325). The tailors fail to reinscribe the space through the act of sleeping, and the city refuses to extend hospitality at the threshold. Government 'hospitality' to the homeless translates into a work camp on an irrigation project, where the unemployed (which does not include Ishvar and Om, but they are nevertheless forced to join the project) are promised 'food, shelter, and clothing' as their salary (332). But given that the inmates of the work camp are there involuntarily, having been forcibly transported as 'human cargo' (326) – with its connotation of slave labour – this hospitality is nothing other than imprisonment, a monstrous version of Dina's initial locking in of the tailors at her flat to keep them from discovering the company whose contracts they labour to fulfil.

The tailors receive the most genuine hospitality at Dina's after their liberation from the work camp by Beggarmaster, a liberation that Beggarmaster refers to as *his* 'hospitality' (366), for which he charges fifty rupees a week, per person, per year. Unlike Beggarmaster, the railway policeman, and the nightwatchman, Dina carefully refuses payment in exchange for hospitality, as this transaction would erode her own position in relation to her landlord. Significantly, the tailors take up residence on Dina's veranda, a space both attached to the flat and not quite a part of it. When Dina has grown to accept the tailors as part of her family and agrees to allow Om's future wife to live with them, she emphasizes the transformation of the veranda by dividing it with a curtain for the anticipated newlyweds' privacy. This gesture also gives the tailors some kind of jurisdiction, even if only through occupation, over the makeshift rooms.

This positive occupation of a liminal space has precedent in *Such a Long Journey*'s pavement artist. Disgusted by the wall that separates Khodadad Building from the road, used 'like a wholesale public latrine' (16) at night, Gustad 'invites' the artist to devise a mural to 'fix that stinking wall' (181) by covering it with 'holy pictures' (182). The artist wishes to represent 'assorted religions and their gods, saints and prophets': 'I always like to mix them up, include a variety ... Makes me feel I am doing something to promote tolerance and understanding in the world' (182). David Williams argues that 'the wall is neither as holy nor as ecumenical as it first appears, since its saintly face masks a more divisive purpose: to preserve the Parsi in his self-sameness and hierarchical privilege, and to protect him from the threat of difference, of Otherness itself' (60). But as a 'cluster of symbols,' the wall alters during the narrative from its original function as 'protection and reduction ... shut[ting] out the outside world' (Bharucha, 'When Old' 63). In my view, it is crucial that Gustad acquiesces to the artist's desire to inaugurate the wall, which 'reduces contact with the Indian reality' (Bharucha, 'When Old' 63), with images of the Hindu deities Brahma, Vishnu, and Shiva, rather than Zarathustra. Although Gustad rationalizes the artist's decision on the grounds that 'this triad would have a far-reaching influence in dissuading the urinators and defecators' (*Such* 183), implying, as Williams points out, a scapegoating of non-Parsis fouling the wall, the wall becomes something larger than Gustad's initial intention. The original desire to 'free [the wall] of malodour' (183) and mosquitos is achieved, but the text underscores the range of 'holy countenances on the wall' (184) instead and the 'shrine for all races and religions' it comes to represent, particularly crucial for a nation whose identity is multiply constituted: 'A good mixture like this is a perfect example for our secular country' (214).

Gustad thus indirectly extends hospitality to the world's religions and to the pavement artist himself: 'I am planning to build a small shelter for myself. With your permission, sir' (287). The acts of painting the wall, of offering hospitality in both artistic and religious terms, become enshrined as the artist paints a version of the wall upon the wall itself: 'It's now a sacred place, is it not? So it rightfully deserves to be painted on a wall of holy men and holy places' (288). The wall transcends Gustad's project, as demonstrated following its destruction by municipal government order for a road-widening scheme. The artist thanks Gustad – 'I am very grateful to you for providing me with the wall's hospitality' (338) – as though the wall has acted as the host, and Gustad its intermediary. The wall's destruction to widen the road, and the expropriation of Dina's flat to make way for luxury apartments, signals a pessimism about the power of hospitality when figures of authority and ownership can assert their interests to the fullest. However, these texts encourage sympathy with the forces of hospitality in Dina's home and at the wall, underscoring the indictment of economic and state power and their effects on community.

Healing and Hospital/ity

Like Ondaatje's and Shields's works, Mistry's texts engage with the intersection of healing and hospitality. But hospitals carry very different connotations in Mistry's texts, complicating their equation with hospitality and extending the borders of healing spaces into the home. Hospitals often become suspect in Mistry's fiction. In *Such a Long Journey*, the hospital functions in the context of a larger healing industry. Following Gustad's accident, the water-seller at the scene demands payment: 'The man has had an accident. So? He will pay the ambulance and the doctor and the hospital, to get mended. Why should I be the only one left out?' (59). The water-seller competes for the patronage of Gustad-as-patient. But the hospital is also a place to avoid, not a place of healing at all, as the exchange among Dilnavaz, Gustad, and Dinshawji about Roshan's illness indicates:

'What about doctor?'
   'Saying idiotic-lunatic things. That we are not giving proper rest and diet. Blaming us! Wants to put Roshan in hospital. Everyone knows what happens in hospital. Blunders and blotches, wrong injections, medicine mix-ups.'
   Dinshawji nodded in agreement. 'Go to a hospital when you are ready to die, is what I always say.' (194)

Here, healing within the home is preferable to the last resort of the hospital 'that leads to death' (Foucault, *Biopolitics* 52). Dinshawji's comment proves prescient: both he and Jimmy Bilimoria will die in hospital. Bilimoria's death in a prison hospital in particular emphasizes a lack of hospitality and healing in the 'biopolitical diagram' that is 'capable of assuming many different physical shapes' (Wallenstein 37, 35), and here collapses two modes of architecture into one. The absence of hospitality is underscored by the fact that Gustad needs to be approved as a visitor – 'Whether hospital, jail cell, solitary' (266) – before visiting his former neighbour. *A Fine Balance* invokes similar assumptions about hospitals, although from a dubious source at the irrigation project work camp, when 'the foreman admonishe[s] the injured': 'Doctor sahab is looking after you so well. What more do you people want? If we took you to a hospital, you think you'd be better off than here? Hospitals are so overcrowded, so badly run, the nurses will throw you in filthy corridors and leave you to rot. Here at least you have a clean place to rest' (360). Unlikely to convince either the injured workers in the text or the reader about the quality of work-camp hospitality, the foreman, implicated in the state's bio-power, nevertheless throws the hospitality of hospitals in doubt.

The government's corruption of hospitality, both in refusing hospitality at the thresholds of the city space and in claiming a kind of imprisonment *as* hospitality, becomes particularly sinister through the enforced sterilization campaign. The beginning of the novel presents an ideal of healing through Dina's father, whom she views as 'some kind of god who gave people good health, who struggled against illness, and who, sometimes, succeeded in temporarily thwarting death' (16). Although the text offers no reason to doubt that Dr Shroff is a good doctor, this portrait of medical ethics, significantly, invokes the past. In the context of the Emergency, doctors collude in government hostility and caste violence at the sterilization camps: '. . . the doctors seem to have forgotten their age-old professional ethics by "confusing" sterilization with castration,' as in the Thakur's retribution against Om; further, 'hospitals follow standing orders to put down the cause of any death during [the] Emergency as "accidental"' (Misra 188–189, 190), as suggested by the reporting of Ashraf's death. The sterilization camps reveal the state's violence against the poor through the administrator's rhetoric of population control: 'We have to be firm with the doctors . . . If it is left to them to fight the menace of the population explosion, the nation will drown, choked to death, finished – end of our civilization. So it's up to us to make sure the war is won' (*Fine* 534). Here, the function of biopolitics is clear insofar as the camps respond to an attempt to 'rationalize the problems posed to governmental practice by phenomena characteristic of a set of living beings forming a population: health, hygiene, birthrate, life expectancy, race' (Foucault, *Biopolitics* 317). But whereas, in a Foucauldian reading, 'such institutions as the medical clinic are not coercive in the violent or authoritarian sense because they are readily accepted as legitimate and normative at the everyday level' (B.S.

Turner, 'Foreword' xiv), the sterilization camps are, precisely, violently coercive. If Hana's experience in *The English Patient* leads her to reject the war hospital ethos in favour of a hospital ethos, the administrator here suggests that medical staff are soldiers whose duty is to violence, not care.

Both hospitality and healing, therefore, emerge not through the nation-state but through private relationships and domestic spaces. Just as Dina's flat becomes a space of hospitality, so too it becomes one of healing, beginning with her application of balm to Om's painful arm. Although Dina benefits from an improvement in Om's health and capacity to work, Ishvar recognizes the significance of Dina's act: '... she applied the balm for you ... it's the applying I want you to remember' (314). Dina's willingness to touch Om overrides her distaste for the tailors: '... the thought of their bodies in her bathroom still made Dina uncomfortable' (387). While applying the balm, she notes Om's 'salty-sour odour' (313) but persists in the act of touch, a bodily hospitality. Dina's acts of healing signal the development of a more ethical relationship between her and the tailors. She continues to help Om by supplying the medicine to rid him of worms, but crucially, this help accompanies a closing gap between Dina and the tailors, as exemplified by her ceasing to give them segregated dishes (389).

Family Matters also demonstrates a tension between hospitals and healing at home, although this novel more carefully ascribes political and economic factors to the conditions of the hospitals themselves. At Parsi General, where Nariman is treated after breaking his ankle, the assistant Mr Rangarajan assures him, 'This is a really good hospital ..., a five-star hotel compared to some,' and describes his previous work 'at a government hospital in Indore. What a truly dreadful place. Rats running everywhere, and nobody getting upset about it' (53). Although Mistry's work often identifies the government as an obstacle, at best, to hospitality and healing, Rangarajan invokes the economics behind the poor conditions at a public facility. The comparison between Parsi General and a five-star hotel suggests that a high quality of hospitable healing comes at a greater price, confirmed later, following Nariman's death, when 'all his medicine bottles [are] taken away from his dressing table, for donation to the charity hospital' (448).

Much of the novel focuses on the economic toll that Nariman's care takes on his family, particularly through Roxana's constant, anxious reallocation of money in envelopes reserved for household necessities. Healing at home does not presuppose a greater degree of hospitality, as demonstrated not only through Coomy, content to destroy her house (and enlist her enthusiastic but incompetent neighbour Edul to assist her unwittingly), rather than continue caring for her stepfather, but also through Yezad's bristling at his father-in-law's presence. Yezad refuses to allow anyone but Roxana to help Nariman with his bodily functions, inflicting great discomfort on Nariman when Roxana is unavailable. In an argument with Roxana, Yezad defends his sisters: 'At least they don't treat our home like a hospital' (221). This outburst reveals a fracture in the integration of healing at home and hospitality, emphasized when Yezad tells Roxana, 'I didn't marry you for the honour and privilege of nursing your father' (221).

Like Dina in relation to the tailors, Yezad gradually becomes more hospitable towards Nariman, and more involved in his care, overcoming his revulsion through touch when he feeds Nariman his tea, trims his nails, and shaves his beard: 'He realized this was the first time he had sat close to his father-in-law since his arrival months ago' (392). Unfortunately, this moment of ethical touch does not repeat itself: Jehangir's epilogue reveals that having moved into Chateau Felicity after Jal's addition of Yezad's and Roxana's names to the flat ownership documents so they will 'feel completely secure, not feel [they] are just guests' (416), Yezad takes this role of host to its fullest, most patriarchal conclusion as master of the house. Yezad polices the space of the flat according to his adoption of orthodox Zoroastrianism. He refuses not only to sanction Murad's relationship with a non-Parsi girl but also to allow Roxana access to some parts of the flat while she menstruates: 'The decree states that Mummy must not enter the drawing-room at all while she has her period. She will sleep in the spare bedroom on those days, and avoid the kitchen. The cook will take her meals to her' (462). Although not an issue of healing per se, the fact that Yezad's demands are generated by a change in Roxana's body suggests that something is wrong with her. Further, Roxana's monthly banishment to other parts of the flat perpetuates Yezad's earlier concern with purity when he barred his sons from assisting with Nariman's care, as well as his refusal to engage in touch, by Othering Roxana and serially rejecting her, while denying her the authority of host position herself.

Mistry's domestic settings, often within Parsi communities, act as microcosmic representations for larger national or sub-national groupings. As John McLaren writes of *Such a Long Journey*, '... family and friendship ... become metonyms for society and nation' (50). In both that novel and *Family Matters*, medicine acts as a metaphor for healing the problems of the body politic, the 'bodily corruption' (Morey 129) of illness running parallel to national and municipal problems. During the Indo-Pakistan war in *Such a Long Journey*, Dr Paymaster refers to Bangladesh as a patient: 'Correct diagnosis is half the battle. Proper prescription, the other half. Injection of the Indian Army, I said. And so the critical moment is past. Road to recovery ... Now if only we could cure our internal sickness as quickly and efficiently as this external sickness, we could be one of the healthiest countries in the world' (305). Later on, Dr Paymaster 'describe[s] meticulously how, from the very top, whence all power flowed, there also dripped the pus of putrefaction, infecting every stratum of society below':

> ... imagine, he said, that our beloved country is a patient with gangrene at an advanced stage. Dressing the wound or sprinkling rose-water over it to hide the stink of rotting tissue is useless. Fine words and promises will not cure the patient. The decaying part must be excised. You see, the municipal corruption is merely the bad smell, which will disappear as soon as the gangrenous government at the centre is removed. (313)

Of course, the municipality is responsible for destroying the wall that represents India's secular ideal. In *Family Matters*, Mr Kapur also uses the patient metaphor to articulate his affection for Bombay and his anxiety about threats to its diversity:

> This beautiful city of seven islands, this jewel by the Arabian Sea, this reclaimed land, this ocean gift transformed into ground beneath our feet, this enigma of cosmopolitanism where races and religions live side by side and cheek by jowl in peace and harmony, this diamond of diversity, this generous goddess who embraces the poor and the hungry and huddled masses, this Urbs Prima in Indis, this dear, dear city now languishes – I don't exaggerate – like a patient in intensive care, Yezad, my friend, put there by small, selfish men who would destroy it because their coarseness cannot bear something so grand, so fine. (147)

For Kapur, Bombay's greatness lies in its hospitality: 'In her heart there is room for everyone who wants to make a home here'; 'Within this warp and weft is woven the special texture of its social fabric, the spirit of tolerance, acceptance, generosity' (145). Like the pavement artist in *Such a Long Journey*, Kapur attempts to construct a model of diversity and tolerance by celebrating 'all festivals: Divali, Christmas, Id, your

Parsi Navroze, Baishakhi, Buddha Jayanti, Ganesh Chaturthi, everything ... We are going to make a mini-Bombay, an example to our
neighbourhood' (145–6).

Ultimately murdered by Shiv Sena thugs, Kapur falls prey to one
of the forces responsible for the unravelling of his dream of Bombay.
Bombay's hospitality requires healing, particularly with the rise to
power of the Shiv Sena, a group that looms over Mistry's Parsi characters
concerned about the increasingly exclusive definition of India through
Hindutva: 'The Collectors' refers to the Shiv Sena riots, the tenants of
Firozsha Baag 'remember[ing] [Dr Mody] for the gate which would
keep out the rampaging mobs' (87); *Such a Long Journey*'s Dinshawji
frets about 'that bloody Shiv Sena, wanting to make the rest of us into
second-class citizens' (39); and *Family Matters* repeatedly invokes the
violent threat Shiv Sena poses, both through the Babri Mosque riots
(141) and the fact that the party 'polluted the police. And now Shiv
Sena has become the government' (142). In power in Maharashtra,
Shiv Sena wields the authority of the host, seeking to alter the house of
Bombay to make it less hospitable and eradicate what Kapur praises:
'Bombay makes room for everybody. Migrants, businessmen, perverts,
politicians, holy men, gamblers, beggars, wherever they come from,
whatever caste or class, the city welcomes them and turns them into
Bombayites' (338).

Canadian Migrations

Kapur's exaltation of Bombay's hospitality resonates with claims made
for Canada's multiculturalism, particularly in the clashes between official policy, ideals, and lived reality. Although Mistry's texts mostly take
place in Bombay, the depictions of Canada in some *Tales from Firozsha
Baag* stories and *Family Matters* contribute much to the representation
of hospitality, accommodation, and tolerance in his work. *Tales from
Firozsha Baag* deals with migration to Canada most prominently in the
stories 'Lend Me Your Light,' in which Kersi Boyce, having migrated
to Toronto, negotiates his relationship to both his brother Percy, a local
activist in India, and their childhood friend Jamshed, who has rejected
India in favour of the United States; 'Squatter,' in which Nariman
Hansotia narrates the experience of Sarosh's migration to Toronto and
subsequent inability to 'become completely Canadian' (162), signalled
by his failure to adapt to Western toilets; and 'Swimming Lessons,'
which presents Kersi not only as the narrator of the story but also as

writer of the collection as a whole, the stories his means of communicating with his parents in India.

These stories explore multiculturalism and the relationship between nation and habitation. In 'Lend Me Your Light,' Kersi describes 'the segment of Toronto's Gerrard Street known as Little India' in a letter to Jamshed: 'I promised that when he visited, we would go to all the little restaurants there and gorge ourselves with *bhelpuri, panipuri, balata-wada, kulfi,* as authentic as any in Bombay' (189). Kersi attempts to counter Jamshed's disavowal of India: 'Bombay is horrible. Seems dirtier than ever, and the whole trip just made me sick. I had my fill of it in two weeks and was happy to leave!' (188). Having relocated to the United States, Jamshed positions himself as an unhappy guest in his nation of origin, and Kersi invites him to partake in the culture of the Indian diaspora as manifested in Toronto's Little India. But as Kersi privately admits, 'I have been there just once. And on that occasion I fled the place in a very short time, feeling extremely ill at ease and ashamed, wondering why all this did not make me feel homesick or at least a little nostalgic' (189). Kersi fails to recreate a sense of home through either Little India or the Parsi Society: 'Many of the guests at these gatherings were not the type who would be regulars at Little India, but who might go there with the air of tourists, equipped with a supply of ohs and aahs for ejaculation at suitable moments, pretending to discover what they had always lived with' (190).

If Kersi wonders why he is not interpellated by Little India or the Parsi Society, regardless of the 'authenticity' of the goods on offer, Sarosh in 'Squatter' blames himself more harshly for his failure to make Canada home. 'Squatter' presents a humorous, exaggerated portrait of the discomforts of attempted assimilation and the state's efforts to manage difference. Sarosh ('Sid,' following his emigration) wishes to join the Canadian cultural host, regarding himself as a failure (and returning to India after ten years as a result) for not effecting a complete assimilation: his bodily functions rebel against his cultural intentions, as Sarosh needs to 'squat' in order to complete a bowel movement. Crucially, 'obtaining his new citizenship ha[s] not helped' (161); the disjunction between citizenship and nationality plays out in his body. Sarosh continues to regard himself as a failed Canadian, as this projection demonstrates:

The absence of feet below the stall door, the smell of faeces, the rustle of paper, glimpses caught through the narrow crack between stall door

and jamb – all these added up to only one thing: a foreign presence in
the stall, not doing things in the conventional way. And if the one outside
could receive the fetor of Sarosh's business wafting through the door, poor
unhappy Sarosh too could detect something malodorous in the air: the
presence of xenophobia and hostility. (163)

'Squatter' articulates 'a *resistance* to hegemonic practices' (Heble, 'Foreign'
54), despite the fact that 'Sarosh-Sid certainly doesn't find his predicament empowering as he perches uneasily on the toilet rim' (Morey 155).
Because Sarosh should not be required to assimilate, his self-definition
as a failed Canadian reflects an unjust definition of Canadianness itself.
His 'internalization of racist discourses' (Eustace 34) causes Sarosh both
physical and cultural discomfort; but despite his conscious attempts
to suppress it, Sarosh's body valorizes his Indian experience, rejecting this self-imposed (though culturally circumscribed) definition of a
Canadian host.

The solution offered by the 'Multicultural Department' demonstrates how Canada's official multicultural policy has failed to redefine Canadianness in a truly hospitable way. The suggestion that
Sarosh undergo an operation to have '[a] small device, *Crappus Non
Interruptus* . . . implanted in the bowel' (169) indicates that, according
to official discourse, there is something wrong with Sarosh's foreign
body, not with his perception that he must fully assimilate. Doctor
No-Ilaaz ('no remedy' [Eustace 36]) fails to offer healing as he attempts
to restore Sarosh to the status of a more productive worker, his struggles
repeatedly making him late for his job. The fact that the doctor tries to
prevent 'the consequences' of his condition from becoming 'serious as
far as [Sarosh's] career is concerned' (164) reflects a biopolitics in which
'health is a form of policing which is specifically concerned with the
quality of the labour force' (B.S. Turner, 'Foreword' xv). Moreover, the
doctor admits that the device will not make Sarosh's difference disap-
pear but, rather, will exacerbate it: 'You will never be able to live a
normal life again. You will be permanently different from your family
and friends because of this basic internal modification. In fact, in this
country or that, it will set you apart from your fellow countrymen'
(169). Sarosh would lose the ability to assume host status anywhere,
his body continuing to present a difference to be managed, ultimately
indicating that 'Canada's multicultural machinery' (Eustace 35) cannot effectively ensure Sarosh's integration into the body politic.

'Swimming Lessons' further undermines the notion of Canada as a welcoming nation and exposes the limits of official multiculturalism when the racist boys at the pool insult Kersi: 'As I enter the showers three young boys ... emerge. One of them holds his nose. The second begins to hum, under his breath: Paki Paki, smell like curry. The third says to the first two: pretty soon all the water's going to taste of curry' (246). The boys' use of the 'epithet that reduces all people from the subcontinent into a dismissive contraction' (Malieckal 372) betrays an aggressive anxiety about the constitution of Canadian society (the population 'pool') altering as a result of non-white immigration. At the same time, Kersi's father's response to the stories indicates how immigration might be culturally valued and, indeed, is suggestive for how we might read Mistry's own reception, as the immigrant perspective accrues some kind of exchange value: '... *if he continues to write about such things he will become popular because I am sure they are interested there in reading about life through the eyes of an immigrant, it provides a different viewpoint; the only danger is if he changes and becomes so much like them that he will write like one of them and lose the important difference*' (258–9). Immigrant difference, then, may be considered positive by the host culture; but there is also a risk of fixing this difference, refusing to allow a dynamism in both the cultural host position and the negotiation of multiple identities. If he 'becomes popular,' must he persist in offering his difference to the dominant culture for approval, assessment, and definition? Kersi's father's assumption that ethnic-majority Canadians are in the position to judge his son's work betrays the danger of looking to the dominant majority for legitimacy. As Sharmani Patricia Gabriel argues of 'immigrants like Sarosh' (and, I would suggest, Kersi),

> ... they do not see that their assimilable difference is in fact a valuable commodity: it is a signifier of the heterogeneity of Canadian national identity. Their inability to consider themselves 'completely Canadian' reflects the underlying premise of Canadian multiculturalism that considers ethnic subjects mere 'squatters' ... , not rightful or legitimate inhabitants of the national space of Canada. (35)

By gesturing towards dominant Canadianness as the judge of Kersi's experience, Kersi's father implicitly valorizes how that dominant Canadianness would assess his son's claims to belonging and reinscribes Kersi's position as guest, at best, or squatter, at worst.

In *Family Matters*, Canada appears as a present absence, the location of Yezad's failed attempt to emigrate. If Canada has been a 'fantasy' (125) prior to his application, Yezad's experience of hostility at the Canadian High Commission demonstrates that the idea of Canada, and its claims to hospitality, is not simply a fantasy, but 'a gigantic hoax' (235). Despite his knowledge of Canadian history, politics, and literature, Yezad's application fails when he cannot demonstrate knowledge about Canadian sports: 'What's a power play? Do you know what it means to deke? What's an icing penalty? Tell me the difference between the CFL and the NFL. How many franchises in the NHL? How is lacrosse played?' (234). Yezad cannot immigrate to Canada and become a Canadian citizen because he does not meet Canadian 'national' requirements, in the form of knowledge about Canada's 'national' sports. Denied hospitality outside Canada's borders, the Chenoys are not even allowed to be guests.

Yezad's application letter to the Canadian High Commission has made similar claims for Canada that Kapur makes for Bombay: 'The generosity of the Canadian dream makes room for everyone, for a multitude of languages and cultures and peoples. In Canada's willingness to define and redefine itself continually, on the basis of inclusions, lies its greatness, its promise, its hope' (231). Yezad extols the virtues of 'Canada's multicultural policy, a policy that in the beauty of its wisdom did not demand the jettisoning of the old before letting them share in the new' (231). But like Kapur, Yezad is overly optimistic about the convergence of ideal and reality for the accommodation and celebration of difference. Having previously praised the multicultural policy, his experience of being refused entry recalls the extent to which Canada's multiculturalism has always been a hoax, as he castigates the Immigration Officer for 'abusing Indians and India, one of the many countries your government drains of its brainpower, the brainpower that is responsible for your growth and prosperity' (235). Like Mireille Rosello, Yezad acknowledges that welcoming immigrants for the purpose of bolstering a nation-state's fortunes is not truly hospitable. Further, Yezad's incredulity that the Japanese-Canadian Immigration Officer could have so little compassion for hopeful immigrants recalls the 'racism and xenophobia' directed at Japanese-Canadians 'in Canada, where they were Canadian citizens, put in camps like they were prisoners of war' (235). Astonished at his mistreatment by an individual, Yezad also foregrounds how Canada has failed, historically, to accord host status to ethnic-minority families, even those born within its borders. Although

Canada has figured as the place of escape from Bombay, Canada's failures to live up to its own fantasy of hospitality sorely undermine its claims to a just society in comparison to India. Mistry's representations of Bombay therefore both implicitly and explicitly offer comparisons with Canada, his site of habitation and of the production of his texts, particularly surrounding issues of claims to legitimate belonging and the negotiation of hospitality and difference.

Reception, Celebration, and the Negotiation of National Identity

Mistry's frequent use of Bombay as his narrative setting, with only occasional, brief forays into representing Canada, has not impeded the development of a large Canadian – indeed, Western – readership for his work. Mistry emerged, and has continued to be positioned, as a traditional storyteller whose straightforward prose facilitates the engagement of the Western reader. Reviews of Mistry's work repeatedly return to the same claims: beginning with *Tales from Firozsha Baag*, Mistry received acclaim for offering 'the good old-fashioned pleasure of diverse characters lovingly observed and vividly brought to life that only a skilled storyteller can provide' (Schapiro 5C). Many reviewers have compared Mistry to Charles Dickens and declared that Mistry's work has more affinities with the nineteenth-century novel than with contemporary fiction, foregrounding the fact that 'Mistry's characters dominate his work' (Battersby 9). Reviewers also describe Mistry's prose style in consistently basic terms, such as 'graceful, simple prose,' 'technically conservative' (Ross, 'Mistry's Dark World' C1), 'stately and strangely workmanlike' (Battersby 9), 'unpretentious' but 'technically accomplished' (Foran, 'Mistry Still' J6). Critics often contrast Mistry with Salman Rushdie, distinguishing the writers' diverging stylistic ambitions: Mistry's writing is 'less hyper, . . . less given to flashy virtuoso display, more open to genuine wonder and sorrow at the ways people manage to endure' (Mojtabai 29); and another critic claims, 'In the heyday of magic realism and everything that comes with postmodernism, it takes courage to go back to the traditional way of novel writing' (Shah 115). Although Martin Halliwell invokes both Dickens and Rushdie, arguing that Mistry draws his characters 'with a gentleness of touch rarely found' (205) in the other two writers, such comparisons betray an expectation that an Indian diasporic writer might have more in common with Rushdie's postmodern magic realism, an assumption thwarted by Mistry's apparent connections to nineteenth-century fiction, implicitly valorized in some reviews for accommodating a wider readership.

That Mistry's narrative setting has not pre-empted a Western read-ership may be partly due to the perception of his works' authenticity, exoticism, and universalism, consistently invoked in reviews. The high-profile criticism Mistry received from Germaine Greer for his portrayal of Bombay in *A Fine Balance* – 'It's a Canadian book about India. What could be worse?' (quoted in 'Mistry Miffed' E7) – has not been echoed, on the whole, by reviewers in the West. The authenticity claimed for Mistry in most Western reviews – 'no matter how many of these events beggar our belief, far less our experience or understanding, it is impos-sible to question [Mistry's] authenticity' (MacDougall 13) – resembles some Indian responses. Although some Indian critics express concerns about Mistry's 'diasporic time warp' (Bharucha, *Rohinton Mistry* 206) or his 'tilt[ing] the balance in favour of the western reader who likes to see a bleak picture of India' (Dodiya 71), others insist that despite Mistry's migration to Canada, he 'writes most authentically about his experi-ence in India' (Pandit 16); he is 'an insider to Firozsha Baag, Bombay, and his vignettes are naturally totally authentic' (Ramaswamy 54); and he 'emerges as a true Indian writer, for the scenes, the situation, the characters and even the language reflect the typical Indian culture vividly' (Myles 91).

These assertions of authenticity suggest not only the 'stamp of approval' (Foran, 'Mistry Still' J6) that Mistry has admitted he seeks from Indian readers but also that Western readers can be satisfied that they are reading the 'real' India, an 'exotic' country from their point of view. Mistry's Indo-Canadian identity complicates his relation-ship to exoticism. Current associations with exoticism derive from the nineteenth-century connotations of 'stimulating or exciting dif-ference, something with which the domestic could be (safely) spiced' (Ashcroft, Griffiths, and Tiffin 94). But since the exotic is also 'not my own' (Todorov 264), the position of both Mistry and his Western read-ers fundamentally underpins the dynamic of the exotic in his works. In many ways, Mistry does not write about that which is not his own; India does not present the 'extreme foreignness' (Célestin 4) associated with exoticism. But the attribution of the exotic to Mistry suggests that Western readers do not claim him as someone belonging to their culture. For some, Mistry's national identities mean his work is always already exotic: as one American reviewer claims of *Such a Long Journey*, '... the novelist himself is an exotic: Rohinton Mistry, Bombay-born but a resident of Toronto since 1975, a standout among the influx of immi-grants that has so enriched Canadian culture in the past decade or two' (Drabelle D3). The *Jerusalem Post*'s review identifies the novel's 'Gujarati and Hindi phrases' as 'add[ing] an exotic flavor to the writing' (Di'Antonio), indicating that 'safe spicing' of literature. The *Globe and Mail*'s Val Ross acknowledges the exotic's inherent relativity when she invokes Rushdie's response to the novel as 'the first book of fact-based fiction in the Indian literary tradition' and concedes that 'one society's exotic fantasy is another's realistic reportage' ('Governor-General's'). However, Ross presupposes that society is homogeneous, raising the question of whether Mistry does not belong to Canadian society if he appears to be exotic to Euro-Canadian readers.

Exoticism does not impinge upon the consumption of Mistry's work, of course, and reviewers often claim a universalism for his fiction. The *Washington Post* states that *Such a Long Journey* 'conjure[s] up a world that looks exotic but strikes recognizable chords of middle-class aspiration' ('New' X12), presumably accessible for the newspaper's readership. The thrill of the exotic might be tempered by reviewers' reassurances that readers of any nationality can appreciate Mistry's fiction: of *A Fine Balance*, one American reviewer insists that its 'spellbinding narrative allows us to peek into the particular, but never misses the point of elevating things to the universal,' relying on 'a compassionate realism that evokes many aspects of human emotions' (Uppala 2E). Unsurprisingly, humanism and universalism often intersect in Mistry's reception, as *Scotland on Sunday*'s review of the same novel indicates: 'A humanist novel, it is polemical without hectoring or posturing ... It could be objected that this account allows only one side, a single analysis of a complex human tragedy. But this misses the universality, the permeating force of what is portrayed in terms that lay bare the potential for evil, as well as for sacrifice and greatness in every one of us' (Adair 13). Mistry himself has acknowledged the attractions of his work's exoticism and universalism: 'I'm sure there is some appeal to read about India for people who have not been to India ... But I think there is also a universal appeal. Everyone can identify with the character who struggles against great odds' (quoted in Nichols 15A).

The frequent association of Mistry with realism dovetails with claims for his authentic portrayals of India, and a traditional writing style. As David Williams describes *Such a Long Journey*, 'Technically, there are very few risks, and very few discoveries, in the use of a limited third-person narrator ... Narrative omniscience ... becomes a larger mark ... of the reassuring sense of an author-God' (62). But the assignation of realism to Mistry's work may be insufficient. There are some affinities between the reception of Mistry and Carol Shields, as both writers focus on the domestic, and both can be read as aesthetically 'unchallenging' or 'not-so-challenging' (Archer, 'Plain' 14). Indeed, although many critics identify Mistry's realist tendencies, several highlight his writing's postmodern aspects, just as critics focus on either Shields's ostensible aesthetic simplicity or her postmodern experimentation. Mistry not only exhibits 'a postmodern understanding of the relationship between language and the material world' (Tokaryk 3), but he also engages in metafiction, for instance, in *Tales from Firozsha Baag*'s 'postmodern trick' (Albertazzi, 'Passages' 65) that identifies Kersi as the author of the stories. As Morey contends, 'If this writing can be classified as realism at all it is a kind of self-conscious, "implosive" realism: a post-colonial "metarealism" perhaps' (169). Further, although Mistry has been 'taken to resuscitate the humanist traditions of the realist novel' (Moss, 'Can Rohinton' 157), and widely celebrated for not producing 'what has come to be viewed as a postcolonial novel of resistance' (157–8), *A Fine Balance* demonstrates humanism's failure, as Laura Moss argues: 'Things have fallen apart; the universalist paradigm can not hold' (163). Noting that the back-cover blurb of the American edition privileges a humanist and universalist reading of the text, Moss counters that this view 'decontextualize[s], dehistoricize[s] and ultimately depoliticize[s] the realism in the novel' in order to 'make it more palatable for a general American public' (163), as it no doubt would for a general Canadian or, indeed, international public. Like Shields, Mistry can be read straightforwardly, allowing his readership to proliferate globally; however, Mistry is not *only* a realist writer, as his metafictional, 'metarealist' aspects indicate. His technique may have been mistaken as conservative, but it does not follow that he has produced ideologically conservative texts.

Nevertheless, references to realism, authenticity, universalism, and exoticism dominate reviews of Mistry's work. His insertions into both the exotic and the universal resonate with Canadian anxieties about Mistry's national and cultural status. Canadian newspaper coverage of Mistry has consistently mentioned that he has yet to set one of his books in Canada (beyond a few short stories). Of *Tales from Firozsha Baag*, nominated for the Governor General's Award for English-language fiction in 1987, Mistry expressed surprise at the collection's Canadian reception: 'When I saw the book was so readily appreciated ... I could never quite decide whether it was because, one, multiculturalism is in fashion, or two, it was a case of let's encourage this poor guy from India or, three, because the writing is good' (quoted in Allemang D1). Mistry's invocation of multiculturalism before projecting ethnic-majority Canadians' views of him as 'this poor guy from India,' as opposed to a Canadian of twelve years, demonstrates that official multiculturalism has failed to expand the definition of Canadianness.

Tales from Firozsha Baag's Governor General's Award nomination has been described as 'a landmark' (Parameswaran 184), and Mistry was positioned by some as part of a growing representation of ethnic-minority writing in Canadian literature. Amin Malak's review of the collection in *Canadian Literature* declared, 'Canadian literature has gained a fresh and distinctive voice. Mistry, together with such talented writers as Michael Ondaatje, Joy Kogawa, and Neil Bissoondath, opens exciting new vistas that expand the Canadian imagination beyond familiar Anglo-European motifs towards Oriental and Third World dimensions' (103). Enacting hospitality by advising readers that Mistry is 'a writer to watch and welcome' (103), Malak also suggests that Mistry's work extends the borders of Canadian culture. The invocation of Ondaatje invites a telling comparison, for he and Mistry have received diverging critical responses to their works, particularly in Canada. As in the case of Ondaatje, Mistry's work was celebrated early in his career, and his first Governor General's Award–winning text did not take place in Canada. But reviewers do not fixate on Ondaatje's non-Canadian settings to the same degree as they do on Mistry's. The response to Mistry's award suggests that the definition of Canadian culture may not have expanded as much in popular perceptions – however much it may have in Malak's, who is writing for an academic journal – as it ought to have since Diefenbaker's outburst at *The Collected Works of Billy the Kid*. Marke Andrews writes in the *Vancouver Sun*, 'When Rohinton Mistry won the Governor-General's Award ... for his first novel, some people wondered aloud why the Brampton, Ont., writer didn't write about his adopted country, Canada' ('Author's Imagination' C7). As Mistry has stated, 'There was a sense of mild reproach when my novel came out – the assumption was that now this chap was in Canada I would write about that. A logical transition, but I fooled them. I'm more drawn to Bombay at the moment' (quoted in Guttridge 29). Although Mistry's Bombay settings have been included in Canadian literature's increasing tendency 'to move abroad [and] the national introversions which have occupied us politically are now indistinguishable in our fiction,' the fact that the award-winning *Such a Long Journey* 'has no Canadian content at all after the publisher's imprint' (T.L. Craig 21) has continued to agitate many reviewers.

Surprisingly, the Canadian immigration plot of *Family Matters* went largely unexamined in Canadian newspaper reviews. Only the *Ottawa Citizen*'s Paul Gessell foregrounded this narrative, warning, 'Be wary about coaxing Rohinton Mistry, one of Canada's most beloved and decorated authors, to write about his adopted country instead of his native India: The results could be brutal' ('Mistry' J1). Gessell claims that Mistry, 'according to the rules of the game . . . should be the poster boy for Canada's multiculturalism policy and not one of its harshest critics': 'Mistry should be eternally grateful for the opportunities Canada offered him, an immigrant with few prospects from the Parsi minority of India who, after only three books to his credit, was elevated to the top ranks of the international literary world' (J1). The policy has had some impact on Mistry through McClelland and Stewart's multicultural funding for publicizing *Such a Long Journey* (see Young 90). But Gessell does not stipulate for what, exactly, Mistry should be 'eternally grateful,' though it may be the national celebrations of 'Canada's two main literary prizes, the Giller and the Governor-General's Award' (J1).

Mistry credits his move to Canada with his becoming a writer ('That has been the redeeming factor' [quoted in Gessell, 'Mistry' J1]), and certainly the state has been involved, even at arm's length, in financial support and celebration, directly through his Canada Council Explorations grant and Governor General's Award, and indirectly through McClelland and Stewart's funding. But Gessell's assignation of Mistry as 'poster boy' for state-sponsored multiculturalism raises disturbing questions about hospitality and Gessell's perception of Mistry's Canadianness. Derrida writes that

> . . . to be what it 'must' be, hospitality must not pay a debt, or be governed by a duty: it is gracious, and 'must' not open itself to the guest [invited or visitor], either 'conforming to duty' or even . . . 'out of duty' . . . For if I practice hospitality *'out of* duty' [and not only *'in conforming with* duty'], this hospitality of paying up is no longer an absolute hospitality, it is no longer graciously offered beyond debt and economy, offered to the other, a hospitality invented for the singularity of the new arrival, of the unexpected visitor. (*Of Hospitality* 83, brackets in original)

Gessell comes dangerously close to according Mistry the role of ungrateful guest, and to replicating the position of reviewers who complain about Mistry's 'refusal' to set his books in Canada. In this way, Canada's hospitality to Mistry, its invitation to become 'one of us,' is inauthentic, for Gessell implies, despite his somewhat tongue-and-cheek writing, that Mistry owes Canada more than he cares to admit: not only representation within his fiction, but also representation in a better light than that offered by *Family Matters*. In failing to do so, Gessell and other critics imply, Mistry refuses to 'pay up.'

What Gessell does not state in his roll-call of honours that testify to Mistry's success in Canada is that Mistry's having 'racked up several other honours at home and abroad, including the short list for Britain's Booker, the ultimate plum in English-language literature' (J1), might itself constitute Mistry's 'paying up.' Again, Ondaatje provides a fruitful comparison: *The English Patient* includes little overt representation of Canada, but critics were not as anxious about this setting as they tend to be with Mistry's. Ondaatje's varied settings over the course of his career have not seemed as threatening as Mistry's consistent return to Bombay in his fictions. The reinvocation of Bombay in Mistry's work appears to provoke the kinds of anxieties raised in recent years in Canada about dual citizenship. By returning to Bombay in all of his texts, and not engaging as much with Canada as many Canadian reviewers would like, or indeed in the manner that they would like, Mistry might be guilty of having 'divided loyalties,' his preference for Bombay as setting seemingly suggesting that he wishes to remain a guest in Canada rather than become one of the hosts – or, worse, that he is content to 'squat' without paying Canada his cultural dues. Thus, Kersi's father in 'Swimming Lessons' proves incorrect, as many critics appear to tire of the 'important [and valuable] difference' that Mistry offers.

Nevertheless, Mistry's work has been celebrated both within and without Canada, Bombay settings and all. Although his first Governor General's Award nomination, for *Tales from Firozsha Baag*, celebrated a text whose trajectory moved towards engagement with Canada through Kersi's stories of migration, Mistry's Governor General's win came for *Such a Long Journey*, 'the first novel by an Indian immigrant to win' the award (D. Williams 57). It also won the Smith Books / Books in Canada First Novel Award. Despite the fact that the novel does not mention Canada, its anointing by these Canadian prizes interpolated it into Canadian literature. Given critics' frequent comparisons of Mistry and Dickens, the Governor General's Award win seems anomalous in light of Shields's claim that this prize looks to celebrate innovative texts that reinvent fiction, although Mistry's play with realism suggests more subtle readings of his technique undermine the Dickens comparison. But the Governor General's Award jury, like many reviewers, described Mistry's writing as old-fashioned: Sharon Butala, who selected *Such a Long Journey* as her first choice, stated that 'the writing reminded her of Charles Dickens'; conversely, Kenneth Radu complained that the novel was 'hampered by an antiquated prose style' (quoted in 'Mistry Wins' F8). In these terms, Mistry's win reflects not an expanding definition of fiction but perhaps an expanding definition of a Canadian text.

Media coverage of Mistry's win points to a growing significance of immigrant writers to Canadian literature ('Mistry's award for Such a Long Journey confirms immigrant writers as a major force on the Canadian literary scene' [Demchinsky D1]) as well as to Mistry's contributing to Canada's multicultural identity ('Governor-General's Awards winners reveal a remarkable regional and multicultural range' [Ross, 'Mistry's Journey' C1]). There was, therefore, a sense that Canadian culture could, indeed, redefine itself, and that state-sponsored multiculturalism was part of that redefinition. However, despite the fact that Canadian literary prizes awarded to immigrant writers interpolate these writers into Canadian culture, the complaints about Mistry's settings throughout his career from several Canadian reviewers demonstrate a lack of consensus about the effectiveness of this interpolation.

It would be a mistake, however, to declare that Mistry's Bombay-set texts have nothing to say to or about Canada. Not only do Mistry's Bombay settings offer 'a migrant representation of India' (Herbert 13), but the constitution of Canadianness also requires further probing here. Such statements as 'this word "Canadian" has to mean something . . . , it means that a given work reflects this place, Canada, one way or another' and '[Mistry] can write a Canadian novel any time he wishes. But as yet, he hasn't done so' (McGoogan, 'More' F2) ignore Mistry's concern with the forging of community out of difference, a concern shared with Ondaatje's *The English Patient* and particularly evident in both *A Fine Balance*'s ad-hoc family in Dina's flat and the multi-faith wall in *Such a Long Journey*, described by one reviewer as 'multiculturalism with a vengeance' (Marchand, 'A Tale' K13). While it would be simplistic to insist that Mistry 'really' writes about Canada when he portrays Bombay, this question of setting is more nuanced and complicated than reviewers and critics acknowledge: not only is the site of production significant, with Mistry declaring, '. . . it is very important to me that the act of writing takes place here. I cannot imagine myself in a room in any other city, in another other country, writing' (quoted in Richler, *My Country* 443), but Mistry's representation of community and difference also resonates with significant Canadian concerns. Mistry's '[speaking] out against cuts to Ontario's social-welfare programs' (Ross, 'Mistry's Dark World' C1) at McClelland and Stewart's launch of *A Fine Balance* demonstrates an overlapping concern with the disenfranchised in India as represented in the novel and the effects of Mike Harris's 'common-sense revolution' as well as with the suspension of rights under Indira Gandhi's Emergency and the violent suppression of protest by the Ontario government.

Mistry's recreation of the Emergency partly echoes Canadian political and economic questions current during *A Fine Balance*'s production. Further, given that Mistry's first book, *Tales from Firozsha Baag*, was published the year the Reform Party was created in Canada, Mistry's consistent critique of Shiv Sena's racist 'Maharashtra for Maharashtrians' platform operates along a continuum with Reform's anti-immigration and ethnocentric policies. If hospitality implies healing, *Family Matters'* narrative about the cost of care provides an instructive contrast between India and Canada. Although one reviewer, invoking universalism, asserts that *Family Matters* 'could easily take place in [Mistry's] adopted home, Toronto – or anywhere, for that matter' (Kubacki C12), that is not, in fact, the case: Canada's state-sponsored health care means that Nariman's family would not have been left to their own devices to such an extent; further, as Mistry himself has noted, in Canada 'there are options: nursing homes or seniors' apartments for those who can afford them' (Smulders 29). However, cuts to health care in Canada and the qualification of 'those who can afford' these options also mean that *Family Matters* could operate as a cautionary tale, reminding Canadians of what is at stake in the drive towards increasing privatization and the off-loading of responsibility for care from the state to the family.

Journalists who dispute Mistry's Canadianness fail to address the fact that Mistry is not the only Canadian of Indian origin. To declare that 'Mistry's *Such a Long Journey*, which is set in India, might well be the best novel written by a Canadian in 1991. That doesn't make it a Canadian novel, because the book does not speak expressly to Canadians' (McGoogan, 'More' F2) not only ignores the links between Mistry's Bombay and Mistry's Canada, but it also effectively writes him out of the Canadian nation, along with every other Indo-Canadian. Ken McGoogan here reinforces the boundaries of nation and habitation, fixing them in a way that excludes immigrants from participating in and altering the host culture, and implicitly reifying the dominance of a British, colonizing identity as that which is Canadian.

To declare *Such a Long Journey* the best English-language Canadian fiction of 1991 through the Governor General's Award and *A Fine Balance* the best English-language Canadian fiction of 1995 through the Giller Prize therefore announces these texts' importance to Canadian culture, subverting the equations quoted above. Both these novels won the Commonwealth Writers' Prize after first winning the regional prize for the Caribbean and Canada (and not, crucially, for Europe and South Asia), emphasizing at this supranational level the interpolation of Mistry within Canadian literature. *Such a Long Journey* further contributed to Canadian culture, and celebrated Canadian culture at that, through its overwhelmingly faithful 1998 film adaptation, directed by the Icelandic-Canadian filmmaker Sturla Gunnarson, which won three Genie Awards, for best actor (Roshan Seth), editing, and sound editing. As was the case with the film adaptation of *Swann*, however, this adaptation did not bestow upon its source text the enormous after-life granted to *The English Patient* after Minghella's version. Indeed, when *Such a Long Journey* was 'finally . . . on screen in Toronto theatres' (Kirkland 44), the Genies had already been broadcast, illustrating how the awards often introduce audiences to Canadian films that have not yet arrived in cinemas, and may not appear on many Canadian screens. Like *Swann, Such a Long Journey* was a Canada-U.K. co-production, and, as with Benson Gyles's film, Canadian journalists assessed the Canadianness of Gunnarson's adaptation. Gunnarson himself declared the film to be 'classically Canadian': 'It was made by a Canadian born in Iceland, who's married to an Indian woman born in Canada, based on a novel by an author from Bombay who lives in Brampton. The novel has a Canadian voice. Rohinton could not have written it if he'd never left India' (quoted in Stoffman, 'Bombay' B1). In asserting the film's Canadianness, Gunnarson gestures towards the context of production – '[Mistry] needed distance to reflect on his roots, to write with that kind of clarity' (quoted B1) – as well as Canada's immigrant population and ideals of multiculturalism.

Not everyone, however, was convinced by either the film or its Canadianness. The *Toronto Star's* Peter Howell, despite complimenting 'this U.K.-Canada co-production' as 'a technical marvel, praiseworthy for the skill of Gunnarson and his crew in filming East Indian actors in the noisy streets of Bombay – and negotiating with both police and gangsters for the right to do it,' also criticizes the busy narrative and its reliance on historical background, presented on three title cards, which Howell argues 'demands a lot of its audience right off.' Howell punctures the film's Canadianness by claiming, '... it's a sizeable international production which we can pretend is Canadian, and in today's Hollywood North, good intentions and flag-waving go a long way.' We can only *pretend* to recognize the film's Canadianness, Howell implies, because although 'many people still stand in awe at the notion that Canadians actually make movies,' it 'doesn't seem to matter if the movies have little or nothing to do with Canada, although we are constantly told of the need for "Canadian voices" in our cinema.' Without explicitly saying so, Howell suggests that this Bombay-shot and -set film, directed by an Icelandic-Canadian and based on a novel by an Indo-Canadian, does not constitute any 'Canadian voice.'

Regardless, Mistry's Bombay narratives would continue to find celebration within Canada. Although *A Fine Balance* was not nominated for a Governor General's Award, it won the Giller Prize, and with a more sweeping narrative than its predecessor, it seems to have fit Noah Richler's covert identification of the Giller as the award for English-language Canada's Best Big Book. The largeness of *A Fine Balance* is comprised not only of its physical size (ranging from 600 to more than 700 pages, depending on the edition), its multi-generation narrative, and its expansive geographical sweep of India in its setting, but also its impressive international, as well as national, afterlife.

Mistry has received a number of international awards, including his Commonwealth Writers' Prizes as well *A Fine Balance*'s Winifred Holtby Memorial Prize and Los Angeles Book Prize. But his three Booker Prize nominations have most powerfully influenced his Canadianness as negotiated by the Canadian media. When *Such a Long Journey* lost the Booker to Ben Okri's *The Famished Road* in 1991, the year prior to Ondaatje's win, the Canadian Press used this *lack* of winning the prize to emphasize Mistry's Canadianness: 'Toronto writer Rohinton Mistry has joined the ranks of other Canadian authors, such as Margaret Atwood and Robertson Davies, who have been nominated but failed to win the coveted Booker Prize for literature' ('Nigerian-born' F3). Mistry was thus anointed as a Canadian, on par with these canonical Canadian figures, and the valuing of *Such a Long Journey* was transferred from the literary prize (which surely would have been celebrated in Canada had Mistry won) to national culture and Mistry's interpolation within it.

As with the response to Ondaatje's depiction in British media as a Sri Lankan who happens to live in Canada, Canadian journalism has often, in the face of international counterclaims about Mistry's identity, leapt to the defence of Mistry's Canadianness, demonstrating the incoherence of assumptions about Canada, Canadianness, and multiculturalism when contrasted with the concern over Mistry's settings. For Mistry to circulate in the global cultural marketplace both increases Canadian cultural power and suggests a need to police Canadianness, given some extranational media's tendency to conflate national identity with nation of origin. In order to claim Mistry as 'one of us,' some Canadian reviewers and critics have credited Canada with enabling Mistry's representations of India:

> It would be wrong to think that Mistry's Canadian perspective and Canadian experience have played no part in his depiction of Bombay. We can't tell exactly ... how that perspective and experience has shaped his fiction, but we can sense it in the very atmosphere of his narrative. Could Mistry make the same detached and almost clinical observations of his home town if he hadn't absorbed the difference that Brampton, Ont. makes? Not likely. In a sense, Mistry's Bombay is as much Canadian content as a novel about lacrosse players. ('Making' F3)

This simile poses problems, given the rejected immigration application in *Family Matters*, where Yezad is refused because of his lack of knowledge of Canadian sports. But it is not only Canadian critics who claim that Canada enables Mistry's Bombay, for some Indian critics have made similar arguments: '... perhaps he is able to achieve this authenticity as he has distanced himself by emigrating to Canada so that he can produce the effect of an insider/outsider to a scene every detail of which is etched and engraved in his mind' (Ramaswamy 54). Rukmini Bhaya Nair claims that Canada, through its low profile, 'off the beaten tracks of the Anglo-American world,' provides 'a neutral observation post, an ideal non-aligned country of the mind for the realist writer who can here stand back and achieve that exact perspective' (14). Ironically, this Canada-enabled authenticity also leads some critics to declare Mistry 'a true Indian writer' (Myles 91).

The possibility of Mistry being claimed as an Indian writer arises not only in Indian reception of his work, but also through supranational events such as the Booker Prize and Commonwealth Writers' Prize. Philip Marchand's coverage of the Commonwealth Writers' Prize in 1992 invoked the British projection of Ondaatje's identity following the Booker Prize, stating of Mistry, 'Fortunately, nobody at the awards ceremony . . . referred to Mistry as a "Parsi author domiciled in Brampton"' ('Our Authors' K13). But the Canadian administration of that year's Commonwealth Writers' Prize surely played a role in Mistry's being accorded Canadianness. Conversely, the Booker Prize and its British coverage often reinscribes Mistry's Indian identity: the *Sunday Times* referred to *Such a Long Journey*'s author as 'an unknown, Bombay-born, Canadian-based banker' (Walsh), keeping the poles of nation and habitation separate.

But it was not until the 2002 Man Booker shortlist, with its inclusion of three Canadian writers, that the British media really foregrounded Mistry's identity. The initial surprise of the triple Canadian nomination of Yann Martel, Rohinton Mistry, and Carol Shields gave way to debates about whether these writers were 'really' Canadian. In the *Guardian*, Fiachra Gibbons, distinguishing between nationality and citizenship, declared, 'Remarkably, half of the shortlist is made up of Canadians, or at least writers who have Canadian passports, led by Chicago-born Carol Shields, who made the last six once before, with the Pulitzer-winning Stone Diaries' (13). Several Canadian journalists responded to British qualification of these authors' Canadianness by contesting both literary and national valuing, replaying more heatedly the debates that had surrounded Ondaatje following his Booker Prize. Accusing British journalists of snobbery and 'sour grapes,' Canadian newspapers made snide remarks about 'the sad state of "English" literature' ('Canadians' A18). Although Canadian articles on Martel, Mistry, and Shields allude to their birthplaces, the discussion of nationality from outside the country was perceived as a *dismissal* of Canadian nationality. Bruce Wallace's description of the three 2002 Man Booker–nominated Canadians illustrates the implications drawn from British characterizations of Canadian nationality:

> Shields, Martel and Mistry were all born outside Canada. Though they have spent most of their adult lives in that big block of often snow-covered geography north of the United States, as Canada tends to be viewed from Europe, some churlish British critics have questioned the validity of their literary passports, as in the BBC's description of them as 'three Canadian-based writers.' ('Critics' D5)

Wallace thereby ascribes stereotypical perceptions of Canada from outside the country to dismantle what outsiders might have to say about Canada and Canadianness.

In fact, the furore included discussion about the make-up of Canadian nationality from British sources. 2002 Man Booker chair Lisa Jardine linked concerns of national literary style to the nation's population by declaring, 'There is no writing that is identifiably Canadian because what is distinct about the literature coming from there is its diversity' (quoted in Wallace, 'Critics' D5). Jardine invokes multiculturalism and national hospitality in her characterization of Canadian literature and its relationship to the nation: 'There is an immigrant-driven nature to it, a cultural welcoming to Canadian writing that looks to being an alternative voice from elsewhere. That's always been the lifeblood of writing: those who write from the margins speaking to the cultural centre ... There's an openness to a range of voices in Canada' (quoted D5).

As Jardine's comments suggest, the debate about Martel's, Mistry's, and Shields's Canadianness not only afforded the Canadian media the opportunity to reclaim these writers, to incorporate them within a celebration of Canadian culture and its international circulation, but it also provided a platform for celebrating official Canadian multiculturalism in a way that effaced the realities of Canadian racism and xenophobia. Paul Gessell, canvassing Canadian cultural figures to discuss the triple Canadian Man Booker nomination, quoted Gerald Lynch as follows: 'Canada has always been a nation of immigrants and, therefore, much of our literature has been produced by immigrants ... The difference now is that many Canadian writers are from Asian, African or Caribbean countries rather than from Britain and Europe. To characterize these writers as less than Canadian is "racist"' ('Wot's This?' J1). Lynch's invocation of immigration partly demonstrates a divergence in Canadian and British conceptions of nationality. The relative newness of the Canadian nation-state, and its dependence, subsequent to colonization, on immigration for the purposes of nation-building, might explain a greater willingness in Canada to accommodate multiple national identities; for Canadians to have come from elsewhere is possible, even ordinary. But this argument unravels in light of what goes unstated in Gessell's article, namely, the fact that many *Canadians* would not consider immigrant writers to be 'really' Canadian, and specifically, immigrant writers who do not correspond to perceptions of the ethnic majority; indeed, Canadian journalists' anxieties about Mistry's settings, including Gessell's own contribution to this discussion, do not appear in the nationality debates with the British media. Thus, the Canadian media, with reference to British descriptions of Martel, Mistry, and Shields, displaced issues of xenophobia onto the

British press, who presumably denied or failed to understand Canada's history of immigration and its official multicultural policy.

In the *Globe and Mail*, Charles Foran asserted, 'Choose Canada, and you are Canadian' ('As Canadian' D6), eclipsing the fact that the Canadian state holds the position of power of choice, that it wields the power to invite immigrants within its borders and the power to reject them, as *Family Matters* emphasizes. Further, absent from debates about Canadian nationality surrounding Martel, Mistry, and Shields are acknowledgments that these three authors do not, in fact, provide the same *kind* of example: quite simply, neither Martel nor Shields complicates Canadianness through racial difference. Mistry's immigration from India involves different configurations of Canadian identity than Martel's and Shields's locations of birth, as dominant constructions of Canadianness are less accommodating of the negotiations of Mistry's racialized identity. In response to debates about Shields's nationality, the setting of her Man Booker–shortlisted *Unless* 'almost entirely in Canada' ('Making' F3) underscored her Canadian credentials, particularly after *The Stone Diaries'* and *Larry's Party's* border crossings. Canadian debates about Mistry's settings, however, already indicate that Mistry is not considered the 'same' kind of hyphenated Canadian as Shields.

The Canadian response to the British media suggests that Mistry has always been welcome in Canada as a Canadian writer, that he has not only been invited in and been granted citizenship, but also become a host through his works' contribution to Canadian literature particularly and Canadian culture generally. Their external sanctioning through multiple Booker Prize nominations has prompted celebrations of Canadian culture within Canada. Thus, the exchange of guest for host status has been appropriated by the official version of Canadianness, which not only benefits from this external celebration of Canadian cultural products but also perpetuates the idea of Canada as defined by its hospitality, even as *Family Matters*, the Man Booker–nominated novel that contributed to the beginning of this transatlantic debate, exposes Canada's inhospitality.

Popular Celebrations

Despite Mistry's Commonwealth Writers' Prizes and multiple Booker nominations, his work has received the most overwhelming reception as a result of Oprah Winfrey's talk-show book club, an event that not only raised questions about literary value, but also contributed to a further negotiation of Mistry's Canadianness, this time in a popular context, through the People's Choice poll of the first Canada Reads competition.

When Winfrey chose *A Fine Balance* for her book club, Mistry's acceptance was notable, given that the author of Winfrey's last selection, Jonathan Franzen, expressed his reservations about *The Corrections'* inclusion within what has been perceived to be the 'schmaltzy,' 'one-dimensional' (quoted in Italie) Oprah's Book Club canon. On the one hand, critics viewed *A Fine Balance* as a departure from Winfrey's usual choices, calling it 'a rare highbrow selection' ('A World'), 'unsentimental' (Italie), 'probably the only literary choice the populist entertainment diva made' (Rajghatta). On the other hand, Mistry consented to the Book Club's apparatus, responding in the affirmative to Winfrey's questions 'Do you want to come to dinner? Do you want the label on your book?' (quoted in Stoffman, 'Canadian's Novel' D5).

The label raises questions for the circulation of Mistry's text. In contrast to Franzen's protest – 'I see this as my book, my creation, and I didn't want the logo of corporate ownership on it' (quoted in Striphas 132) – Mistry asserted that '... the logo doesn't change the story underneath' (S. Martin, 'Oprah' A18). But the Oprah brand, like 'the Governor-General's Award logo, the Giller Prize logo, the Booker shortlist logo' (quoted in 'Mistry Loves' D19), which, as Mistry emphasized, have previously appeared on his texts, interpellates a particular audience, and a different audience than the prize logos. As Cecilia Konchar Farr notes, '... when Farrar, Strauss put the Oprah seal into the cover art of Franzen's *The Corrections*, it became a different book. It became a mass-produced, popular choice rather than a marker of distinction and taste. And elite readers began to insist on unmarked covers' (88). Despite the disinterpellation of elite readers, the Oprah brand functions like a prize, popularizing literature to increase sales, and it seems to do so more successfully than the prizes themselves. Following Winfrey's selection of *A Fine Balance*, 'more than 750,000 paperback copies [were] printed to accommodate the anticipated rush on the title in North American alone' (S. Martin, 'Oprah' A18), of which 500,000 sold (see Morey xiii). One Indigo spokeswoman declared that Mistry 'deserves to have world-wide recognition and I am hoping this will have that effect' (quoted in S. Martin, 'Oprah' A18), suggesting his Commonwealth Writers' Prizes and Booker nominations had not achieved what booksellers anticipated Winfrey's attention would. Mistry was hailed as 'the first Canadian writer to be chosen for Oprah Winfrey's book club' ('Mistry Loves' D19), another example of external validation conferring legitimacy upon the nation's culture. Within Canada, Oprah's Book Club was credited with 'caus[ing] his audience to virtually double' ('Rohinton Mistry Signs').

Did Mistry become a middlebrow writer by having been 'Oprah-sanctified' (Umrigar D7), 'canonis[ed] courtesy the mistress of middle-brow,' and granted 'paperback stardom' (Prasannarajan 66)? *Family Matters* was published after the televised Book Club appearance, and its reviews inserted Mistry into the middlebrow category. James Grainger, declaring the novel 'undeniably readable,' also accuses Mistry of using 'the language of paperback genre writing' (D12). Another reviewer claims, 'Mistry is openly writing melodrama' (Elie 127). Mistry's reviews over the course of his career have tended to find his work both senti-mental and unsentimental in reasonably equal measure, demonstrating a lack of consensus and the fact that Mistry's style 'engages both the populist and the intellectual markets simultaneously' (Buzacott M7). Indeed, as Grainger claims, 'Mistry's writing ... has always walked a fine line between pathos and melodrama' (D12). On the whole, most critics responded positively to *Family Matters*, but the majority pre-ferred the large-scale narrative of *A Fine Balance*, disappointed by the intimate scale of the later novel: 'What's missing – and what the reader acutely misses – is Mistry's accustomed scope' (Vowles M18). But reviewers betray a sense that this scale of *Family Matters* translates into a novel of less significance. Its domestic focus, along with the Oprah-branding and Winfrey's 'massive middlebrow readership' (Aubry 351), contributes to Mistry's insertion into the middlebrow category, given that the Oprah audience 'encompasses the barely middle class, the less educated, the ubiquitous audience member who hasn't "read a book since high school," as well as the privileged, the college graduates, the stay-at-home soccer mom longing for intellectual stimulation' (Konchar Farr 2). The constitution of Winfrey's audience (and thus members of the Book Club) means that the 'Oprahfication' of literature, via the Book Club, has connoted 'a perceived excess of emotionality; the populariza-tion of suffering, public confession, therapy, and self-help; the privileg-ing of image over depth; a lack of intellectualism; and, more generally, the debasement of culture' (Striphas 114). Given that '"Oprah" is an abstract label under which more or less unique books can be ren-dered commensurable' (115), the 'Oprahfication' of the Book Club's selected authors appears to have detracted from Mistry as a unique author, and 'debased' the cultural value of his work. If the middlebrow negotiates the posited disjunction 'between pleasing a larger audience and gaining literary respect' (York 176), it seems that for Mistry, post-Oprah, the constitution of that larger audience played a considerable role in diminishing the respect Mistry had previously enjoyed.

Significantly, *Family Matters* was not nominated for either the Governor General's Award or the Giller Prize, though it did win the Kiryama Prize and received Mistry's third Booker nomination. The absence of nomination for the Canadian national awards may stem from the increased association of Mistry with the middlebrow. However, the overlooking of *Family Matters*, identified in one review as 'one of the angriest books of 2002' by virtue of its failed migration plot and its exposure of the empty 'rhetoric of multiculturalism' (Kröller 159), may also suggest an unwillingness on some level to license Mistry's transgression. Donald C. Goellnicht's overview of the emergence of Asian-Canadian writing posits that the focus of many South Asian–Canadian writers 'on the past in a distant place that still haunts them, ... rather than writing novels about racism and discrimination *in Canada*, may also help to explain why it has been easier for their works to get published by mainstream publishing houses such as McClelland and Stewart' (15). Goellnicht implies that 'the spectacular success of Rohinton Mistry' (15), despite complaints about his Bombay settings, may have been *facilitated* by his not grappling with issues of racism in Canada, that his work has been deemed 'the kind of "acceptable" and "exotic" writing that the white literary establishment has tended to elicit and reward from ethnic minority writers' (15–16). Although Ondaatje's *In the Skin of a Lion* was celebrated despite its concerns with Canadian racism, its historical setting is crucial for a comparison with *Family Matters*, which, unlike Mistry's two previous novels, is set contemporaneously to the time of its production. While Goellnicht does not mention *Tales from Firozsha Baag*'s critique of Canadian racism, his observations of what allows immigrant writers' success may partly explain the embracing of texts like *A Fine Balance* by so many Canadian readers.

Although Mistry's 'angry book of 2002' received no recognition from the main Canadian prizes, in the same year, *A Fine Balance* was in contention for the inaugural Canada Reads competition. Although it lost to *In the Skin of a Lion*, *A Fine Balance* won the parallel People's Choice competition. Considering that Canada Reads selects a book for the nation to read together, the popular selection of *A Fine Balance* suggests that Canada Reads' audience had less trouble viewing Mistry as a Canadian writer than some reviewers have done, given 'the People's' preference for Mistry's story of Bombay over Ondaatje's Toronto narrative. These Canadian readers thereby problematized the view of journalist Connie Woodcock: 'A Fine Balance is an excellent book ... but it's set in 1970s India. A book that speaks to Canadian experience it's not' (C5). Woodcock replicates McGoogan's definition of Canadians that would exclude those of Indian origin, but the People's Choice suggests otherwise. However, given that Mistry's Canadian readership nearly doubled following his selection by Winfrey, the Oprah brand likely affected and effected this celebration of Mistry's text; thus, American cultural imperialism bore some responsibility for popularizing Mistry in his own nation.

If Winfrey's selection of *A Fine Balance* stemmed partly from the events of 11 September 2001, and 'Americans understand[ing] they have to look outside themselves, to understand other cultures' (Stoffman, 'Canadian's Novel' D5), ironically, Mistry suffered the fallout from the attacks during his *Family Matters* promotional tour, the American leg of which he cut short after being repeatedly subjected to racial profiling at U.S. airports, despite his Canadian citizenship and the absence of his nation of origin from the list of 'suspect' countries. Given that even the United States' official guidelines for searching and detaining passengers did not justify Mistry's treatment, this series of incidents was unambiguously racist. Regarded as an unwelcome, threatening guest below the border, Mistry chose to avoid the United States, and Canadian officials, particularly then–citizenship and immigration minister Denis Coderre ('With friends like that, you don't need enemies' [quoted in 'Coderre']), protested the American treatment of ethnic-minority Canadians on the grounds that all Canadians should be treated equally at the border, the threshold that distinguishes between us and them along citizenship lines, but now also divided between threatening and non-threatening Canadians according to their skin colour. As one American editorial insisted, 'By discriminating among Canadians, the United States is telling the rest of the world that citizenship is, essentially, worthless' (Bayoumi 1C).

Mistry's international celebration has no doubt contributed to Canadian cultural power, but there is a greater anxiety about Mistry's national identity as opposed to his citizenship, given his focus on Bombay and an exclusive, narrow definition of what it means to be Canadian and what constitutes Canadian experience, a failure to acknowledge that 'Canadianness is indeterminate, and its meanings are constantly being renegotiated and rearticulated' (Gabriel 34). When asked about his own sense of identity, Mistry does not declare his Canadianness as readily as Ondaatje and Shields. Although he has stated, 'I don't consider myself an Indian writer. I feel perfectly at ease living in this society' (quoted in Heward, 'Mistry's New' F13), he has also asserted, 'I don't have to decide the question of my identity . . . There are academics and experts out there who will decide my Canadian-ness, my Indian-ness, all the hyphenated combinations. As far as I'm concerned, I'm a writer' (quoted in Coulson C5). As a writer, Mistry implicitly claims a cosmopolitan status: '. . . the world is my audience' (Hancock Interview 146); however, Mistry also suggests that he 'reside[s] within the space of the hyphen' (Kamboureli, *Scandalous* 100) when he claims to be 'forever suspended between the two cultures' (quoted in Foley EE2). Mistry refuses to fix himself as host or guest in either location, his residence within the hyphen's space a residence on the threshold.

Response to Mistry oscillates between suggesting his Canadianness is incomplete (like Sarosh's, perhaps) through his 'failing' to represent Canada in his fiction, and appropriating his international successes. Claiming Mistry as a Canadian in the global cultural marketplace capitalizes on the increase in Canadian cultural currency while betraying an anxiety that that currency cannot appreciate if Mistry does not project himself as 'recognizably' Canadian. Suspended between host and guest positions in Canada, poised on the threshold, Mistry appears to occupy the status of cultural guest worker despite his support and celebration through the Canada Council, Governor General's Award, and Giller Prize; and, indeed, some media responses to Mistry imply that he is a parasite, feeding off the Canadian cultural host and its institutions without paying 'the price for a space, a payment for territory' (Serres 22). Tellingly, unlike Ondaatje and Shields, Mistry has not received the Order of Canada, emphasizing the extent to which hospitality to Mistry has indeed been provisional, perhaps on the expectation that he might eventually 'pay up' and represent Canada, in both senses, for a global audience.

5 'Un Québécois francophone écrivant en anglais': Yann Martel's Zoos, Hospitals, and Hotels

The most recent Canadian writer to win the Man Booker Prize, Yann Martel took centre stage in the international anglophone literary community with his novel *Life of Pi*, which not only beat the other short-listed Canadian novels in 2002 (Mistry's *Family Matters* and Shields's *Unless*) but also became the most successful Booker-winning text to date. Previously considered a writer of experimental fiction, Martel simultaneously consolidated his highbrow credentials through the prize and vastly increased his audience, both inside and outside Canada, through the celebration and reception of his part-philosophical, part-adventure story of a multi-faith Indian boy shipwrecked with a Bengal tiger, and their 227 days spent sharing a lifeboat in the Pacific Ocean.

Just as the Man Booker–enhanced popularity of Martel's novel allowed the text to travel globally, so too the life of the writer has been characterized by frequent travel and significant amounts of time spent outside his 'home' country: Martel was born in 1963 in Salamanca, Spain, where his Québécois parents were graduate students; they moved to Portugal shortly afterwards, and Martel was raised in locations all over the world. His father's academic career took the family to Alaska and Victoria, BC; later, his parents' positions as diplomats led them to Costa Rica, Paris, Ottawa, Spain, and Mexico (see Menzies). Martel attended Trent University in Peterborough, Ontario, and Concordia University in Montreal, where he studied philosophy. He is francophone, but was educated in English, the language in which he has written his five books: the collection of four stories, *The Facts behind the Helsinki Roccamatios* (1993), the title story of which won the Journey Prize; his first novel, *Self* (1996); the Man Booker Prize–winning *Life of Pi*, which was also nominated in 2001 for the Governor General's Award for English-language fiction, won the Hugh MacLennan Award for fiction, and was short-listed for the 2003 Canada Reads competition; *What Is Stephen Harper Reading?* (2009), a collection of letters to the prime minister accompanying fortnightly reading suggestions from Martel; and *Beatrice and Virgil* (2010), his first novel since *Life of Pi*.

Although Martel professes not to be interested in autobiography (see Sielke Interview 14), his writing grapples with issues that run parallel to his unusual upbringing, particularly the experience of displacement in many forms, the disjunction between nation and habitation, and the role of the citizen. That *What Is Stephen Harper Reading?* should address Canadian issues ought not to come as a surprise, but in *The Facts behind the Helsinki Roccamatios, Self,* and *Life of Pi,* Canada is also often explicitly discussed, the object of overt consideration as not only characters' but also the nation's identity come under scrutiny. These fictional texts envision a Canada whose hospitality is provisional: at times ineffective, at other times completely absent when dominant forces seek to limit the boundaries of the Canadian host. Yet Martel also offers moments in which Canada fulfils its hospitable promises, and his work functions through both form and content to expand the borders of Canadianness and its expression. His work engages a syncretism of language and religion that reconfigures established, official models for the negotiation of difference and offers a rethinking of Canadian multiculturalism. For Martel, a radical simultaneity of language and religion insists upon differences that cannot simply be managed by the state and that require more imagination to consider.

As with Ondaatje, Shields, and Mistry, Martel has undergone negotiations of his identity in the international, particularly British, press in the wake of his success and celebration. Whereas the other three writers' immigration to Canada has formed the basis of this negotiation, Martel's international upbringing has prompted a misrecognition of his nationality, one which was heatedly debated following his Man Booker Prize win. Martel's own recruitment into the debate functioned not only to reassure Canada of his Canadianness but also fed into the celebration of Canada as a hospitable space, a celebration not entirely upheld in Martel's own representations of his country. Further, although Anglo-Canadian journalists demonstrated a strong investment in the recuperation of Martel's Canadianness, particularly in the face of British diminishing of Canada's claims to Martel, the response to Martel's Man Booker in the Québécois press presents another negotiation of Martel's identity and the operation of diverging national projects. That Martel has been claimed to represent both Anglo-Canadian and Québécois literature resonates with his textual interest in representing ostensibly clashing affiliations as nonetheless simultaneous.

Narratives of Displacement

Although *Self* and *Life of Pi* offer dramatic, and drastic, narratives of displacement, the first two stories of *The Facts behind the Helsinki Roccamatios* also explore various forms of dislocation. The narrator of the title story, echoing Martel himself, is a philosophy student at Trent University; but little of the narrative has to do with Peterborough or the university. The story focuses on the narrator's friendship with Paul Atsea, a younger student who develops AIDS as a result of a tainted blood transfusion after a car accident in Jamaica. Most of the narrative unfolds in Toronto, where Paul's family lives, particularly the Atseas' house and the hospital. The narrator has moved to Oshawa to be closer to Paul, but he is 'hardly aware of Oshawa' (23), and the narrative occurs elsewhere. Keeping Paul company during his illness, the narrator enters into a hospitality of frustrated and impossible healing. The narrator moves from a guest position ('I used to call ahead and ring at the door when I came to visit') to one that assumes the privileges of the host ('... quickly I was given a key and told I was welcome any hour of the day or night, seven days a week, three hundred and sixty-five days a year' [37]). His relationship of affiliation becomes recoded as filiation: 'It's as though I have three parents now instead of one: Jack pats me on the back and Mary smiles at me and touches my forearm lightly' (37). After Paul's death, it transpires that his nurse has assumed that the narrator is Paul's partner – 'I'm sorry about your boyfriend' (74), she says – emphasizing the narrator's family status even as such an assumption presupposes a connection between HIV contraction and the gay community, a narrative that does not apply to Paul.

The narrator vacillates between the roles of new family member/host, good guest (devoted to Paul and his emotional well-being), and bad guest, just as the spaces of hospitality represented by the Atsea family home and the hospital lose their ability to maintain their status. Paul's father carries out symbolic acts of destruction, burning his Mercedes (6) and taking to 'destroy[ing] something sturdy, like a table or a major appliance' (9) to vent his anger; he thereby dismantles the family home, as though punishing it for failing to have kept the family safe, exposing the myth behind conservative representations of HIV and AIDS and

their 'imagining[s] [of] familial and geographical space ... that appear
to secure the individual body and the nuclear family against contamina-
tion' (Brophy 6). Although the author-narrator of *Life of Pi* observes that
'doctors [are] the current purveyors of magic and miracles' (vii), in 'The
Facts behind the Helsinki Roccamatios,' no such miracles are possible,
and the hospital fails to heal. The hospital in Jamaica has simultaneously worked to heal Paul after the accident and unknowingly facilitated his infection with the HIV virus, the generous, hospitable gesture
of the blood donor unwittingly giving way to a bodily invasion.

The displacement of Paul's contraction of HIV onto Jamaica and away
from Canada is somewhat problematic, as well as unnecessary, given
the Canadian Red Cross tainted blood scandal of the 1980s. In this manner, Martel's story appears to conform to cultural representations of
'HIV infection and AIDS [that] are repeatedly displaced from the home-
space and the nation-space ... and banished to the floating container
of elsewhere' (Brophy 6). However, Martel also presents Canada as a
site of compromised healing insofar as the Toronto hospital, although
it attempts to manage Paul's condition, at times with some success, cannot ultimately cure him: 'I am having this imaginary conversation in
my head with the doctors. "What the hell is all your science for? Do you
know how much money we give you?" I leave the hospital trembling.
"You're FRAUDS!"' (67). Whereas the narrator has previously talked
himself into a kind of optimism, insisting that 'amazing remissions have
been reported. In some desperate cases of cancer, for example. Why not
here?' (50), the 'here' of AIDS is always already a site of impossible healing. Paul's deficient immune system lacks protection, is too hospitable
in its vulnerability to illness. Moreover, Paul's complaint that he is 'sick
of being their guinea pig' (66) suggests that the hospital, in the context
of HIV/AIDS, functions like the eighteenth-century hospitals analysed
by Foucault that treat patients as objects of medical experimentation
(*Clinic* 101). In the absence of a cure for AIDS, the hospital can only offer
an imitation of hospital/ity, rather than real healing, functioning at best
as a hospice, sheltering Paul while he dies. But it has also sheltered
the narrator when he is not at the Atseas', becoming a temporary and
provisional home.

Whereas the narrator's displacement in 'The Facts behind the Hel-
sinki Roccamatios' occurs within the same province, the narrator of
'The Time I Heard the Private Donald J. Rankin String Concerto with
One Discordant Violin, by the American Composer John Morton' is a
Canadian visiting Washington, DC – and indeed, the United States – for

the first time. The narrator (another Trent philosophy student) ostensibly goes to Washington to see a high-school friend, but this friend is so absorbed in his work that the narrator hardly sees him, a guest without a real host, certainly without a guide. Despite Washington's status as the 'capital of the world in a way' (80), the narrator repeatedly underscores the foreignness of his experience: 'I found everything interesting because everything was part of Washington and Washington was new and foreign to me' (80). The narrator distinguishes between the global and the national, suggesting that the nation-state has not become irrelevant despite globalization. The story depends heavily on the invocation of the Vietnam War, in which the Private Donald J. Rankin of the title fought and died, but the narrator repeatedly insists that 'it was a foreign war, an American trauma ... the whole thing was alien to me' (81). Moved to tears later at the Vietnam War Memorial, touching Rankin's name, the narrator nevertheless re-emphasizes that it was a 'stupid war that had nothing to do with me and that I know so little about' (119). In this way, the narrator undercuts his own assignation of 'capital of the world' to Washington and articulates the relationship between Canada and the United States here as one of difference. He remains a guest and underscores this guest status; indeed, he feels 'like an uninvited guest' (94) at the concert whose audience consists largely of Vietnam veterans.

But following the concert, he is granted entry to the bank where John Morton works as a night cleaner: '... he unlocked the door. It had three deadbolts, each requiring a different key. I prepared myself. The door opened' (107). The protection of the bank's premises contrasts sharply with the state of the theatre in such disrepair that it 'look[s] like Beirut' (91). But the text not only makes a clear statement about the privileging of money over art by juxtaposing the theatre in which Morton plays with the bank in which he works, but it also points out that Morton is required to maintain, and protect the safety of, the bank and, by extension, American prosperity, just as he did as a soldier in Vietnam. Yet Morton has recoded his Vietnam experience in ways likely unintended by the politicians who sent him there: as Morton shouts over the noise of the vacuum cleaner, 'THAT'S WHERE I WAS HAPPIEST WITH MY MUSIC. KHE SANH. I KNEW THEN THAT EVERYTHING ELSE WAS A WASTE OF TIME AND LIFE' (113). In this sense, Washington becomes a meeting place for two characters whose points of reference lie elsewhere: the narrator from Canada, perceiving the United States as foreign; John Morton self-identifying through his music and his experiences in Vietnam, rather than the 'home' to which he has ostensibly returned.

Nation, Habitation, and Language

These stories offer numerous references to displaced figures, particularly those for whom nation and habitation do not match. The narrator of 'The Time I Heard' recalls not only 'that Dutch violinist [he] had heard in Montreal' but also Lubomyr Melnyk, '[a] Polish Canadian but living in Sweden but [the narrator] saw him in Peterborough' (93). The repetition of 'but' highlights the series of displacements, both of residence and travel, qualifying the processes by which individuals are identified. The hybrid identity of Polish Canadian echoes that of the fictional Helsinki Roccamatios, created by Paul in the collection's first story. The narrator offers storytelling as a way to keep Paul occupied during his illness, as a means 'not to forget the world, but to remember it, to re-create it' (15); despite his own good health, the narrator envisions himself and Paul, in contrast to the storytellers of Boccaccio's *Decameron*, as 'the sick . . . , fleeing a healthy world' (14–15). Although the narrator tells the reader explicitly, 'Now, understand that you're not going to hear the story of the Helsinki Roccamatios' (18), the discussions about the storytelling itself reveal that although they remain themselves within Ontario, the narrator and Paul allow their storytelling to incorporate displacement through their selection of characters. As the narrator says of Paul's decision to name their fictional family, 'I wasn't very keen about that one. Not very realistic. I would have chosen a more Scandinavian-sounding name, like Karlson or Harviki. But Paul insisted the Roccamatios were a Finnish family of Italian extraction' (17). The narrator admits that Helsinki provides an attractive location for their narrative because 'neither . . . had been there and [they] knew next to nothing about the city' (17); moreover, the fact that they are to focus on 'contemporary and Western' narratives, 'so that cultural references would be easy' (15), suggests that to some extent, they will simply map Canadian narratives onto the Helsinki they imagine. In his characterization of the fictional family, Paul implies that Italian-Finnish is as plausible or 'realistic' a hyphenate identity as any multiple Canadian identity born of displacement.

In *Self*, the disjunction of nationality and location emerges as a truism: 'It is one of the ironies of travel in the late twentieth century that, unless you make special efforts or are lucky, if you go to England you will meet Australians, if you go to Egypt you will meet Germans, if you go to Greece you will meet Swedes and so on' (135). Self, the protagonist, like Martel, undergoes numerous shifts in habitation. Self is 'born in 1963, in Spain, of student parents' (3) and 'change[s] schools, languages, countries and continents a number of times during [his] childhood' (9). Self begins school in San José, Costa Rica, at a kindergarten that 'operate[s] in English' (18), despite the fact that he speaks French with his family. But Self's parents recode this disjunction of nation and habitation, of language of education and mother tongue, as something that anchors his Canadianness:

'Tu seras bilingue. Même	You'll be bilingual. Even
trilingue,' qu'ils me dirent.	trilingual,' they told me.
'Très Canadien.'	'Very Canadian.' (18)

Canada's official bilingual and multicultural policies lead Self's parents to suggest that, in fact, Self inhabits his Canadian identity precisely through these displacements. Further, the text goes beyond the official versions of Canadian multiplicity. The Canadian Multiculturalism Act of 1988 pledges both to 'preserve and enhance the use of languages other than English and French, while strengthening the status and use of the official languages of Canada' (*Canadian Multiculturalism* n.p.), a move that betrays the Act's refusal to allow a genuine reconstitution of the Canadian cultural host position. But Self's parents assert not only bilingualism in French and English but also trilingualism as 'très Canadien / very Canadian,' thus exceeding the parameters of officially sanctioned multiplicity.

For Self, language constructs his identity and parcels up his daily life:

So it was that, by a mere whim of geography, I went to school in English played outside in Spanish and told all about it at home in French. Each tongue came naturally to me and each had its natural interlocutors. I no more thought of addressing my parents in English than I did of doing arithmetic in my head in French. English became the language of my exact expression, but it expressed thoughts that somehow have always remained Latin. (18–19)

The linguistic hyphens proliferate, becoming more complicated throughout the narrative. Again, like Martel, Self lives for a time in Paris, and later explains (when Self has become female): '. . . unfortunately my Quebec accent has never been very good for having lived in France as a child' (238). If Self's languages define her identity, and have made her 'very Canadian,' her French does not correspond to

Canadian French as she discovers in Montreal, her Québécois heritage absent from her pronunciation: 'On occasion, when I made the *faux pas* of addressing a nationalist Québécois in English and was replied to in French, which would bring out my French French, I went from being *une maudite anglaise* to being *une maudite française*' (238). Self should be a linguistic host in both English- and French-speaking Canada, but finds she is accorded foreignness at 'home,' where she did not grow up. In contrast to Derrida's confession that 'an accent – any French accent . . . – seems incompatible . . . with the intellectual dignity of public speech' (*Monolingualism* 46), it is precisely Self's 'French French' that undermines her in public in Quebec, as the dignity of her claims to being Québécoise is attacked.

That she should encounter hostility from a nationalist Québécois also underscores the fact that the geography called Canada contains within it multiple national projects, and that the imagining of the Canadian nation is not coterminous with the imagining of the Québécois nation. Further, despite Self's parents' definition of 'very Canadian / très Canadien' as bilingualism, 'even' triligualism, Self has found, as an adolescent male in Ottawa, an 'Anglophone intolerance that reigned in the capital of my country during the years that I lived there, where those who spoke two languages were despised by those who spoke only one (and poorly at that)' (72). Self has suffered the disjunction between official policy and lived reality, the assertion of Canadian culture's bilingualism and the hostility of the dominant group towards linguistic multiplicity. That this hostility should be manifested in Ottawa, in particular, undermines the claims for a multiple Canadian host, demonstrating the fracture between official claims and lived relations as 'the [linguistic] other as nearest neighbour' (Derrida, *Monolingualism* 37) disrupts the twin fictions of Canada's monolingualism in practice and its celebration of official bilingualism. Unlike Ondaatje's *In the Skin of a Lion,* which takes place decades before Canada's adoption of a bilingual policy and demonstrates state enforcement of Anglo supremacy, Self is born the year that the Royal Commission on Bilingualism and Biculturalism begins. In this way, Self might be considered symbolic of Canada's official reinvention of itself in policy terms while testifying to the failure of the policy to extend the borders of Canadianness in linguistic practice.

If linguistic multiplicity characterizes Self, his upbringing has also unfolded within cosmopolitan spaces, particularly at the multinational and multiracial school in Paris, where none of the students' nation and habitation match. The school is 'attended mostly by children of diplomats and foreign business executives' (46), and therefore, to a certain extent, composed of young citizens of the world. However, the text presents this multiplicity from a child's point of view, with a child's perception of racial difference: '. . . there was a large contingent of dark blacks, middle blacks, pale blacks, dark browns, milk-chocolate browns, pale browns, yellows and olives among the freckled whites, the English transparent veiny whites, the Australian tanned whites and the just plain boring whites' (47). Although this description, as Smaro Kamboureli notes, 'reduce[s] . . . to a matter of skin pigmentation . . . a visual repertoire that delights the narrator with its interminable possibilities' ('Limits' 954), the narrator's consonance here with the *child* Self's perspective explains the revelling in both the range of skin colour and in the litany itself. The comparison of one girl's, Gora's, 'shimmering soft brown' (*Self* 47) skin to Nestlé chocolate milk powder suggests that 'empathy . . . operates as both consumption and simulation' (Kamboureli, 'Limits' 954); Self observes that Gora's skin has 'a quality of yellow-reddishness that Nestlé's just doesn't' (47). But if 'in the child narrator's mind the untranslatability of Gora's difference is attributed to his tool for simulation, the particular brand of chocolate he uses' (Kamboureli, 'Limits' 954–955), the child narrator, crucially, deems Nestlé inadequate and discards the brand (which in recent years has been accused of unethical global business practices) as an appropriate index. The gap between the child's perspective replicated in the narrative and the otherwise adult narrative voice offers an ironic, even if playful, distance between the text and the child's perspective. Clearly, racial difference is not a matter of chocolate milk powder, yet the child's list of different kinds of blacks, browns, yellows, olives, and whites disrupts the binaries with which racialized bodies and identities are constructed by adults.

Although racial politics appear to be 'irrelevant to the school's interracial student body, an assumption that posits the school as an imagined community, one presumed on the students' essential similarity' (Kamboureli, 'Limit' 955–6), ability plays a major role of differentiation through the reference to the 'Irish cripple' and 'a British pasty white [who] was a touch mentally retarded' (*Self* 47). Self argues that these white individuals constitute the *most* difference from the rest of the student body on the basis of ability rather than their race. The ironic gap between the (child) narrator's statements and the position of the text complicates the impression of the irrelevance of racial politics: not only does the description of the school come from the perspective of a child, but, most significantly, it does so from the perspective of a *white* child. We have no reason to believe that Gora, called 'shit-coloured' because she is 'snooty' (47), would agree with Self, but we *are* told that Self unapologetically refers to her as such, allowing the text to undermine Self's attempts to present the school as racially harmonious. Similarly, the 'Irish cripple' and the labelling of the 'touch mentally retarded' boy as 'Nigger,' and then, following the lesson in 'Martin Luther King, the American Deep South and the Civil Rights Movement' (47), simply 'moron' invites the reader's objection. The fact that the school offers a history lesson in response to the use of the word 'Nigger,' a lesson based on the politics of another country, the United States, rather than the location of the school, France, is also ironic, as it fails to account for the articulation of racism in the present narrative location. Finally, the section's title, 'ON THE CURRENCY OF THE WORDS "NIGGER" AND "FUCK"' (46), as well as the fact that the discussion of race precedes a discussion of the schoolyard usage of 'fuck,' suggests that racial issues only interest the child narrator insofar as they present opportunities for uttering taboo words. But if the weight of racial politics behind the words used by the children escapes the child Self, it does not escape the reader.

Despite the cosmopolitan space of the school and the plethora of international locations in which Self grows up, Self nevertheless consistently returns to Canadianness as a marker of identity; Self's sex may change twice in the novel, but his/her Canadianness remains constant. Whereas the narrator of 'The Facts behind the Helsinki Roccamatios' explicitly complains about Canadians and their proximity to American values, insisting in the midst of Paul's illness that 'this country reeked of insipidity, comfort and insularity. Canadians were up to their necks in materialism and from the neck above it was all American television' (11), both the narrator of 'The Time I Heard' and Self discover distinctions between Canada and the United States while travelling outside Canada. Self encounters some U.S. soldiers stationed at a NATO base in Turkey, and is told, '... there was no difference between Americans and Canadians' (150):

I was at a loss for words. I searched among the icons of the Canadian *Gestalt* – maple syrup, beavers, niceness, the Queen, no guns – for an essential difference, an originality, something to war-of-1812 about. But the only irrefutable difference I could come up with was that I *wanted* to be different. I looked at my hegemonic comforter and I thought,

Je ne veux pas être comme	I don't want to be like
toi, je ne veux pas être comme	you, I don't want to be like
toi ...	you ... (150–1)

The slippage between Canadian and American sameness and differ-ence confounds Self's attempt to produce a significant, concrete distinction between the two; however, the *desire* to be different, the refusal of affiliation with the United States, in itself produces difference. Further, as Ruth, Self's lover and travelling companion notes, 'You can't be American, you don't have an American passport. And you speak French in Quebec' (152). For Ruth, citizenship, as signalled by the passport, makes a difference, as does the official linguistic construction of Canada, in opposition to the United States' projection of unilingualism. That Self should articulate her desire to be different simultaneously in both French and English enhances her refusal to self-identify as American.

Self later explains to Tito that as 'the daughter of diplomats ... [she] carried [her] roots in a suitcase, but the suitcase was originally put together in Quebec, though [she] didn't feel strongly about that' (251). Although 'a quintessential cosmopolitan subject, or tourist *par excellence*' (Kamboureli, 'Limits' 944n12), Self nevertheless finds an anchor in citizenship. When Self wakes up a woman on her eighteenth birthday, her response elides any serious consideration of the spontaneous sex change and favours the assertion and implications of national citizenship instead:

> I got up in the morning, stood naked in front of the mirror looking at myself and thought, 'I'm a Canadian, a woman – and a voter.'
> It was my birthday. I was now eighteen years old. A full citizen. (108)

This invocation of citizenship and its attendant rights occurs in Portugal, not Canada, emphasizing a primacy of national identity regardless of location. The eight brief sentences that constitute chapter 2, which concludes the novel, make no reference to sex but follow details about age, weight, height, hair and eye colour, and blood type with the information: 'I am Canadian. I speak English and French' (331).

The juxtaposition of the final two sentences might be read as an equation: that Self's languages testify to Self's Canadianness, just as the rejection of American identity has unfolded in both of Canada's official languages. But the novel includes several languages other than English and French, not only the Spanish that Self learns as a child but also the Czech of Marisa's family, the German that Marisa also speaks, and the Magyar spoken by Tito's family. As a Canadian text that represents all these languages (and not always providing translation), *Self* implicitly extends the linguistic borders of Canadian culture beyond bilingualism into multilingualism. Moments when translation is absent offer further production of difference, as do occasional contradictory translations. Although the parallel French and English texts tend to be direct translations of each other, there are some exceptions. Immediately preceding Self's assertion of Canadian citizenship in Portugal, she has the following thoughts about language:

... Je	... I
savais que je pensais en	knew that I was thinking in
français, ça au moins, c'était	English, that much I knew
sûr. Mon identité était liée à	right away. My identity was
la langue française.	tied to the English language.
(107)	

The meaning of the two texts completely contradicting each other, Self apparently thinks – in the same moment – in both French and English, her identity simultaneously tied to both. She articulates this equivalence despite the discrepant French and English meanings. This syncretic relationship to language is even more imaginative than the 'in-between' spaces of a hybridity based on *'neither the One ... nor the Other'* (Bhabha 41). Self does not think in *either* French *or* English, but *both* French *and* English, the linguistic simultaneity, even when expressing the opposite meaning, offering a radical reconsideration of language and identity – even more radical, it seems, than Self's spontaneous sex changes. Although Self's sex changes constitute the text's most obvious and spectacular examination of difference, Self inhabits either a male body or a female body. With language, however, using the technique of the parallel columns, the text produces simultaneous assertions of difference.

Whereas Derrida writes, 'In a sense, nothing is untranslatable; but *in another sense*, everything is untranslatable; translation is another name for the impossible' (*Monolingualism* 56–7), the translation in the example above offers both the impossible and possibility. In fact, in this passage, there is no translation, but syncretic claims to different languages instead, insofar as 'commonsense opposites occu[r] in the same text, a difference within unity that by contradiction opens spaces of creativity'

(Schäfer 42). The simultaneous French and English operates as a 'paradox of phenomena that seem to contradict each other in commonsense knowledge, forcing the reader to go back and read over again' (42), particularly at the moment of Martel's contradictory articulations of Self's selfhood through language in French and English. But instead of 'this unbearable discord . . . coincid[ing] with true subjectivity: not the exclusion of the Other, but the dialectical tension between Self and Other' (42), Martel offers a character – Self – that embodies *both* languages appearing in 'unbearable discord': the tension occurs *within* the Self.

However, although Self's linguistic simultaneity posits a more radical idea of Canadian bilingualism, and the text's linguistic multiplicity expands the definition of Canadianness, the novel also underscores the racial hierarchy embedded in the dominant construction of Canadian identity. If Self, as a child in his Parisian school, has deemed race irrelevant, his complicity in violent racism as an adult when he attacks a Native man in Saskatoon offers a retroactive indication that the child Self's assertions about race are hardly adequate. Following the rape and second sex change, Self violently beats a Native man in Saskatoon, writing over gendered violence with racialized violence. If Self wants 'to kill the whole human race' (323), he quite specifically targets a Native man who, Self admits, 'could do [Self] no harm' (322). Self refers to the Native man as an 'Indian,' which, in Kamboureli's view, signals the text's complicity with the racism of the violent act represented ('I don't think "Indian" operates at once as a sign of racist representation and a critique of it' ['Limits' 959]); in contrast, I suggest that neither Self's description of the Native man nor the violence he does to that man is endorsed by the text itself.

Self may be the narrator, but I suggest that it would be a mistake to read this text's position to be an uncritical legitimation of Self. Rather, Self's act of violence against the Native man, both in terms of the narration itself and the act narrated, operates in relation to the text's emphasis on Self's bilingualism, itself a reflection of Canada's two original European colonizing powers. As a woman, Self has been disempowered by her experience of rape. *Self* does not simply offer a 'psychological script according to which the abused becomes abuser' (Kamboureli, 'Limits' 958), but also underscores the fact that the Canadian identity Self's bilingualism confers is predicated upon imperial conquest. As this scene in the novel demonstrates, the Canadian social hierarchy privileges white women over Native men. Further, the underside of Self's embodiment of bilingual Canada constitutes a continuing legacy of colonization. The character of Self is, then, also the 'Self' in national allegorical terms, who not only forges an identity in opposition to the Other, but also violently subjugates the Other.

The text's engagement with bilingualism operates in multiple ways, with implications for both the Canadian and Québécois nations and Aboriginal peoples, invoked through Self's act of violence in a manner that underscores the perpetuation of colonization. *Self* foregrounds the relationships among language, nation, and state: Martel prefaces his novel with acknowledgments in parallel French and English texts that are not translations of each other, the French version thanking 'le conseil des arts et des lettres du Québec' and the English thanking 'the Arts Award Section of the Canada Council' (n.p.). Only one individual is thanked in both French and English columns, with others thanked separately. Martel thereby frames his novel with this untranslated linguistic simultaneity, gesturing towards separate state bodies funded by the Quebec and Canadian governments, both of which have contributed to the production of this text, and both of which might lay claim to this text as part of their respective national cultural projects.

Life of Pi also begins with an acknowledgment of the Canada Council, but as part of the semi-autobiographical yet fictional Author's Note, in which the 'Martel-like writer' (Stratton 5) or 'author-narrator' (Cole 23) of the text explains how he came to write the novel. The thanks that conclude the Author's Note vacillate between fiction (the characters of Mr Adirubasamy, a friend of Pi's family in India, two Japanese officials, and one Japanese businessman) and reality, as represented by Moacyr Scliar, author of *Max and the Cats* – later the focus of a well-publicized but quickly dismissed plagiarism controversy – and the Canada Council. The author-narrator concludes his Author's Note by '*express[ing] my sincere gratitude to that great institution, the Canada Council for the Arts, without whose grant I could not have brought together this story . . . If we, citizens, do not support our artists, then we sacrifice our imagination on the altar of crude reality and we end up believing in nothing and having worthless dreams*' (x-xi).

The Author's Note constitutes a curious preface precisely because of its blending of fact and fiction, and of the conflation of the author-narrator who interviews Pi in the text with the author Martel himself. It is, of course, usual practice for writers to thank their sources of support in their acknowledgments, and for Canadian writers the Canada Council often features in these thanks that preface their texts, as it does with Martel's *Self*. However, we have already entered the fiction of *Life of Pi* by the time Martel and/or his fictional counterpart acknowledges the Council. By moving the acknowledgments into the narrative and aligning citizenship with cultural production, Martel not only writes into the author-narrator's story the context of production but also privileges this context of production as part of the story itself. Thus, the Canada Council becomes integral both to the existence of the novel *Life of Pi* and its narrative, just as Martel infuses citizenship with cultural significance.

Migration, Religion, and the Syncretic

Where *Self* engages with questions of citizenship, particularly Canadian citizenship, through an examination of bilingualism, *Life of Pi*'s Author's Note, which signals the production of cultural work as a duty of citizenship, gives way to a narrative that focuses largely on a non-national space: the lifeboat Pi shares with a Bengal tiger named Richard Parker following the sinking of the *Tsimtsum*. But as Mercedes Díaz Dueñas emphasizes (253), *Life of Pi* tells a story of emigration, one in which the actual journey is not only difficult, as in the other Canadian texts she invokes for comparison (such as *Alias Grace, Jade Peony,* and *No Great Mischief*), but also forms the bulk of the story. Before embarking on the ill-fated journey, Pi begins to consider himself in Canadian terms. He is a 'future Canuc[k],' a 'Winnipegge[r] at heart already' (100). Mr Okamoto's report that concludes the end of the novel asserts that Pi is an 'Indian citizen' (354), which is technically true at this point, Okamoto having visited Pi in a Mexican hospital before he completes his journey to Canada. But Pi has already declared himself an Indo-Canadian at sea when he announces his intentions to tame Richard Parker: 'THE PI PATEL, INDO-CANADIAN, TRANS-PACIFIC FLOATING CIRCUUUUUSSSSSSSSSSSS!!!' (183). In addition to being a common articulation of identity to refer to Canadians of Indian ancestry, the hyphenate 'Indo-Canadian' represents the fact that Pi is still in transit, his Indo-Canadianness resting on his rather imprecise 'Trans-Pacific' location. By the time Pi arrives on shore in Mexico, he has no intention of returning to India, the journey having marked him already as an immigrant to Canada, despite the fact that he has yet to arrive, his welcome incomplete.

To a certain extent, Pi has embodied some ideals of the Canadian nation. Similar to Self, who operates simultaneously in French and English, Pi subscribes to three religions – Hinduism, Islam, and

Christianity – in a plurality that confounds his Pondicherry community. Thus, Pi shares with Self a syncretism, but one of religion rather than language. As Christopher Balme explains, 'syncretism,' as a term, has a long history of association with religion: 'the fusing of philosophical or religious doctrine' in the sixteenth and seventeenth centuries, giving way to 'the connotation of doctrinal confusion'; a 'pejorative taint' maintained in nineteenth-century religious historiography 'to describe various manifestations of religious fusion'; followed by a continued pejorative use 'to designate "hybrid," "impure" religious phenomena' (10). Where syncretism in religious discourse has traditionally tended to be regarded with suspicion, *Life of Pi* delights in incongruous simultaneity and syncretism. For instance, Pi's atheist biology teacher and his Sufi baker friend, professing divergent beliefs, have the same name, Satish Kumar:

> These are common names in Tamil Nadu, so the coincidence is not so remarkable. Still, it pleased me that this pious baker, as plain as a shadow and of solid health, and the Communist biology teacher and science devotee, the walking mountain on stilts, sadly afflicted with polio in his childhood, carried the same name. Mr. and Mr. Kumar taught me biology and Islam. Mr. and Mr. Kumar led me to study zoology and religious studies at the University of Toronto. Mr. and Mr. Kumar were the prophets of my Indian youth. (67–8)

Although the name's attribution to two different men clearly resonates with a Saussurean reading of a single signifier with multiple signifieds, Pi's insistence upon 'Mr. and Mr. Kumar' also underscores a syncretism through these men with opposing theologies sharing the same name.

When the pandit, imam, and priest meet Pi and his family by chance and realize he has been practising all three religions, they each protest that Pi singularly ascribes to their own religion, seeking to clarify what appears to them as religious confusion on Pi's part and to redress what they see as the 'unbearable discord' between their faiths. However, an unwitting simultaneity forges connections between them. Pi's father implores the priest, pandit, and imam, attempting to persuade Pi to choose one religion, to desist from their arguments:

> Father raised his hands. 'Gentlemen, gentlemen, please!' he interjected. 'I would like to remind you there is freedom of practice in this country.'
> Three apoplectic faces turned to him.

'Yes! Prac*tice* – singular!' the wise men screamed in unison. Three index fingers, like punctuation marks, jumped to attention in the air to empha- size their point.

They were not pleased at the unintended choral effect or the spontane- ous unity of their gestures. Their fingers came down quickly, and they sighed and groaned each on his own. (75–6)

Although this chapter concludes with Pi's punchline, 'That was my introduction to interfaith dialogue' (77), this sequence does not simply lapse into irony. The priest's, pandit's, and imam's insistence upon sin- gularity emerges simultaneously, in unison, undermining their claims to exclusivity. In articulating their disagreement, these three men prove to be the same despite their difference, and Pi reads their simultaneity as a justification of his religious syncretism.

The posited discord arises not only from impressions of incommen- surability between religions but also from politically charged assig- nations of Otherness. The pandit condemns Islam and Christianity as '*foreign* religions,' despite both the centuries-old presence of these religions in India and the fact that both the imam and the priest are 'native Tamils' (75). Later, Pi's father insists that Islam is 'totally for- eign to our tradition. They're outsiders' (83), limiting the construction of the Indian host. (He is more hospitable to Christians, however, claim- ing India 'owe[s] them good schools' [83].) Pi's syncretic embracing of Islam and Christianity alongside Hinduism may be read as 'one of the positive results of what has been the fundamentally destructive process of direct or indirect colonisation and cultural imposition' (Balme 9).

Later, when Pi is an adult in Canada, his house in Toronto, like the wall in Mistry's *Such a Long Journey,* serves as a shrine to all three religions, with pictures and statues of several Hindu gods, the Virgin Mary, a cru- cifix, and a cloth that bears '*a single Arabic word, intricately woven, four letters: an* alif, *two* lams *and a* ha. *The word* God *in Arabic'* (51). Although the signs of multiple religions in the Toronto house serve 'as an indica- tion of that hybridity which multicultural societies all over our global- ized world ... tend to produce' (Wolf 107), they particularly suggest that Pi's multicultural ideal diverges from its state-sponsored versions: instead of individuals and groups of differing faiths co-existing harmo- niously, these faiths co-exist within Pi himself. His hyphens proliferate, as he might be identified as a Hindu-Muslim-Christian Indo-Canadian. If multiculturalism in its official capacity, as Kamboureli suggests, func- tions to manage difference, Pi privileges sameness in his adherence to

Hinduism, Islam, and Christianity, arguing that all three permit him 'to love God' (76). But again, like Self, Pi insists upon the simultaneity of both/and, rather than the opposition of either/or: when his father insists of Islam and Christianity that Pi 'must be either one or the other,' Pi demands to know, 'Why can't I be both?' (80), and embodies difference that is unmanageable. Thus, Pi offers what Balme describes as 'inventive syncretism,' which 'assumes a view of cultural change that is fundamentally dynamic, that presupposes openness and a creative utilisation of disparate, heterogeneous cultural products' (9). Pi's openness, or hospitality, to multiple religions does not so much allow him to forge a new hybrid faith, '*something else besides*' (Bhabha 41), but rather insists upon a scarcely imaginable, unruly unity of the three together.

Animals and Accommodation

Just as Pi rejects either/or thinking in favour of both/and through his multiply constituted religious affiliation, so too he articulates his realization that he must tame Richard Parker as 'not a question of him or me, but of him *and* me. We were, literally and figuratively, in the same boat. We would live – or we would die – together' (181). On the lifeboat, of course, difference arises through species rather than nation, religion, culture, or language; the presence of Richard Parker offers a 'confrontation with the other' (Martel, Sielke Interview 20), but not a human Other. Although issues of accommodation and attempts at mastery arise as the taming of Richard Parker necessitates a hierarchy of power to keep Pi alive, the novel's use of animals to explore questions of accommodation does not begin with the lifeboat. The narrative of Pi's family's zoo in Pondicherry offers instances of cohabitation that resonate, through anthropomorphic analogy, with struggles to accommodate difference in human society.

Life of Pi both encourages and discourages connections between the animal world of the zoo and human social structures, partly because of 'Pi's tendency to humanize the animals that surround him – despite the zoological knowledge that affords him insight into the drawbacks of such a tendency' (Cole 28). If '*Animalus anthropomorphicus*, the animal seen through human eyes,' is 'more dangerous' (*Life* 34) than humans, who can be destructive to the zoo environment, Pi's narration offers substantial and significant anthropomorphic analogy, both to describe animal habitat in ways that an audience without zoological knowledge will understand and to comment on the shortcomings of human

society's attempts to negotiate difference. For instance, Pi both introduces the possibility of comparing a zoo with a hotel and dismisses
the posited likeness through anthropomorphosis: 'In many ways, running a zoo is a hotelkeeper's worst nightmare,' given the animal-guests'
demands for free lodging and food, housekeeping, dietary restrictions,
and their display of sexual proclivities (14–15). Pi draws a firm distinction here between the animal and the human by illustrating animal
behaviour as unacceptable, unwelcome in a human context. Hospitality
in this imagined hotel is compromised, not by the charging of guests
for accommodation and services, but rather by a lack of profit for the
owner-host (with the animal-guests' refusals to tip), coupled with the
animal-guests' refusal to act as good guests.

However, anthropomorphic analogy in this text does not exclusively
function to point out the inappropriateness of equations between animal and human society. In his defence of zoos, Pi appeals to humans'
need for a home to illustrate his argument:

> If you went to a home, kicked down the door, chased the people who lived
> there out into the street and said, 'Go! You are free! Free as a bird! Go!
> Go!' – do you think they would shout and dance for joy? . . . The people
> you've just evicted would sputter, 'With what right do you throw us out?
> This is our home. We own it. We have lived here for years. We're calling
> the police, you scoundrel.'
>
> Don't we say, 'There's no place like home?' That's certainly what ani-
> mals feel. (18–19)

At this point, Pi closes the gap between humans and animals, and
his subsequent assertion that 'animals are territorial' (19) potentially
includes the human within the category of the animal, which would
thereby alter the terms of distinction to that between human and 'non-
human animals' (Tiffin, Introduction xii).

Although Pi explains the links between human and non-human animals through their mutual need of accommodation, the text also offers
moments when non-human animals behave better than humans, particularly in their negotiation of difference. Pi describes the peaceful coexistence of a rhinoceros and a herd of goats in the Pondicherry Zoo:

> Rhinos are social animals, and when we got Peak, a young wild male, he
> was showing signs of suffering from isolation and he was eating less and
> less. As a stopgap measure, while he searched for a female, Father thought

of seeing if Peak couldn't be accustomed to living with goats. If it worked, it would save a valuable animal. If it didn't, it would only cost a few goats. It worked marvellously. Peak and the herd of goats became inseparable, even when Summit arrived. Now, when the rhinos bathed, the goats stood around the muddy pool, and when the goats ate in their corner, Peak and Summit stood next to them like guards. The living arrangement was very popular with the public. (29)

Mr Kumar, Pi's atheist biology teacher, reads this non-human animal coexistence as a template for how human animals should interact, and be governed: 'If we had politicians like these goats and rhinos we'd have fewer problems in our country. Unfortunately we have a prime minister who has the armour plating of a rhinoceros without any of its good sense' (29). Mr Kumar thereby suggests that the cohabitation of the rhinoceros and the goats demonstrates a hospitable, inter-species accommodation that exceeds the inter-ethnic accommodation in Indian society under Indira Gandhi.

The text's most extended example of inter-species accommodation unfolds on the lifeboat, through the relationship between Pi and Richard Parker. At the level of narrative, of course, Pi needs to tame the tiger in order to stay alive, just as he needs to begin to kill and eat fish and turtles in order to feed both himself and the tiger. We might argue that in his taming of Richard Parker, Pi, despite his ordinarily subscribing to vegetarianism (which necessarily lapses while he is a castaway), participates in a 'speciesism' that presupposes 'a "natural" prioritisation of humans and human interests over those of other species on the earth' (Tiffin, Introduction xv). Although Pi's speciesism may be tempered by his insistence that in his relationship with Richard Parker, it is 'him *and* me' (181), both/and rather than either/or, as John Simons contends, 'All representations of animals are ... a facet of the speciesism which bedevils the human relationship with the non-human' (87). Further, Helen Tiffin argues that speciesism constitutes the repetition of 'the racist ideologies of imperialism on a planetary scale' (Introduction xv) through the constructions of Self and Other. Pi's representation of his relationship to Richard Parker, 'the tiger with a human name, an anthropomorphic trope writ large' (Cole 28), potentially offers an illustration of the relationship between human Selves and Others, and attempts an accommodation of difference.

The lifeboat is the object of a struggle over territory as Pi attempts to become master of the space and of the tiger in his attempt to stay alive, as if the lifeboat is Pi's rightful 'home.' At some points, Richard Parker seems already domesticated, '*catlike*': 'He looked like a nice, big, fat domestic cat, a 450-pound tabby' (180), a kind of oversized pet. As Tiffin notes, 'Pets ... have a semi-human status' ('Foot' 18), largely because of humans' refusal to eat their pets, no doubt because domesticated pets are 'at home' with their owners; however, Richard Parker is *not* domesticated at this initial point in their lifeboat narrative, and could easily undo Pi's attempted mastery of the space through his superior strength. But while Pi seeks to master the animal, he also loses a marker of his human status, namely his clothing: 'Clothing would be proper to man, one of the "properties" of man. Dressing oneself would be inseparable from all the other forms of what is proper to man' (Derrida, 'Animal' 373). Pi gradually becomes naked as his clothing 'disintegrate[s], victims of the sun and the salt': 'For months I lived stark naked except for the whistle that dangled from my neck by a string' (213). At this point, only the marker of his taming of Richard Parker, the whistle, distinguishes him from his non-human animal companion.

Pi has assumed the position of master in both the power to tame and the power to represent through his narration. But Richard Parker's abandonment of him once they reach Mexico undermines Pi's authority as the one who represents. The fact that Pi, with an 'anthropomorphic lament' (Cole 29), bemoans how 'Richard Parker ha[s] left [him] so unceremoniously' (*Life* 316) demonstrates that Pi wishes to have been both the mastering human animal, successfully taming Richard Parker and exerting power over him, and Richard Parker's equal, both to claim the position of master of the house with all the authority that implies and to have Richard Parker thank him, through some kind of recognition, for his hospitality. But Richard Parker's disappearance from the narrative identifies Pi's understanding of him as 'a perceptual strategy' (Cole 30), rather than any claim to truth or accuracy. As Pi describes the tiger's taking leave of him:

He passed directly in front of me on his way to the right. He didn't look at me ... At the edge of the jungle, he stopped. I was certain he would turn my way. He would look at me. He would flatten his ears. He would growl. In some such way, he would conclude our relationship. He did nothing of the sort. He only looked fixedly into the jungle. Then Richard Parker, companion of my torment, awful, fierce thing that kept me alive, moved forward and disappeared forever from my life. (315–16)

Pi attempts to write Richard Parker into a narrative in which the tiger refuses to participate. Pi exposes the limits of his understanding and his ability to read Richard Parker, and the tiger does not give his consent to Pi's narrative or his version of their relationship. Derrida asks 'what to respond means, and whether an animal ... ever replies in its own name' ('Animal' 379). 'Richard Parker,' of course, is not the tiger's 'own name,' but rather the name of a human animal. In intertextual terms, 'Richard Parker' is both the name of a sailor in Edgar Allan Poe's *The Narrative of Arthur Gordon Pym*, itself a shipwreck narrative, and the name of the chief mutineer on the *Bounty*. Within Martel's text, 'Richard Parker' is a hunter, his name mistakenly attributed to the tiger 'because of a clerical error' (146), rather than the tiger's name of 'Thirsty' (148); yet neither is 'Thirsty' the tiger's 'own name,' for that is the name with which the hunter 'baptize[s]' (147) the tiger. 'Richard Parker's' disappearance from the narrative therefore suggests that Pi has never been able to read the tiger adequately, that he has consistently positioned the tiger in relation to his Self, reading the tiger as his companion not just for his sense of Self, but for his very survival. 'Richard Parker,' however, refuses to respond, and his abandonment of Pi indicates that despite Pi's efforts to accommodate the tiger, his insistence upon 'him *and* me,' Pi's version of the Other has never been legitimate.

Multiculturalism and the 'Horrible Story'

The narrative of Richard Parker's abandonment of Pi offers a resistance of the Other to the representation of the Self. But Pi's narrative of Richard Parker is not the only story on offer. The second version of the shipwreck story that Pi relates to the Japanese Ministry of Transport officials offers human counterparts to the lifeboat animals in the first version: a Taiwanese sailor with a broken leg stands in for the zebra, Pi's mother for the orang-utan, the ship's French cook for the hyena, 'which means [Pi's] the tiger!' (346), as Mr Chiba concludes. In Pi's second version, the Poe allusions particularly resonate, as *Pym*'s Parker suggests cannibalism as a solution to starvation, and is subsequently killed and eaten (Poe 90). In Pi's story, the cook eats the dead sailor's body and murders Pi's mother, prompting Pi to kill the cook, when the officials refuse to believe his story about Richard Parker: 'We want a story without animals that will explain the sinking of the *Tsimtsum*' (336). Pi asks the two officials which version is 'the better story, the story with animals or the story without animals?' (352), to which Mr Okamoto and

Mr Chiba respond that the first version, with the tiger, is the better story, the violent, human story declared to be 'horrible' (345).

We receive no criteria for assessing the better story, apart from the question of what the listeners 'prefer' (352). But the second version, deemed not to be the 'better story,' presents a narrative of failed inter-racial and intercultural relationships. Given how this second version of Pi's story contrasts with the villa community in Ondaatje's *The English Patient*, for instance (which also comprises three men and a woman in the aftermath of violence and upheaval), the second story not only pres-ents a failed, deeply unethical relationship between Self and Other, but also a violently failed multiculturalism. In this way, that the 'better story' should write out Otherness between humans altogether, preferring inter-species Otherness instead, and pre-empt the possibility of interra-cial and intercultural violence keeps the multicultural possibility intact.

The novel offers not simply 'an oblique thumbs-up to the young, multiculturally transformed middle power that is Canada today' (Ball 99), but rather many competing versions of multiculturalism in its movement towards a more radical multiculturalism than that on offer by the state. Firstly, Pi's description of himself and his brother, waiting for their move to Canada, as feeling like 'two animals [who] were being shipped to the Canada Zoo' (98), although it does match the narrative of selling the zoo's animals and continues the text's use of anthropomor-phic analogy, also introduces one discourse of critique of official mul-ticulturalism. If Pi and Ravi are to be animals in the Canada Zoo, they will be marked as different, as exotic spectacle, and, indeed, 'managed' by inhospitable national constructions, in addition to being treated as second-class citizens. Secondly, however, Pi's syncretic ascription to three religious faiths presents another kind of multiculturalism, one that produces unexpected results and cannot fit neatly into the usually anticipated patterns of the Canadian mythical 'mosaic.' But the failed multicultural story of cannibalism also acts to insist that *some* kind of multiculturalism is necessary.

Indeed, if the story of failed multiculturalism constitutes the 'worse' story, it is not a story that Pi seems to have encountered following his arrival in Canada. Unlike *Family Matters'* Yezad, who is never granted entry to Canada, Pi is not only allowed in, but also unambiguously wel-comed, the recipient of a healing hospitality in two North American locations: 'Mexican and Canadian officials opened all doors for me so that from the beach in Mexico to the home of my foster mother to the classrooms of the University of Toronto, there was only one long, easy corridor I had to walk down. To all these people I extend my heart-felt thanks' (318). Although Pi 'miss[es] the heat of India,' he 'love[s] Canada. It is a great country much too cold for good sense, inhabited by compassionate, intelligent people with bad hairdos' (6). Despite the arduous, tragic physical journey of emigration, Canada figures here as a hospitable nation, one that, the novel implicitly suggests, accommo-dates Pi's multiple faiths in ways his nation of origin has not.

And yet, this Canada also offers only a partial solution to the trauma of personal upheaval through migration. Pi asks,

> Why do people move? What makes them uproot and leave everything they've known for a great unknown beyond the horizon? Why climb this Mount Everest of formalities that makes you feel like a beggar? Why enter this jungle of foreignness where everything is new, strange and difficult?
>
> The answer is the same the world over: people move in the hope of a better life. (86)

This passages identifies immigration with the stripping of a sense of self-worth; if Pi's physical experience of migration through the ship-wreck has been astonishingly, unusually difficult, he also asserts that the psychological experience of migration more generally is equally difficult, tantamount to a 'jungle of foreignness' – on par, perhaps, with sharing a lifeboat with a Bengal tiger. Pi's experience of a waiter's con-tempt in an Indian restaurant in Canada underscores a hostility towards migrants interpellated as embarrassing guests:

> The first time I went to an Indian restaurant in Canada I used my fin-gers. The waiter looked at me critically and said, 'Fresh off the boat, are you?' I blanched. My fingers ... became dirty under his gaze. They froze like criminals caught in the act. I didn't dare lick them. I wiped them guil-tily on my napkin. He had no idea how deeply those words wounded me. (8)

Elsewhere, Pi feels like a welcome guest in a Canadian hotel that pro-vides, like most other Canadian hotels, a copy of the Bible:

> The first time I came upon a Bible in the bedside table of a hotel room in Canada, I burst into tears. I sent a contribution to the Gideons the very next day, with a note urging them to spread the range of their activity to all places where worn and weary travellers might lay down their heads, not just to hotel rooms, and that they should leave not only Bibles, but

other sacred writings as well. I cannot think of a better way to spread the faith. No thundering from a pulpit, no condemnation from bad churches, no peer pressure, just a book of scripture quietly waiting to say hello, as gentle and powerful as a little girl's kiss on your cheek. (230)

Given Pi's religious syncretism, it is difficult to determine whether 'the faith' in this passage is Christianity, any faith with 'sacred writings,' or Pi's own multiply constituted faith. Considering the hotel setting, this passage does, to some extent, work to undermine the assumption of Christianity within Canada. While Pi focuses here on the effectiveness of using scripture to proselytize, Christian guests appear to be, implicitly, more welcome than others, a welcome that Pi seeks to expand through his advice to the Gideons. Although Pi explicitly praises Canada and its hotels for their hospitality, the text also demonstrates a slippage between hospitality and hostility and the exclusive configurations of the host position. Pi ruptures singularity through his syncretic faith, subtly demanding a new multiculturalism, a better story than the official policy the state has to offer.

Reception and Celebration: The U.K., Canada, and Quebec

In the context of Martel's career, *Life of Pi* has also emerged as the 'better story,' the one that readers have preferred to his earlier, less conventional, and more challenging texts, particularly *Self*, as well as to his most recent novel, *Beatrice and Virgil*. In *Life of Pi*'s semi-autobiographical Author's Note, the author-narrator announces, '*In the spring of 1996, my second book, a novel, came out in Canada. It didn't fare well. Reviewers were puzzled, or damned it with faint praise. Then readers ignored it*' (v). This declaration clearly invokes *Self*, although it exaggerates reviewers' reactions to the novel. Martel may have disavowed his first novel (claiming, when Faber and Faber reissued the text following the success of *Life of Pi*, 'It has a very new cover but don't let that trick you into thinking it's good' [quoted in Cornwell B24]), but at the time of *Self*'s release, as with *The Facts behind the Helsinki Roccamatios*, reviewers' responses in both Canada and the U.K. were generally positive, praising Martel's innovation and intelligence, if occasionally cautioning him against 'cleverness for its own sake' (Whiteside 11). Unlike Shields and Mistry, Martel was unambiguously aligned with highbrow fiction, his aesthetic experiments obvious and frequently noted. One reviewer of *The Facts behind the Helsinki Roccamatios* labels Martel 'an innovator with a Calvino-like concern for technique' (E. Henderson D19), while another declares the collection 'freakishly well written' (L. Henderson D17). *Self,* despite some qualified praise and concerns about 'thin ... interiorization' (J. Thomas C20), constituted 'a courageous attempt at an experimental novel' (Bunce 18), 'an exhilarating piece of fiction, ... bold and original' (Foran, 'Martel Novel' I1), 'wild, strange and sometimes dreamlike' (Rengger 24).

Granted, the sales for Martel's first two texts pale greatly in comparison to the Man Booker Prize–boosted *Life of Pi,* and *Beatrice and Virgil* seems unlikely to match the success of its predecessor. Martel's 'intellectual fun' (T. Adams 15) in *Life of Pi* does not compromise its status as an 'enormously lovable novel' (Jordan 10), and therefore a 'better story' that is perhaps less demanding than Martel's other works. Margaret Atwood's review, which privileges the 'boy's own adventure' ('A Tasty Slice') aspect of the novel, signals the ways in which *Life of Pi* is more accessible to a wider audience: 'wacky, but not intimidating and experimental' (Payne, 'When Greatness' 9), as another reviewer put it. Indeed, Martel was a guest on Martha Stewart's television program, although this foray of Martel's into popular culture has been far less commented on than Mistry's Oprah appearance, implying, somehow, that Martel's highbrow credentials have remained more intact. Yet the 2010 publication of *Beatrice and Virgil,* coupled with its response of disappointment from critics, introduces an additional lens through which to read *Life of Pi*'s success, for not only does *Beatrice and Virgil* comment upon the *Life of Pi* phenomenon, but reviewers' positions on the later novel also demonstrate concerns about straying too far from the middlebrow. *Beatrice and Virgil* tells the story of Henry L'Hôte, a French-Canadian writer who, having grown up all over the world, writes in English, whose second novel, which 'featured wild animals' (29), was a prize-winning bestseller, and who 'liked zoos. It was where he'd started his career, in a way' (113). Following a traumatic meeting with his publishers, who refuse to allow him to publish his next book as a 'flip book,' comprised of an essay and a novel about the Holocaust, published together and meeting in the middle, Henry moves with his wife to an unnamed city outside Canada. Henry is a cosmopolitan guest in the city (reflected through the doubled etymology of L'Hôte, meaning both host and guest) and a parasite in relation to a taxidermist who sends him a copy of Gustave Flaubert's story 'The Legend of Saint Julian Hospitator' and seeks assistance in the writing of a play about a monkey named Virgil and a donkey named Beatrice – an allegorical work, it seems, about the Holocaust, as the animals walk across a striped shirt, trying to find ways to talk about 'the Horrors' (136). After a series of meetings, Henry admits to his wife that the taxidermist's writing allows Henry to 'ge[t] ideas off him' (117). Much of Martel's short novel is taken up with the Beckett-like play, the action involving Henry himself ending abruptly and violently as Henry is suddenly an unwelcome guest, the taxidermist an inhospitable host, when it dawns on Henry that the taxidermist is a 'stinking old Nazi collaborator' (190). Henry refuses to take the play when it is offered to him, and the taxidermist stabs him, though not fatally. The novel itself ends with a section entitled 'Games for Gustav,' a series of ethical dilemmas relating to the Holocaust, the title of which refers both to Flaubert and the name of a dead human body in the taxidermist's play.

The early part of the *Beatrice and Virgil* focuses on the frustrations of Henry's attempts to represent the Holocaust in a form (the flip book) he thinks appropriate. Ultimately, Martel's novel is not about the Holocaust but precisely about the impossibility of representing it. Nevertheless, the uncomfortable subject matter of *Beatrice and Virgil*, its self-reflexivity, and metafictional elements have attracted the ire of many reviewers, most especially those who expect a novel more on the lines of *Life of Pi*. Reviewers have attacked the novel as being 'often perverse' (Kakutani C1), 'dimly appalling' (Lasdun Review 10), 'self-indulgent' and 'self-congratulatory' (Chakravarty), an 'awkward medley of comedy, tragedy and fantasy' (Leggatt Books 12). Yet because many aspects of *Beatrice and Virgil* have appeared in Martel's earlier works, reviews of the most recent novel indicate a great deal about how *Life of Pi* has been read. The philosophical, religious, and ethical debates about *Life of Pi*, as well as the earlier novel's metafictional discussion, have much in common with *Beatrice and Virgil*'s concerns with morality and representation. Readers who recoil from *Beatrice and Virgil* indicate that *Life of Pi*'s pleasures lie in its 'boy's own story' elements, rather than those aspects of the text – its philosophical dimension and aesthetic play – that have recurred throughout Martel's oeuvre. If *Beatrice and Virgil* is, like Shields's *Larry's Party* or Mistry's *Family Matters*, positioned as a kind of 'disappointing' aftermath text, Martel's novel not only has been more vehemently rejected by reviewers but also diverges from Shields's and Mistry's work insofar as *Beatrice and Virgil* is not more, but less, middlebrow than *Life of Pi*. As is claimed of *Self* in *Life of Pi*, most of the positive reviews of *Beatrice and Virgil* tend to damn it with faint praise: it is 'not without merit, [but] slighter and stranger' (Wigod C6); its 'bleak, cold intellectual world' (McPhee 16) constitutes a betrayal of the popular readership Martel acquired through *Life of Pi*. If Martel is 'a global commodity' (Oliveira D8) thanks to his second novel, unhappy reviewers suggest that *Beatrice and Virgil* can only fail in the global cultural marketplace, unlikely as it is to attract 'the average fan of *Pi*' (Basilières n.p.). Thus, *Beatrice and Virgil*, in itself and its reception, emphasizes the particular positioning of *Life of Pi* by readers, reviewers, and prize judges. The Man Booker Prize jury of 2002 pointedly announced that they were not interested in '"pretentious, portentous and pompous" novels' and instead were seeking 'quieter or more popular books' (Alberge 3). The fact that *Life of Pi*, considered to be 'populist on account of its universality or accessibility' (Celyn Jones 19), has become 'the most popular Booker prizewinner ever' (quoted in Hartley, 7) signals its adaptability to the marketplace in ways that have eluded Martel's other works. Like Henry L'Hôte's successful second novel, *Life of Pi* is 'set to turn . . . into a movie' (3), directed by Ang Lee, which promises even further circulation and global commodification, as well as recirculation of Martel himself as the author of the novel on which a high-profile film is based.

If *Life of Pi*'s enormous success has been partly due to its Man Booker recognition, the 'Booker effect' on *Life of Pi* in Canada has been easy to detect, given that the novel was published by Knopf Canada in 2001, a year prior to the Man Booker win. The initial print run of 10,000 copies of *Life of Pi* sold out, and the novel was nominated for the Governor General's Award for English-language fiction, but did not win. When Noah Richler claimed the *Life of Pi's* Man Booker meant 'the G-G's will enjoy some residual light' ('Not Much Ado' AL1), he also identified the Man Booker as a guest authority in Canadian culture, one which bolstered the Governor General's Award, despite *Life of Pi*'s loss to Richard B. Wright's *Clara Callan* (the Giller had ignored Martel's novel altogether). More tangibly, *Life of Pi*'s sales skyrocketed following the Man Booker, using the amended British edition first published by Canongate. Unlike *The English Patient*, then, with its Booker nomination announced prior to publication in both Canada and the U.K., *Life of Pi*'s domestic and international circulation are clearly separate, with the novel's international celebration rejuvenating domestic readership and reception. On the heels of the Man Booker win, *Life of Pi* was shortlisted for the Canada Reads competition, ultimately losing to Hubert Aquin's *Prochain épisode / Next Episode*. However, as Canada Reads judge Will Ferguson insists, 'Canadians already *are* reading *Life of Pi*' (R1); the novel did not need the publicity that might have been provided by winning the competition.

With a narrative that unfolds largely in the Pacific Ocean, *Life of Pi*, as one British reviewer noted, 'could almost be set nowhere' (Payne, 'Weird Bunch' 12), raising once again the spectre of celebrated Canadian literary texts that do not explicitly present Canada in any extended way. For some Canadian reviewers, this spoke to a general trend of contemporary Canadian literature, one that seems to be remarked upon as though for the first time, as evidenced by the ten-year gap between Mistry's *Such a Long Journey* and *Life of Pi*. The relative absence of Canada itself from *Life of Pi* no doubt contributed to the Canadianness controversy that erupted surrounding the identities of Shields, Mistry, and Martel following the 2002 Man Booker nominations. Martel, like his character Self, claims to carry his 'roots in a suitcase' (Marchand, 'Author as Explorer' L10), his Canadian nationality transported all over the world as he followed his peripatetic parents. Significantly, however, British reviews of Martel's first two books contain no qualifications of Martel's Canadianness, as though the increased stakes presented by the Man Booker Prize in determining the viability of national literatures through international competition made the assignation of identity part of the competition itself. Following the Man Booker's spotlight on Martel and his fellow Canadian nominees, Canadian journalists seemed at pains to prove Martel's Canadian credentials. Paul Gessell declared that Martel should not be addressed as 'Senor Martel,' warning, 'Do not raise the Spanish flag if he gets to mount the winner's podium,' and described Martel as 'almost shout[ing] into the telephone' when he declared in an interview, 'Of course I am Canadian' ('Wot's This?' J1). Despite these strenuous objections to qualifications of his Canadianness, however, some British newspapers continued to refer to Martel as a 'naturalised Canadian' (Reynolds 8) and a 'Spanish novelist now resident in Canada' (Harrington 5).

Life of Pi's 'nowhere setting' has found a more explicit incarnation in *Beatrice and Virgil*, almost as though Martel is deliberately playing with such characterizations of his, and his second novel's, lack of Canadianness, in that *Beatrice and Virgil* refuses to name its primary setting. Martel tells us that Henry is from Canada (17), but gives no further details. Following his publishers' rejection of the flip book, Henry 'convince[s] Sarah,' his wife, that 'they need a change of scenery' (20), and they 'mov[e] abroad': 'They settled in one of those great cities of the world that is a world unto itself, a storied metropolis where all kinds of people find themselves and lose themselves. Perhaps it was New York. Perhaps it was Paris. Perhaps it was Berlin. To that city Henry and Sarah moved because they wanted to live to its pulse for a time' (21). We never know either which Canadian 'scenery' Henry needs to exchange for 'abroad,' or which metropolis is this destination, where Henry lives as 'a resident alien' (21). Although it is clear that like his enormously successful second novel, with its publishers in different countries and readers around the world, Henry can travel anywhere, 'anywhere,' in this instance, consists of locations that are exactly alike in the fact that they are metropolitan centres away from his home country. In *Beatrice and Virgil*, there is simply Canada and not-Canada, thereby emphasizing not only Henry's nationality but also Martel's.

It seems unlikely that anyone other than a Canadian writer would, for example, foreground Canadian domestic politics in a world history of the twentieth century, as Martel does in 'The Facts behind the Helsinki Roccamatios,' juxtaposing early twentieth-century Canadian federal elections and the development of new strains of wheat with the First World War and the death of Lenin in his historical backdrop to the stories of the Roccamatios to which the reader is not privy. But while there is no need to 'prove' Martel's Canadianness, the implications of his representations of Canada in light of his national and international reception and celebrations are worth probing. It is striking that whereas Martel's narrator in 'The Facts behind the Helsinki Roccamatios' can utter such explicitly anti-Canadian statements as 'I developed a loathing for Canada, Canadians and things Canadian, a loathing which still has not left me entirely,' given, among other things, 'Canada's policy on Central America, on native issues, on the environment, on Reagan, on everything' (11), without any comment from reviewers, Rohinton Mistry's 'failure' both to represent Canada and to represent it in a good light has been read as his refusal to give Canada its due. Martel's transgressions of the nation-state appear to be more licensed than those of Mistry; however, the fact that *Life of Pi*, which represents Canada as hospitable, the nation that welcomes a shipwrecked, homeless, orphaned Indian boy, has become Martel's most popular text, in Canada as elsewhere, perhaps speaks to the ongoing desire to legitimate many Canadians' belief in our own hospitality.

In many ways, Martel should be, as Gessell would have it, a 'poster boy' for Canada, for he is bilingual in both of Canada's official languages; indeed, although he wrote the text of *Life of Pi* in English, its dedication, to Martel's parents and brother, appears in French (n.p.), and he thanked them in French at the Man Booker ceremony. Despite having lived all over the world, a figure of cosmopolitan travel, Martel nevertheless embodies one official version of Canada; his bilingualism performs the function of a national cultural passport. To Martel's assertion that Canada is 'where I come home to ... this is the place where I speak the languages' (quoted in 'Canadians Write' A18, original ellipsis), an *Ottawa Citizen* editorial responded, 'And that is why we can proudly call [him] all our own' (A18). Significantly, in the wake of Martel's Man Booker success and the debates about his nationality, Canadian journalists did not revisit *Self*'s indictment of hostility to bilingualism in Ottawa.

Martel reassures us that *Life of Pi* is 'very Canadian' (quoted in Higgins A3). But his own characterization of Canada following the Man Booker win tapped into some anxieties about Canada and its national culture. In a comment that has since been frequently quoted, Martel characterized Canada as 'a vast country so that inspires you. It's also the greatest hotel on Earth: It welcomes people from everywhere' (quoted A3). This boundless hospitality suggested in Martel's declaration celebrates Canada as hotel and as 'a true nation of immigrants' ('CanLit' A14). But given that a hotel is also 'somewhere you pass through, where the encounters are fleeting, arbitrary' (Clifford 96), the metaphor also has generated some anxiety about the Canadian nation: as one editorial put it, 'Is a nation more than a convenient way-station?' ('Canada's Winning Words' A10).

Although Martel has since explained his 'silly off-the-cuff remark' as his intention to express the fact that 'Canada has the variety of peoples of a hotel' (quoted in Richler, *My Country* 450), the image deserves further discussion in relation to hospitality. The hotel metaphor underscores a national hospitality, and implies that all Canadians (not just Pi in his hotel room) are guests with equal claim to the host position of Canadian culture and its definition. This notion is extremely problematic with regards to Aboriginal peoples, unjustly treated as unwelcome guests (attested to in Martel's own fiction through Self's violence towards a Native man). Canada as hotel is built by settler-invaders on indigenous peoples' lands, denying Aboriginal peoples the position of host despite their prior claims. The metaphor of the hotel for the hospitable nation becomes further complicated if we consider the working of the hotel itself. As mentioned in chapter 3, hotels merely provide imitations of 'the signs of generosity' (Rosello 34), hardly genuine hospitality in the first place. While denying indigenous peoples the power of host,

Canada as hotel imitates hospitality to immigrants, and it does so at a price, but one not really experienced by Pi in Martel's prize-winning novel. As such, Martel's celebration of Canada says more than he perhaps intends.

Martel also declared that 'in many ways Canada is the world' (quoted in Higgins A3), like the 'great meeting place' (quoted in Gombu A23) that has also been claimed for this country. But when asked if he 'consider[s] [him]self a citizen of the world' (Sielke Interview 30), Martel has replied, 'No. I'm Canadian. I don't believe there are citizens of the world. Everyone is from somewhere, rooted in a particular culture. We're also citizens of the languages we speak. Some people speak many languages – I speak three, I'm a citizen of English, French and Spanish – but no one speaks World. World is not a language' (30). In contrast to Derrida, who claims that 'citizenship does not define a cultural, linguistic, or, in general, historical participation,' Martel argues here for a linguistic citizenship, a 'being-at-home . . . in language' (*Monolingualism* 14–15, 17). Insisting upon his Canadianness, despite his cosmopolitan travel, Martel undoes the threat latent in his characterization of Canada as a hotel, declaring it his home.

Martel moved to Montreal as an adult, his first extended residence in the province of his parents (although he now lives in Saskatoon). While he has been inserted into Canadian culture, and his position within that culture has been defended by the Anglo-Canadian press, Martel's identity as both a Québécois and a Québécois writer has equally been negotiated. On the one hand, as winner of the Hugh MacLennan Prize for English-language Quebec fiction for *Life of Pi*, a prize sponsored by the Quebec Writers Federation, whose mandate is 'to promote and encourage English language writing and writers in Québec' ('About the QWF' n.p.), Martel was declared to be part of English-language literary culture in Quebec. On the other hand, however, Martel's recognition within Quebec was not limited to the English-language literary community. Indeed, if Ondaatje was lauded as Canada's first Booker Prize winner, Martel was hailed in the francophone press as 'le premier Québécois . . . à remporter le Booker Prize, l'une des plus prestigieuses distinctions littéraires du monde anglo-saxon' (Bégin A1). Québécois coverage of Martel's Man Booker nomination and win demonstrates the slippages between citizenship and language, and sub-national, national, and transnational cultures. Québécois articles about Martel explained for their readers the significance of the Booker Prize, with one piece referring back to the Booker's original model in order to contextualize the award: 'On estime que le Booker Prize est, pour le Commonwealth, l'équivalent du Goncourt' (Lepage, 'Booker Prize' C1). Through the Man Booker, Martel became '[l']écrivain anglo-québécois le plus célèbre sur la planète' (Fugère L2), whose prize constituted 'un évènement majeur pour la littérature québécoise' (Guy F2).

How, then, was the francophone Martel, who writes in English and has lived outside of Quebec for most of his life, inserted into the category of 'la littérature québécoise?' As Gil Courtemanche noted in an earlier article on *Self*, Martel's family 'est une des plus vieilles familles du Québec' (87). If Martel carries his roots in his suitcase, these roots nonetheless find legitimation through the Martels' *pure laine* history. Further, the fact that his father, Émile, is a Governor General's Award–winning French-language poet as well as translator adds to this sense of Yann Martel being part of a lineage embedded in Québécois culture. However, journalistic coverage of Martel also devotes considerable attention to rehearsing the reasons behind his writing in English rather than in French and the fact that he, like his character Self, is 'un Montréalais qui parle français avec un accent parisien' (Courtemanche 86). Jean Fugère describes Martel's accent in less specific, more cosmopolitan terms, as an 'accent qui n'appartient qu'à lui, l'accent de celui qui s'est frotté à bien des cultures' (L2). In Québécois newspaper articles, and subsequently in *Beatrice and Virgil*, Martel explicitly acknowledges the potential implications of his (and Henry's) choosing to write in English: in the novel, Henry explains his writing in English as '*un hasard*' (22); as Martel has acknowledged elsewhere, this 'hasard' could be considered 'malheureux d'un point de vue symbolique – un francophone qui écrit en anglais, je sais que ça sonne mal. Mais ça n'a rien à voir avec une assimilation dans mon cas' (quoted in Bégin A1). Further, Martel attempts to distinguish English as a literary language from English as a tool of political domination: 'Quand j'écris en anglais, c'est la langue de Shakespeare et d'Hemingway, pas dans celle de Ronald Reagan ou de l'assimilation des Québécois ... Je suis francophone et j'en suis fier, je défends le fait français' (quoted A1). Similarly, Martel has been quoted in the English-language press as stating, 'I'm not an anglophone. I speak Wolfe's language – but I identify with Montcalm' (quoted in Abley, 'Filling' A1). As discussed in relation to *Self*, the text's bilingualism both insists upon expanding dominant definitions of Canadianness and implicitly explores the colonial implications of Canada's official bilingual policy. But Martel's evocation of an anti-bilingual Ottawa also demonstrates the hierarchy within the imperial powers and their colonial legacies. In invoking Wolfe and Montcalm, in particular, he draws attention to the historical subjugation of French Canadians and the privileging of the English language and British-based culture that persists, in practice, to this day.

Martel's overt identification as a francophone no doubt has functioned to close any perceived gap between himself and Québécois culture. Chantal Guy recounts a poll taken in December of 2002 by members of *La Presse* to determine 'ce qui constituait à leurs yeux, "l'évènement littéraire de l'année"': 'En fait, il n'y a qu'une seule réponse qui fait l'unanimité: l'attribution du prestigieux Booker Prize à . . . un Québécois francophone écrivant en anglais' (F2). Perhaps even more striking than this unanimity is, as Jocelyne Lepage notes, the lack of outcry at Martel's not having written in French:

> Les temps changent. Quand le Booker Prize a été attribué cet automne à l'écrivain québécois francophone qui écrit en anglais, Yann Martel, personne ne s'est levé debout, ni n'a écrit dans les journaux, pour crier que Martel n'appartenait pas à la culture québécoise, comme cela avait été le cas il ya quelques années pour . . . Celine Dion, sans accent aigu sur le e, qui chantait en anglais. ('L'écrivain' F2)

The comparison between Martel and Dion offers important distinctions. Part of the reaction to Dion's development of a career in English is largely due to the fact that she began her singing career in French and chose to pursue the anglophone market, whereas, as the francophone press consistently points out, Martel's writing in English continues a logical trajectory that begins with his childhood education in English.

But significantly, the celebration in Quebec of Martel's Man Booker Prize unfolded in the context of the fact that many journalists who covered the story had not yet read the novel, for the French translation, *L'histoire de Pi*, executed by Martel's parents, was not published until August of 2003: '. . . il a été traduit en 41 langues, depuis le chinois, jusqu'à l'islandais en passant par l'estonien, le serbe, le thaïlandais, l'espagnol . . . Il ne manquait que le français' (Lepage, 'Yann Martel' C1). After the publication of the French translation, the first print run of 14,000 copies had nearly sold out by the end of its first week in circulation (see Bérubé C3).

In terms of Québécois culture, the publication of the French translation of *Life of Pi*, and indeed, the coverage of both the Man Booker

and the subsequent sales success of *Life of Pi* in the global marketplace, attracted a great deal more attention than did the Canada Reads
selection of *Prochain épisode* by the 2003 Canada Reads competition.
Although the selection of Aquin's book and the fact that it sold 18,000
copies in English Canada as *Next Episode* did not go entirely unnoticed
by the francophone press, the novelty of the emergence of Aquin as
'best-seller au Canada anglais!' (Richard A7) appears to have had much
less resonance and significance than the sensation caused by Martel,
despite the Canada Reads panel's sense that the choice of Aquin was
a notable selection in terms of relations between Quebec and Anglo-
Canada: as panellist Denise Bombardier stated, 'Il y a un avenir pour le
Canada' (quoted in Cayouette 17). Thus, if Aquin's narrative of separat-
ism appears to be more integral to Quebec culture, Martel's text and its
afterlife nevertheless sparked more interest in Quebec itself than the
adoption of Aquin by CBC listeners in Anglo-Canada.

Given that the national(ist) projects of Canada and Quebec are not
coterminous, Martel's explicit identification as both Canadian and
Québécois suggests a kind of syncretism like that present in his character Pi. Martel has stated,

> L'identité peut être multiple, complexe, fluide, selon d'où vient la lumière,
> qui va éclairer une partie du visage, mais aussi créer des ombres ... Quand
> je suis avec des séparatistes bornés, je me sense Canadien. Quand je suis me
> retrouvé parmi des Anglophones, je me sens alors Québécois, puisque le
> français demeure ma langue maternelle, la langue de mon coeur. (Quoted
> in Lessard A2)

This explanation of the oscillations within Martel's identity functions
more along the lines of Self and Other in conceptions of the syncretic
subject. Martel describes a kind of negative interpellation, wherein
anglophones and Quebec nationalists fail to hail him as one of them,
causing him to assert the other part of his identity. But some journalistic
descriptions of Martel that attempt to encapsulate the contradictions
of Martel's identity both replicate the litany of qualifications from 'The
Time I Heard' and offer a syncretic identity: as 'un Québécois francophone écrivant en anglais' (Guy F2), Martel seemingly poses 'unbearable discord,' but works instead to embody inventive syncretism,
equally hospitable to both halves of his identity. As Courtemanche's
answer to the question of whether Martel is 'Canadien ou Québécois?'
indicates, Martel embodies the state of both/and: 'Les deux' (87).

If Martel admits to being 'Quebec's worst nightmare ... a francophone who writes in English' (quoted in Mahoney C14), he is also, in
many ways, the official Canadian dream, a Canadian who embodies
Canada's bilingual policy and insists upon his Canadian citizenship,
as do his characters Self and Henry. However, Canada is not unequivo-
cally celebrated in Martel's work, despite its role as Pi's hospitable
destination in his Man Booker–winning novel. Although Martel has
represented Canada positively, in both senses of representation, particularly through *Life of Pi* and its celebrated afterlife, he has nevertheless
demonstrated the extent to which official policy and lived reality fail to
coincide. He expands the definition of Canadianness by writing multiple languages and identities into his texts. If Canadian multiculturalism is 'a better story,' it is one that would be further improved, Martel
suggests, through assertions of the syncretic, the radically simultaneous
that does not fit into manageable taxonomies or government policies.

Conclusion, or Discrepant Invitations

Although readers' disappointed responses to Yann Martel's *Beatrice and Virgil* have attracted a great deal of attention, less notice has been taken of the book Martel published between his second and third novels, *What Is Stephen Harper Reading?* In *Beatrice and Virgil*, Martel describes Henry L'Hôte's second novel's success with the caveat 'Writers seldom become public figures. It's their books that rightly hog all the publicity' (3), but it is clear that the publication of *What Is Stephen Harper Reading?* depends upon Martel himself having become a public figure through the publicity generated by *Life of Pi;* moreover, Martel's one-sided correspondence with Canada's prime minister, in which he champions the support of the arts and the welfare state in Canada, allows Martel to consolidate his public-figure status. *What Is Stephen Harper Reading?* comprises fortnightly letters sent by Martel to the prime minister, accompanied by a book that Martel suggests Harper should read. Having only received two impersonal responses by Harper's staff since he began this project in 2007, Martel acknowledges that 'it's been a lonely book club' (2). The genesis of Martel's attempt to expand the reading horizons of the prime minister lies in an act of hostipitality: the invitation of fifty Canadian artists to attend a fiftieth-anniversary celebration of the Canada Council at the House of Commons, each representing a particular year of the Council's work (Martel's year is 1991, when he received a grant that enabled him to write *Self*). The hospitality of the invitation is compromised by the hostility of the artists' reception:

> The Minister for Canadian Heritage ... rose to her feet, acknowledged our presence and began to speak. We artists stood up, not for ourself but for the Canada Council and what it represents. The Minister did not speak

for long. In fact, she had barely started, we thought, when she finished and sat down. There was a flutter of applause and then MPs turned to other matters. We were still standing, incredulous. That was it? Fifty years of building Canada's dazzling and varied culture, done with in less than five minutes? (4)

Even worse, Harper 'did not speak during our brief tribute. He didn't even look up. By all appearances, he didn't even know we were there' (4–5). In other words, Prime Minister Harper, as host, completely ignored his guests.

As Harper made explicitly clear during the 2008 election campaign, and as Martel increasingly highlights in the letters that make up *What Is Stephen Harper Reading?*, the state is rapidly losing interest in the arts, even when economic arguments are offered on behalf of the income generation of the (seemingly more economically sensible) 'cultural industries.' If the international celebration of Canadian culture is of benefit to the Canadian nation, the government's cutting of PromArt in 2008 – prompting Harper's infamous statement that '"ordinary people" don't care about arts funding' (Campion-Smith A1) – indicates a jettisoning of state support for artistic production and dissemination. Beginning virtually every package to Harper with the inscription 'To Stephen Harper, / Prime Minister of Canada, / From a Canadian writer, / With best wishes, Yann Martel' (15) in the book in question, Martel declares himself not only an interested citizen of Canada, but also 'a citizen of the arts' who demands 'the right to know what [his] elected leader thinks about reading' (5), for 'if Stephen Harper is informed by literary culture, or indeed, by culture in general, it doesn't show in what he says or does' (9). As many scholars have noted, after decades of essential support for writers and publishers through the Canada Council, cuts to the Council's budget, the disastrous fallout of Chapters' collapse with its 'ripple effect on dozens of small publishers' (van Herk 137), and the increasing foreign ownership of Canadian publishers have damaged book publishing in Canada (see also Godard, 'Notes'; MacSkimming). Leaving the publication of literature in Canada increasingly vulnerable to market forces can only result in the decreased production of Canadian literature. Through the means of his 'lonely book club,' then, Martel attempts to engender in Harper an appreciation of literature. These gifts are explicitly didactic, seeking to teach Harper about a cultural value that diverges from exchange value, particularly in Martel's decision to send the prime minister used copies of the books he selects:

'I have done this not to save money, but to make a point, which is that a used book, unlike a used car, hasn't lost any of its initial value' (24). Half-way through *What Is Stephen Harper Reading?*, Martel announces the criteria on which he bases his selections: the books must be short, because Harper is 'probably busier than most people, and ... probably feel[s] that [he is] more importantly busy'; they must 'speak plainly'; and they must be 'varied ... [and] show [Harper] all that the word can do' (94). Martel's selections are eclectic, comprised of fiction, non-fiction, poetry, drama, graphic novels, and song lyrics, ranging in temporal terms from translations of *The Epic of Gilgamesh*, the oldest recorded narrative, to Steven Galloway's *The Cellist of Sarajevo*, which had not yet been published when Martel sent it to the prime minister.

As previously indicated in his preface to *Life of Pi*, Martel is unfailingly celebratory of the Canada Council, 'that towering institution that has done so much to foster the cultural identity of Canadians' (*Stephen Harper* 2), whereas, as we have seen, other writers have argued the Council is inadequately representative. Martel fleetingly worries about his own representativeness in the kind of canon he creates, taking its pulse on 'the one-year anniversary of [the] book club' and conceding that he has sent 'too many novels, too many men, not enough poetry,' while arguing both that 'it's hard to be representative and impossible to please everyone' and that 'there is time yet' (113). Martel is not attempting to construct a Canadian canon, arguing it is sensible to 'vee[r] away from the Canadian and the contemporary, so that [he] can't be accused of foisting [his] friends upon [his] fellow club member' (11). In this desire not to appear compromised, and in 'jump[ing] across the barriers of borders and languages' (11), Martel not only underscores the cosmopolitanism with which he is frequently associated but also echoes the government's 'arm's length' policy in relation to the Council (a policy that, as Barbara Godard notes, has been threatened itself in recent years ['Notes' 224]). Yet not only does Martel insist that 'if you want to lead, you must read' (10), but he also makes reading an act of citizenship, and consistently addresses Harper as a Canadian (while also addressing him as a Quebecker, maintaining his syncretic status as a member of both of 'our comparatively young nations of Canada and Quebec' [94]). On the one hand, Martel makes humanist claims for literature, wondering how Harper can have empathy if he has never attempted to imagine another person's life and thereby engaging in arguments for the ethical value of literature. Unsurprisingly, Martel suggests that Harper read Northrop Frye's *The*

Educated Imagination, fitting given Martel's insistence that 'literature contributes to ethics by reinforcing tolerance for others' (Goldman, 'Introduction' 811). On the other hand, beyond this general championing of literature as a force for good, Martel also makes particular protests about the status of the arts in Canada, including the cancellation of PromArt, the axing of the CBC orchestra, cuts to the support of small journals, and the government's attempt to tie SSHRC funding to business-related projects.

Although it may not offer the most radical book-club canon, with such weighty figures as Swift, Voltaire, Austen, Tolstoy, Kafka, Woolf, Hemingway, Orwell, Beckett, and Hughes, *What Is Stephen Harper Reading?* addresses crucial questions about the nature of government under neo-liberalism, the future of the arts in relation to the state, the kind of work that literature can do, and the role of what Danielle Fuller calls the citizen-reader ('Citizen'). Despite the pressing nature of these questions, not just in Canada but elsewhere, this book, Martel's first publication after *Life of Pi,* could never win the Booker Prize: (a) it isn't a novel; and (b) it hasn't been published in the U.K., or anywhere outside Canada, for that matter. What this book demonstrates, in addition to its critique of Harper's Conservative government, are the limits of exportable CanLit and the dominance of the novel genre in the global cultural marketplace. Mentioned outside Canada only in passing in reviews of *Beatrice and Virgil, What Is Stephen Harper Reading?* becomes positioned as an inconsequential side-project, a footnote in the career of an extraordinarily best-selling Canadian writer. The fact that Barack Obama's letter of thanks to Martel for writing *Life of Pi* (a favourite of Obama's daughter) has drawn as much, if not more, attention as *What Is Stephen Harper Reading?* (McPhee 16) indicates that perhaps the latter text might have had more international exposure had Martel constructed his book club with the leader of a different nation-state. But that would have been a different book altogether, one in which Martel could not function as citizen-reader agitating for improvement in the material conditions of artistic production in his own country. It is Harper's regressive conservatism that demands Martel's response, regardless of the fact that Canadian political developments have been virtually absent in the international press, unlike those of our powerful neighbour to the south.

Prizing Literature has demonstrated that internationally lauded Canadian writers are not detached from Canadian social reality, even in their work set beyond our national borders; however, it may be the case that those who argue that much of contemporary 'Canadian literature is only "tangentially" Canadian,' with 'nation-bound works ... giving way to those that claim location in the interconnectivity of global space' (Cavell 43) have correctly assessed the reception of such works outside Canada itself. But if one risk of expanding the settings of CanLit outside Canada is that Canadianness becomes invisible to external readers, there are greater risks in Canadian literature adhering too strictly to the game of literary celebration. As Martel acknowledges in a letter to the prime minister, ' ... one of the good things about literary prizes [is that] [t]hey bring attention to books or authors that might otherwise be missed by readers' (125); but, as Martel worries, ' ... if I won, doesn't it mean that someone lost? That's the less appealing part of it, the feeling that you've become a racehorse, that you are competing, that there are winners and losers' (126). In the movement from eligibility to shortlist, shortlist to winner, literary prizes all implicitly enact what Canada Reads, in its *Survivor* format, does explicitly: the discarding of all other 'contenders,' running the risk that 'the fixation with competition and success may only ... benefi[t] the chosen few' (MacSkimming 373). Further, if international prizes wield the most influence in the celebration and circulation of Canadian literature, what of those prizes (such as the [Man] Booker, the Orange) only open to books published in the U.K., thereby drastically reducing the number of Canadian texts eligible? How hospitable can such international prizes be if so many Canadian writers are not invited to participate? And what are the implications of Canadian culture accruing both national and economic capital from the recognition of international prizes that only consider a fraction of what Canadian writers produce?

As I have argued, national literary prizes can declare ethnic-minority writers Canadian by interpolating them into the host culture, but international prizes do a very different kind of work. And although prizes *not* committed to celebrating Canadian literature may be more 'valuable' for CanLit precisely because of their larger pool of competition, there are dangers in looking to these external arbiters to construct a worthy Canadian literary canon. The implications are particularly worrying for Aboriginal writing in Canada. Although in recent years Joseph Boyden has been nominated for the IMPAC Dublin Award for *Three Day Road*, and Eden Robinson's work, nominated for the Governor General's Award and the Giller Prize, has been published in the U.K. by Abacus, there are too many important indigenous writers in Canada who have not been eligible for such prizes as the (Man)

Booker to ignore the risk of overreliance on powerful 'guest' authorities on Canadian culture. In addition to Robinson's nominations for major national awards, several other Aboriginal writers have won national prizes for literature and drama, including Tomson Highway's two Dora Mavor Moore Awards and Chalmers Awards (*The Rez Sisters*, 1987, and *Dry Lips Oughta Move to Kapuskasing*, 1989/1990), Drew Hayden Taylor's Chalmers Award (*Toronto at Dreamer's Rock*, 1992) and Dora Mavor Moore Award (*Only Drunks and Children Tell the Truth*, 1996), Thomas King's Trillium Prize (*The Truth about Stories*, 2004) and McNally Robinson Aboriginal Book of the Year (*A Short History of Indians in Canada*, 2006), and Boyden's McNally Robinson Award (*Three Day Road*, 2005) and Scotiabank Giller (*Through Black Spruce*, 2008). Further, Highway and King have both received the Order of Canada (in 1994 and 2004, respectively), and Governor General's Award nominations have been achieved by Highway (*Dry Lips Oughta Move to Kapuskasing*, Drama, 1989), Daniel David Moses (*Coyote City*, Drama, 1991), King (*A Coyote Columbus Story*, Children's Literature, 1992; *Green Grass, Running Water*, Fiction, 1993), Boyden (*Three Day Road*, Fiction, 2005), Taylor (*In a World Created by a Drunken God*, Drama, 2007), and Canada Reads nominations by King (*Green Grass, Running Water*, 2004) and Boyden (*Three Day Road*, 2006). These national recognitions not only attest to the increasing significance of Aboriginal writing in relation to what is considered Canadian literature but also represent just a small selection of texts produced by indigenous writers in Canada.

If Yann Martel's acknowledgment in *Self* of national funding sources from both Canada and Quebec emphasizes that the Canadian and Québécois national projects are not coterminous, U.S.-based prizes won by Aboriginal writers in Canada (such as Taylor's Native Playwrights Award from the University of Alaska and First Americans in the Arts Award, administered in the United States) remind us that Canadian cultural sovereignty operates at the expense of indigenous sovereignties, that the 49th parallel does not act as a cultural buffer for all citizens in Canada, that nation-state citizenship itself is not an unambiguous or straightforward category of belonging for Aboriginal peoples, many of whose lands are bisected by a colonial boundary. Whereas national literary prizes have interpolated both immigrant and expatriate writers into the national literature, insisting upon their Canadianness by virtue of their celebration, this function in relation to writers such as Thomas King (Cherokee), long-time resident and citizen of Canada, and Joseph Boyden (Métis), now based in New Orleans, depend upon a nation-state border whose colonial logic is one that King, in particular, is often at pains to disrupt and disarm: 'I guess I'm supposed to say that I believe in the line that exists between the US and Canada, but for me it's an imaginary line. It's a line from somebody else's imagination' (quoted in Davidson, Walton, and Andrews 125–6). It is precisely as a Canadian citizen that King 'is supposed to say' that he sides with an Anglo-Canadian nationalism that depends upon Canada's distinction from the United States. This failed interpellation of King negotiates between, on the one hand, his desire to belong to the Canadian nation-state (through the act of taking out Canadian citizenship, as well as running for the NDP in the 2008 federal election), his functioning as a Canadian cultural 'host' as his Canadian prizes and nominations indicate, and, on the other, the fact that from a Native North American perspective, the 49th parallel is deeply problematic, if not invalid, in its attempts to distinguish 'host' from 'guest,' particularly as regards the indigenous peoples of the continent.

Notions of hospitality and celebrated Canadian culture necessarily operate differently – indeed awkwardly, at best – in relation to Canada's Aboriginal peoples, usurped hosts in a settler-invader 'postcolonial' nation-state that has yet to de-colonize. And yet the parameters of the 'host culture' in Canada have largely been drawn by the dominant settler-invader culture, even when national prizes for literature and theatre have included Aboriginal artistic production. Lee Maracle has criticized the 'fort' of Canadian culture, whose 'existence . . . , the laws of this fort, the humanity of it are rarely questioned' (206). Maracle not only invokes Frye's garrison mentality through Canadian writers' 'intellectual incarceration' (206) but also emphasizes the cultural work that has been done, historically, to exclude Aboriginal peoples from the host position, policing the boundaries of Canadianness and its cultural expression (including, in the context of cultural appropriation, representation of indigenous peoples by non-indigenous artists).

If national celebration of Aboriginal culture potentially indicates a greater hospitality of the Canadian cultural 'fort,' the discarding of King's Canada Reads–nominated *Green Grass, Running Water* in favour of Guy Vanderhaeghe's *Last Crossing* in 2004 potentially reveals the limitations of the celebratory project and the work that still needs to be done in order for 'Canadians [to] get out of the fort and imagine something beyond the colonial condition' (Maracle 206). Canada Reads 2004 judge Measha Brueggergosman observed of *Green Grass, Running Water*'s elimination, 'how very Canadian – we don't want anything that challenges us' (quoted in Fuller and Rehberg Sedo 24). Brueggergosman here identifies Canadianness itself as being inhospitable to challenge and revision, whether aesthetic or political. The challenges to a Canadian readership raised by King's novel include the contesting of the Canada–U.S. border's significance for Native North Americans, particularly in Lionel's experiences with the American Indian Movement; indigenous resistance to land expropriation and damaging development, as in Eli's refusal to leave his mother's home in order to facilitate the operation of a dam (echoing Elijah Harper's 'no' to the Meech Lake Accord [Fee and Flick 134]); the critique of Canadian historical and literary figures implicated in colonization through government power and representation (e.g. Clifford Sifton, D.C. Scott, Susanna Moodie, and Archibald Belaney / Grey Owl); a disruption of heteronormativity through the narratives of Moby Jane and Alberta; and, in aesthetic terms, an enormous range of intertextual references comprising Canadian and American literature as well as Native and biblical mythologies, lines written in Cherokee without translation, metafictional reflection on the telling of stories, and the figure of the trickster as Coyote, interrupting the narrative. As Danielle Fuller and DeNel Rehberg Sedo assess the Canada Reads debates generated by King's novel, 'The on-air clashes over the literary merit and political value of King's work revealed a range of anxieties: about the ideological function of fiction; about the position of First Nations communities within the Canadian polity; and the reluctance of most panellists to confront issues of "race" head-on' (24). Although such clashes suggest that King's transgressions may not be licensed, as with all literary prizes, the Canada Reads judges have not, in fact, had the final say, following the delivery of their verdict to readers for assessment. In the case of *Green Grass, Running Water*'s position within Canada Reads, 'the discussion on the website echoed but also interrogated these anxieties, with participants advocating the importance of "listening" to King's delineating of colonization, racism, and resistance' (24). Crucially, the definition of the nation through literary celebration is not completed with the granting of prizes themselves, but with the work that citizen-readers do in response.

In *What Is Stephen Harper Reading?* citizen-reader Martel offers Tomson Highway's play *The Rez Sisters* as an example of what the prime minister must read in order to render him more accountable to the electorate. Although Martel articulates his approval of Harper's government's apology to victims of the residential school system, he also asserts the importance of Native Earth Performing Arts and its influence on the careers of playwrights such as Moses and Taylor, the subtext of which is the need for continuing investment in Aboriginal cultural production. If Martel rails against the increasing corporatization of culture in his letters to Harper, and the danger of allowing state support for the arts to falter, his suggestion of texts that are not novels (despite the fact that, by his own admission, 'too many novels' have been sent to the prime minister) responds to concerns about the rise of the novel at the expense of other genres. As Di Brandt warns in her discussion of the dangers of CanLit's 'going global,' we must 'work very hard to ensure the survival of poetry and drama, the genres most jeopardized in this new commercialized literary economy' (106, 112). On the one hand, as Canada's most celebrated First Nations dramatist, Tomson Highway clearly enjoys an international reputation, as evidenced by the 1988 production of *The Rez Sisters* at the Edinburgh Festival and the 2001 Tokyo production of *Dry Lips Oughta Move to Kapuskasing*. On the other hand, despite the fact that in 1990 critic Denis W. Johnston asserted that 'we will certainly listen to the next play from Tomson Highway. Not only will it be a cultural event, it may also be a play from which we can learn' (263), Highway's play *Rose*, an ambitious musical that constitutes the third instalment of his planned seven-play cycle that began with *The Rez Sisters* and *Dry Lips*, has yet to have a professional production, even in Canada, due to a combination of such factors as the question of whether 'theatres are ready for the vast, immensely diverse and uncompromising theatrical imagination articulated in *Rose*' (Hauck 51) and the material difficulties of theatrical production. In a new literary economy in which the largest and most high-profile prizes are bestowed, more often than not, on not just fiction in general, but the novel specifically, in which 'the coming of age, the very golden age of Canadian literature, both at home and abroad' (Brandt 106) arrived chiefly through the international recognition and circulation of novels by Canadian writers, we risk discarding literature and culture that is produced in Canada that is not as easily marketed, through failing both to support and to celebrate it.

In the context of international literary prizes, discrepant invitations reveal that not all writers are equally welcome. As much as Canada has taken pride in its exportable writers and their cultural as well as economic value, there is only so far that some Canadian literature can travel, whether through subject matter, the economics of publishing, or the global market's hospitality to some writers and genres over others. But citizen-readers cannot afford to dismiss Canadian literature that stays close to home, either in terms of content or circulation, or both, particularly if to do so would be to ignore entire genres and communities of artists given less attention in the global cultural marketplace. While the celebration of Canadian literature on both national and international levels may produce positive effects for some writers of winning texts, the prize economy is not without its potentially harmful consequences. As consumers as well as audience members, citizen-readers must be wary of 'prize cultures that focus upon the definition and creation of a national literature for exclusionary, expropriatory, and marketing purposes' (Scott and Tucker-Abramson 19), both within and outside Canada, if we are to resist the 'discarding' of literature that does not win the most visible, most lucrative literary prize games, or perhaps was not invited to participate in the first place.

If, in some sense, this book has been culpable of a similar discarding through neglect, discussing Michael Ondaatje's fiction, but not his poetry, Shields's novels but not her plays, international prize-winners Mistry and Martel, but not the many brilliant writers who are not published outside Canada, it has intended to suggest neither that only these four writers discussed in detail have been worthy of the international attention they have attracted nor that they are *un*worthy of such celebration. Rather, my aim has been to examine the workings of this 'golden age' of international celebration, circulation, and commodification in relation both to the nation's response to successful 'hyphenate' authors and to the texts themselves. The four writers who have formed the focus of this book – Shields, Ondaatje, Mistry, and Martel – offer very different case studies of celebrated belongings constructed out of international recognition. All four have had their national identities translated for them in both the Canadian and extranational press as a result of their celebration within and outside Canada. All four have attracted high-profile, international celebration that has been recruited for national interests, for the symbolic capital accrued through the winning of or nominations for 'prestigious,' particularly international, prizes ultimately confers cultural value on the nation itself. But this is not to overlook the differences between these writers, their works, their reception, and their relationship to the nation. Not only do these writers inhabit national identities that present different processes and degrees of translation into celebrated Canadians, but they have also been located within diverging fields of production: whereas Ondaatje's and Martel's association with highbrow literature may have facilitated their acquisition of symbolic value through the literary prize, Shields's and Mistry's occasional insertions into the middlebrow alongside the celebration of their texts both questions these aesthetic categories altogether and probes the relationships between symbolic value and the popular. As this book has argued, the popular is not simply a dismissible aesthetic category, but rather both the implicit goal of the literary prize, in general – to render the texts it values more popular – and a key pursuit of the Canadian national cultural project, in particular. That Martel should cast his 'correspondence with (or, more accurately, at)' (Malla F8) the prime minister as a 'book club' in *What Is Stephen Harper Reading?* does not simply reflect ironically on Harper's refusal to participate but also reflects the power of the popular in relation to literary culture.

Celebratory responses in Canada to these writers' international successes have focused on the gains in Canadian cultural currency and its ability to circulate worldwide through the exportability of our literature. This circulation and sense of the national culture increasing in value has at times belied the material difficulties of the Canadian publishing industry. As Charles Gordon notes, 'honors heaped internationally' on Canadian writers should not be 'cited as evidence of a healthy Canadian publishing scene' ('Why' 11). If we consider the timing of the celebration of these writers, in particular, especially the year 2002, which saw the triple Canadian Man Booker nomination as well as the rejuvenated celebration of *In the Skin of a Lion* through Canada Reads, we must also acknowledge the bankruptcy of Stoddart Publishing (at one time Shields's publisher) and General Distributing Services, with disastrous consequences for the Canadian publishing industry, in that same year. Brandt's vision of CanLit's 'golden age,' articulated in 2000, now sounds like an elegiac description of the decade between Ondaatje's and Martel's Booker Prizes.

CanLit's long-standing dependence upon state funding has carried not only material but also ideological implications. The support and celebration of Canadian literature through the Canada Council underscores the position of Canadian writers as the nation-state's licensed transgressors. To a certain extent, challenges presented by literary works to the nation might be subdued, or 'sedated,' by the process of celebration. But responses to some of these writers, either for texts that criticize Canada, or for texts that do not represent Canada at all, suggest that not all writers are equally licensed. For Mistry, in particular, although his international recognition increases Canada's cultural currency, it seems his Bombay settings are read merely as a precursor to the novel that Canadians hope he will write, as though Canada's cultural currency would trade more profitably if Toronto, not Bombay, formed the setting for Mistry's narratives. Mistry, it would appear, is not the same 'one of us' that Shields presented through her 'good' citizenship, one that included her setting most of her narratives in Canada.

If celebrated immigrant writers are welcomed into the cultural host position, there remains some anxiety about Canada's hold on these authors, about whether immigrant writers who transcend the nation through international celebration will be content to remain within Canada's borders and to call Canada home. International recognition thereby provokes the tension between allowing these celebrated writers to act as cultural ambassadors, representing Canada in a global context and cultural marketplace, and the worry that they can do without Canada. In the case of Martel, wrongly identified in the international press as an immigrant to Canada, but the product of an international upbringing, the anxiety focuses on whether Martel, having come 'home' to Canada, will be content to stay, to unpack the suitcase in which he carries his 'roots.' Thus, the increased, but precarious, value for Canada's cultural currency as effected by such international celebrations could suffer deflation if such writers refused to be affiliated with Canada, either through leaving the country or through 'failing' to affirm its significance to them. Cosmopolitanism here seems a kind of threat, relaxing the hold of the nation-state upon the artist who becomes mobile, diminishing the validity of national capital.

Ondaatje, Shields, Mistry, and Martel all probe issues of belonging in their works, through exploring disjunctions between nation and habitation, between citizenship and nationality, the negotiation of host and guest positions, and the possibilities and limitations of cosmopolitanism. They examine the exclusivity with which dominant definitions construct the Canadian cultural host. In doing so, they interrogate these exclusions and work to expand the dominant definition of Canadianness. What these writers have to say about belonging is more complex than the claims made on their behalf by the national press in the wake of their international exposure and exportability. Consequently, more than one thing happens when texts that criticize the nation are also celebrated by it. Canada, as our media would have it, is the hospitable destination that *Family Matters'* Yezad dreams of; but these writers tell us otherwise, that not everyone is invited in, that not all those invited in are allowed to remain, that those who are allowed to remain do not all get to occupy the status of cultural host. If Canadian culture circulates globally through these celebrated writers, it does so in conjunction with their critiques of the nation and its discrepant invitations. Ultimately, as citizen-readers, our role is not so much to decry the co-opting of these critiques as to understand celebratory projects as sites of struggle in which different versions of the nation compete to determine who belongs.

Works Cited

Abley, Mark. 'Author's Intent Is Lost on Australian Voyage.' *Montreal Gazette* 17 Oct. 1992: J1.

– 'Booby Prize.' *Saturday Night* May 1985: 51–6.

– 'Filling a Giant's Shoes.' *Montreal Gazette* 24 Nov. 2001: A1.

'About the CWC.' Internet. <www.crimewriterscanada.com/files/aboutcwc .html> Accessed 17 Jul. 2003.

'About the QWF.' Internet. <http://www.qwf.org/about.html> Accessed 1 May 2008.

Acland, Charles. 'Popular Film in Canada: Revisiting the Absent Audience.' *A Passion for Identity: An Introduction to Canadian Studies.* 3rd ed. Ed. David Taras and Beverly Rasporich. Toronto: Nelson, 1997. 281–96.

Adair, Tom. 'The Stuff of Life, Perfectly Observed.' *Scotland on Sunday* 3 Mar. 1996: Spectrum 13.

Adams, James. 'Shields's Talents Gained World Acclaim.' *Globe and Mail* 18 Jul. 2003: A1, A6.

Adams, Tim. 'Pi Went to Sea with a Bengal Tiger, a Zebra, a Hyena and an Orang-utan. Sorry, No Pussycat.' *Observer* 26 May 2002: Review 15.

Addison, Catherine. 'Lost Things.' *Canadian Literature* 121 (1989): 158–160.

Ahmed, Sara. *Strange Encounters: Embodied Others in Post-Coloniality.* London: Routledge, 2000.

Alberge, Dalya. 'Booker Judges Attack "Pretension and Pomposity."' *Times* (London) 25 Sep. 2002: 3.

Albertazzi, Silvia. 'Passages: The "Indian Connection," from Sara Jeannette Duncan to Rohinton Mistry.' *Imagination and the Creative Impulse in the New Literatures in English.* Ed. M.-T. Bindella and G.V. Davis. Amsterdam: Rodopi, 1993. 57–66.

– Rev. of *Anil's Ghost. Wasafiri* 32 (2000): 74–5.

Allemang, John. 'Winning Writing Contest Changed Mistry's Life.' *Globe and Mail* 11 Feb. 1988: D1.

'American Wins Orange Prize.' *Daily Telegraph* 20 May 1998: 2.

Anderson, Amanda. 'Cosmopolitanism, Universalism, and the Divided Legacies of Modernity.' Cheah and Robbins 265–89.

Andrew, Caroline. 'Multiculturalism, Gender, and Social Cohesion: Reflections on Intersectionality and Urban Citizenship in Canada.' *Reconfigurations: Canadian Citizenship and Constitutional Change.* Ed. Douglas E. Williams. Toronto: McClelland & Stewart, 1995. 316–25.

Andrews, Marke. 'Author's Imagination Engaged by India He Left.' *Vancouver Sun* 23 Oct. 1992: C7.

– 'Writer Urges Colleagues to Put Happiness in Plots.' *Calgary Herald* 16 Oct. 1993: A19.

Angus, Ian. *A Border Within: National Identity, Cultural Plurality, and Wilderness.* Montreal and Kingston: McGill-Queen's UP, 1997.

Anzaldúa, Gloria. *Borderlands / La Frontera.* 2nd ed. San Francisco: Aunt Lute, 1999.

Appiah, Kwame Anthony. *Cosmopolitanism: Ethics in a World of Strangers.* London: Allen Lane, 2006.

Archer, Bert. 'Plain Stories with a Twist.' *Montreal Gazette* 31 May 1997: Books and Visual Arts 14.

– 'The Unstoppable Carol Shields: Pulitzer Prize Caps Stone Diaries Triumph.' *Quill & Quire* Jun. 1995: 29.

Arnold, Matthew. 'The Function of Criticism at the Present Time.' *Lectures and Essays in Criticism.* Ed. R.H. Super. Ann Arbor: U of Michigan P, 1962. 258–85.

Ashcroft, Bill. *Postcolonial Transformations.* London: Routledge, 2001.

Ashcroft, Bill, Gareth Griffiths, and Helen Tiffin. *Key Concepts in Post-Colonial Studies.* London and New York: Routledge, 1998.

Aspinall, Jane. '. . . Meanwhile Back in Canada.' *Quill & Quire* Dec. 1992: 13.

Atkinson, Nathalie. 'The Great Canadian Literary Makeover.' *National Post* 4 Nov. 2006: WP5.

Atwood, Margaret. *Second Words: Selected Critical Prose.* Toronto: Anansi, 1982.

– 'A Tasty Slice of Pi and Ships.' *Sunday Times* (London) 5 May 2002. Nexis UK. Leeds Metropolitan U Lib. 9 Jul. 2007 <http://www.lexisnexis.com/uk/>.

– 'To the Light House.' *Guardian* 26 Jul. 2003: Review 28.

Aubry, Timothy. 'Beware the Furrow of the Middlebrow: Searching for Paradise on *The Oprah Winfrey Show.' Modern Fiction Studies* 52.2 (2006): 350–73.

Ball, John Clement. 'Canadian Crusoes from Sea to Sea: The Oceanic Communities of Douglas Glover's *Elle* and Yann Martel's *Life of Pi.'* Kanaganayakam, ed. 85–103.

Balme, Christopher. 'Inventive Syncretism: The Concept of the Syncretic in Intercultural Discourse.' Stummer and Balme 9–18.

Barber, John. 'How the Book World's Rare Success Story Came to an End in Suburbia.' *Globe and Mail* 30 Dec. 2009: A1.

Basilières, Michael. 'Diderot Derivative: A Novel (?) Poses Puzzles to Convey Angst of the Holocaust.' *Literary Review of Canada* 1 Jun. 2010. Internet. <http://reviewcanada.ca/reviews/2010/06/01/diderot-derivative/> Accessed 16 Jun. 2010.

Bates, J. Douglas. *The Pulitzer Prize: The Inside History of America's Most Prestigious Award.* New York: Birch Lane, 1991.

Battersby, Eileen. 'Ordinary Lives.' *Irish Times* 2 Mar. 1996: Supplement 9.

Bayoumi, Moustafa. 'Immigration: As the Border Tightens, We All Lose Out.' *Charleston Gazette* 24 Nov. 2002: 1C.

Beddoes, Julie. '"Which Side Is It On?": Form, Class, and Politics in *In the Skin of a Lion.' Essays on Canadian Writing* 53 (1994): 204–15.

Bégin, Jean-François. 'Yann Martel remporte le Booker Prize.' *La Presse* (Montreal) 23 Oct. 2002: A1.

Beiner, Ronald, and Wayne Norman, eds. *Canadian Political Philosophy: Contemporary Reflections.* Don Mills, ON: Oxford UP, 2001.

Bemrose, John. 'Best of the Century Fiction.' *Maclean's* 1 Jan. 2000: 241.

– 'Casualties of War.' *Maclean's* 19 Oct. 1992: 71.

Benhabib, Seyla. 'Philosophical Foundations of Cosmopolitan Norms.' *Another Cosmopolitanism.* Ed. Robert Post. Oxford: Oxford UP, 2006. 13–44.

Bennett, Tony. *Outside Literature.* London and New York: Routledge, 1990.

Bentley, D.M.R. *The Gay]Grey Moose: Essays on the Ecologies and Mythologies of Canadian Poetry, 1690–1990.* Ottawa: U of Ottawa P, 1992.

Bercuson, David J. *Maple Leaf against the Axis: Canada's Second World War.* Toronto: Stoddart, 1995.

Bérubé, Stéphanie. 'Pénurie de Pi.' *La Presse* (Montreal) 27 Aug. 2003: C3.

'Bestsellers of 2002.' *Globe and Mail* 28 Dec. 2002: D13.

Bhabha, Homi K. *The Location of Culture.* 1994. London: Routledge, 2005.

Bharucha, Nilufer E. *Rohinton Mistry: Ethnic Enclosures and Transcultural Spaces.* Jaipur and New Delhi: Rawat, 2003.

– '"When Old Tracks Are Lost": Rohinton Mistry's Fiction as Diasporic Discourse.' *Journal of Commonwealth Literature* 30.2 (1995): 57–63.

Bilan, R.P. 'End the Governor General Awards?' *Canadian Forum* Jun.-Jul. 1981: 31–2.

Boswell, Randy. 'Author Shields Wins Big in U.K.' *Ottawa Citizen* 20 May 1998: A3.

Bourdieu, Pierre. *Distinction: A Social Critique of the Judgement of Taste.* Tr. Richard Nice. London: Routledge & Kegan Paul, 1984.

– *The Field of Cultural Production: Essays on Art and Literature.* Ed. Randal Johnson. Cambridge: Polity, 1993.

Brand, Dionne. *Bread Out of Stone: Recollections, Sex, Recognitions, Race, Dreaming, Politics.* Toronto: Coach House, 1994.

– Interview with Dagmar Novak. *Other Solitudes: Canadian Multicultural Fictions.* Toronto: Oxford UP, 1990. 271–7.

Brandt, Di. 'Going Global.' *Essays on Canadian Writing* 71 (2000): 106–13.

Brophy, Sarah. *Witnessing AIDS: Writing, Testimony, and the Work of Mourning.* Toronto: U of Toronto P, 2004.

Brouillette, Sarah. *Postcolonial Writers in the Global Literary Marketplace.* Basingstoke: Palgrave Macmillan, 2007.

Brown, Judith M. *Modern India: The Origins of an Asian Democracy.* Oxford: Oxford UP, 1985.

Brown, Russell. 'The Written Line.' *Borderlands: Essays in Canadian-American Relations.* Ed. Robert Lecker. Toronto: ECW, 1991. 1–27.

Brownrigg, Sylvia. 'Books: Talents to Amaze.' *Guardian* 23 May 1998: Saturday 10.

Bunce, Kim. 'New Paperbacks.' *Observer* 17 Nov. 1996: Review 18.

Buzacott, Martin. 'So Subtle the Seduction.' *Courier Mail* (Queensland) 22 Jun. 2002: M7.

Caine, Sir Michael H. 'The Booker Story.' *The Man Booker Prize* 13–19.

Cairns, Alan C., et al., eds. *Citizenship, Diversity, and Pluralism: Canadian and Comparative Perspectives.* Montreal and Kingston: McGill-Queen's UP, 1999.

Caldwell, Gail. 'Midway in Life's Journey.' *Boston Globe* 14 Sep. 1997: F15.

Caldwell, Rebecca. 'The Great Canadian Book Brawl.' *Globe and Mail* 19 Feb. 2005: R7.

Cameron, Stevie. 'Minding the Books.' *Maclean's* 6 Nov. 1995: 42.

Campion-Smith, Bruce. 'Arts Uproar? Ordinary Folks Just Don't Care, Harper Says.' *Toronto Star* 24 Sep. 2008: A1.

Canada Council. 'Peer Assessment at the Canada Council for the Arts.' Internet. <www.canadacouncil.ca/canadacouncil/user/printthispage .aspx?url=%2fgrants%2 fgrant_policies%2fgq127234205403281250 .htm&language=en#> Accessed 11 Dec. 2003.

'Canada Reads Champion: In the Skin of a Lion.' Internet. <www.cbc.ca/ canadareads/cr_ 2002/skin.html> Accessed 17 Dec. 2003.

'Canada's Winning Words: Be Thankful So Many World-Class Writers Have Chosen to Live Here.' *Ottawa Citizen* 24 Nov. 2003: A10.

Canadian Multiculturalism Act. R.S., 1985, c. 24 (4th Supp.). 21 Jul. 1988. Internet. <http://www.canadianheritage.gc.ca/progs/multi/policy/act_e.cfm> Accessed 4 July 2008.

'A Canadian Treasure.' *Ottawa Citizen* 18 Jul. 2003: A16.

'Canadian Wins U.K. Book Prize.' *Toronto Star* 20 May 1998: D1.

'Canadians Write the Book on Excellence.' *Ottawa Citizen* 24 Oct. 2002: A18.

'CanLit Can Do.' *Kitchener-Waterloo Record* 27 Sep. 2002: A14.

'Carol Shields.' *Times* (London) 18 Jul. 2003: 34.

'Carol Shields 1935—.' *Contemporary Literary Criticism* 113 (1999): 395–448.

'Carol Shields, C.C., O.M., D.Litt., LL.D., M.R.S.C.' Internet. <www.gg.ca/
    Search/ honours_descript_e.asp?type=2&id=3853> Accessed 25 Mar. 2003.

Carter, April. *The Political Theory of Global Citizenship*. London: Routledge,
    2001.

Castles, Stephen, and Alastair Davidson. *Citizenship and Migration:
    Globalization and the Politics of Belonging*. Basingstoke: Macmillan, 2000.

Cavallar, Georg. *The Rights of Strangers: Theories of International Hospitality, the
    Global Community, and Political Justice since Vitoria*. Aldershot: Ashgate, 2002.

Cavell, Richard. 'McLuhan's "Borderline Case" Revisited.' *Comment comparer
    le Canada avec les États-Unis aujourd'hui: Enjeux et pratiques*. Ed. Hélène
    Quanquin, Christine Lorre-Johnston, and Sandrine Ferré-Rode. Paris:
    Presses Sorbonne Nouvelle, 2009. 25–50.

Cayouette, Pierre. 'La résurrection d'Hubert Aquin.' *L'Actualité* 15 Jun. 2003: 17.

Célestin, Roger. *From Cannibals to Radicals: Figures and Limits of Exoticism*.
    Minneapolis: U of Minnesota P, 1996.

Celyn Jones, Russell. 'Read between the Hype.' *Guardian* 22 Oct. 2002: 19.

Chakravarty, Ipsita. 'When It's Over.' *Telegraph* (India) 27 May 2010. Nexis UK.
    U Nottingham Lib. 23 Jun. 2010. <http://www.lexisnexis.com/uk/>.

Cheah, Pheng. 'Given Culture: Rethinking Cosmopolitical Freedom in
    Transnationalism.' Cheah and Robbins 290–328.

Cheah, Pheng, and Bruce Robbins, eds. *Cosmopolitics: Thinking and Feeling
    beyond the Nation*. Minneapolis: U of Minnesota P, 1998.

Clarkson, Stephen. *Uncle Sam and Us: Globalization, Neoconservatism, and the
    Canadian State*. Toronto: U of Toronto P, 2002.

Clifford, James. 'Traveling Cultures.' *Cultural Studies*. Ed. Lawrence Grossberg,
    Cary Nelson, and Paula Treichler. New York: Routledge, 1992. 96–116.

Cockburn, David. 'Light on a Dullard.' *Herald* (Glasgow) 2 May 1992: 19.

Code, Lorraine. 'How to Think Globally: Stretching the Limits of Imagination.'
    Hypatia 13.2 (1998): 73–85.

'Coderre "Annoyed" by U.S. Racial Profiling.' *Canadian Press Newswire* 4 Nov.
    2002. Nexis UK. Leeds Metropolitan U Lib. 4 Jun. 2007. <http://www.lexisnexis
    .com/uk/>.

Coe, Jonathan. 'Books: Quilt with Kindness.' *Guardian* 28 Feb. 1991: 26.

Cole, Stewart. 'Believing in Tigers: Anthropomorphism and Incredulity in
    Yann Martel's *Life of Pi*.' *Studies in Canadian Literature* 29.2 (2004): 22–36.

Colvile, Georgiana M.M. 'Carol's Party and Larry's Shields: On Carol Shields' Novel *Larry's Party* (1997).' *Etudes Canadiennes / Canadian Studies* 49 (2000): 85–96.

Comellini, Carla. 'Michael Ondaatje's *The English Patient:* Why a Patient and a Nurse?' Ondaatje and Lacroix 153–68.

Commonwealth Foundation. 'About Us.' Internet. <http://www.commonwealth foundation.com/about/> Accessed 23 Jan. 2008.

Commonwealth Foundation. 'Commonwealth Writers' Prize.' Internet. <http://www.commonwealthfoundation.com/culturediversity/writers prize/> Accessed 23 Jan. 2008.

Cornwell, Jane. 'Fame Is Just a Bin Away.' *Weekend Australian* 26 Apr. 2003: B24.

Corse, Sarah M. *Nationalism and Literature: The Politics of Culture in Canada and the United States.* Cambridge: Cambridge UP, 1997.

Coulson, Sandra. 'Identity? I'm a Writer, Mistry Shrugs.' *London Free Press* (London, ON) 17 Apr. 2002: C5.

Courtemanche, Gil. 'Du côté de chez Yann.' *L'Actualité* 1 Dec. 1996: 86–7, 89.

Craddock, E.J. 'Publishing: Why the Booker Prize Is Bad News for Books.' *Times* (London) 7 Oct. 1985: 15.

Craig, Amanda. 'Daisy Loses Herself among the Flowers.' *Independent* 11 Sep. 1993: 30.

Craig, T.L. Rev. of *Such a Long Journey. University of Toronto Quarterly* 62.1 (1992): 21–2.

Cryer, Dan. 'An Indian Escapes the White-Man's World.' *Newsday* 18 Sep. 1989: II 6.

Cunningham, Frank. 'Could Canada Turn into Bosnia?' *Cultural Identity and the Nation-State.* Ed. Carol C. Gould and Pasquale Paquino. Lanham, MD: Rowman & Littlefield, 2001. 31–55.

Curtis, Quentin. 'Home Is a Foreign Country.' *Independent on Sunday* 13 Sep. 1992: Review 24–5.

Davey, Frank. *Canadian Literary Power.* Edmonton: NeWest, 1994.

– *Post-national Arguments: The Politics of the Anglophone-Canadian Novel since 1967.* Toronto: U of Toronto P, 1993.

Davidson, Arnold E., Priscilla L. Walton, and Jennifer Andrews. *Border Crossings: Thomas King's Cultural Inversions.* Toronto: U of Toronto P, 2002.

Deibert, Ronald J. *Parchment, Printing, and Hypermedia: Communication in World Order Transformation.* New York: Columbia UP, 1997.

Demchinsky, Bryan. 'Rohinton Mistry Wins Governor-General's Award for Fiction.' *Montreal Gazette* 4 Dec. 1991: D1.

Derrida, Jacques. *Adieu to Emmanuel Levinas.* Tr. Pascale-Anne Brault and Michael Naas. Stanford: Stanford UP, 1999.

- 'The Animal That Therefore I Am (More to Follow).' Tr. David Wills. *Critical Inquiry* 28.2 (2002): 369–418.
- *Given Time: I. Counterfeit Money.* Tr. Peggy Kamuf. Chicago: U of Chicago P, 1992.
- 'Hostipitality.' *Angelaki* 5.3 (2000): 3–18.
- *Monolingualism of the Other; or, The Prosthesis of Origin.* Tr. Patrick Mensah. Stanford: Stanford UP, 1998.
- *Of Hospitality: Anne Dufourmantelle Invites Jacques Derrida to Respond.* Tr. Rachel Bowlby. Stanford: Stanford UP, 2000.
Di'Antonio, Robert. 'A Compelling Story in Graceful Language.' *Jerusalem Post* 8 May 1991. Nexis UK. Leeds Metropolitan U Lib. 1 Jun. 2007 <http://www.lexisnexis.com.uk/>.
Díaz Dueñas, Mercedes. 'The Postmodern Twist in Yann Martel's *Life of Pi*.' *Figures of Belatedness: Postmodernist Fiction in English.* Eds. Javier Gascueña Gahete and Paula Martín Salván. Córdoba: Servicio de Publicaciones de la Universidad de Córdoba, 2006. 247–57.
Dirda, Michael. 'In the Maze of One Man's Life.' *Washington Post* 14 Sep. 1997: Book World 1, 10.
Dobson, Kit. *Transnational Canadas: Anglo-Canadian Literature and Globalization.* Waterloo, ON: Wilfrid Laurier UP, 2009.
Dodiya, Jaydipsinh. *Perspectives on the Novels of Rohinton Mistry.* New Delhi: Sarup & Sons, 2006.
- ed. *The Fiction of Rohinton Mistry.* New Delhi: Sangam, 1998.
Donnelly, Pat. 'Ondaatje Makes It Five.' *Montreal Gazette* 28 Nov. 2007: D1.
Dorminey, Bruce. 'The Patient in Italy.' *Globe and Mail* 11 Nov. 1995: C1, C4.
Doyle, John. 'Thank God, the Giller's Got Mary Walsh to Host.' *Globe and Mail* 4 Nov. 2003: R2.
Drabelle, Dennis. 'Sojourn to the Subcontinent.' *Washington Post* 27 Jun. 1991: Book World D3.
Dvořák, Marta, and Manina Jones, eds. *Carol Shields and the Extra-ordinary.* Montreal and Kingston: McGill-Queen's UP, 2007.
Elie, Paul. 'Off Balance.' *Village Voice* 8 Oct. 2002: 127.
Emery, Sharyn. '"Call Me by My Name": Personal Identity and Possession in *The English Patient*.' *Literature / Film Quarterly* 28.3 (2000): 210–13.
English, James F. *The Economy of Prestige: Prizes, Awards, and the Circulation of Cultural Value.* Cambridge, MA: Harvard UP, 2005.
- 'Everyone's a Winner.' *Guardian* 21 Apr. 2007: Review 3.
- 'Winning the Culture Game: Prizes, Awards, and the Rules of Art.' *New Literary History* 33 (2002): 109–35.

English, James F., and John Frow. 'Literary Authorship and Celebrity Culture.' *A Concise Companion to Contemporary British Fiction.* Oxford: Blackwell, 2006. 39–57.

The English Patient. Screenplay by Anthony Minghella. Dir. Anthony Minghella. Prod. Saul Zaentz. Miramax, 1996.

Erickson, Bonnie H. 'What Is Good Taste Good For?' *Canadian Review of Sociology and Anthropology* 28 (1991): 255–78.

Eustace, John. 'Deregulating the Evacuated Body: Rohinton Mistry's "Squatter."' *Studies in Canadian Literature* 28 (2003): 26–42.

Everett-Green, Robert. 'Hereafter Pays Off for Telefilm.' *Globe and Mail* 26 Mar. 1998: C2.

'Farewell to a Heroine.' *Toronto Star* 18 Jul. 2003: A22.

Fee, Margery, and Jane Flick. 'Coyote Pedagogy: Knowing Where the Borders Are in Thomas King's *Green Grass, Running Water.' Canadian Literature* 161–162 (1999): 131–9.

Ferguson, Will. 'Secrets of a Book Panelist.' *Globe and Mail* 12 May 2003: R1.

Fernando, Basil. 'Disappearances: Why Western-Based Human Rights Groups Have Not Been Able to Play a Significant Role in the Prosecution of Offenders.' Internet. <www.ahrchk.net/hrsolid/mainfile.php/2001vol11no08/1182/> Accessed 10 Jan. 2003.

Feschuk, Scott. 'My Canada Doesn't Include Skin of a Lion.' *National Post* 24 Apr. 2002: AL6.

Finkle, Derek. 'A Vow of Silence.' *Saturday Night* Nov. 1996: 90–8, 138.

Foley, Dylan. 'Tale Tries to Grasp Life in Bombay.' *Denver Post* 22 Dec. 2002: EE2.

Foran, Charles. 'As Canadian As.' *Globe and Mail* 19 Oct. 2002: D5, D6.

– 'Martel Novel Will Delight and Infuriate.' *Montreal Gazette* 18 May 1996: I1.

– 'Mistry Still Looks to India for Stamp of Approval.' *Montreal Gazette* 7 Dec. 1991: J6.

Foucault, Michel. *The Birth of Biopolitics: Lectures at the Collège de France, 1978–79.* Tr. Graham Burchell. Basingstoke: Palgrave Macmillan, 2008.

– *The Birth of the Clinic.* Tr. A.M. Sheridan. 1973. London: Routledge, 2003.

Freeman, Alan. 'The Queen and the Old Colonial.' *Globe and Mail* 10 Mar. 2004: R1.

Frow, John. *Cultural Studies and Cultural Value.* Oxford: Clarendon P, 1995.

Fuentes, Carlos. *Latin America: At War with the Past.* Toronto: CBC Enterprises, 1985.

Fugère, Jean. 'L'histoire de Pi: Rigueur, l'humour et magie.' *La Presse* 12 Oct. 2003: L2.

Fuller, Danielle. 'Citizen Reader: Canadian Literature, Mass Reading Events and the Promise of Belonging.' British Association of Canadian Studies conference. Cambridge University: 7 Apr. 2010.

- 'Listening to the Readers of "Canada Reads."' *Canadian Literature* 193 (2007): 11–34.

Fuller, Danielle, and DeNel Rehberg Sedo. 'A Reading Spectacle for the Nation: The CBC and "Canada Reads."' *Journal of Canadian Studies* 40.1 (2006): 5–36.

Gabriel, Sharmani Patricia. 'Interrogating Multiculturalism: Double Diaspora, Nation, and Re-Narration in Rohinton Mistry's Canadian Tales.' *Canadian Literature* 181 (2004): 27–41.

Gass, William H. *Finding a Form*. Ithaca, NY: Cornell UP, 1996.

Genette, Gérard. *Paratexts: Thresholds of Interpretation*. Tr. Jane E. Lewin. Cambridge: Cambridge UP, 1997.

George, Rosemary Marangoly. *The Politics of Home: Postcolonial Relocations and Twentieth-Century Fiction*. Cambridge: Cambridge UP, 1996.

Gerstel, Judy. 'Men Missing: Swann Adaptation Loses Dynamics.' *Toronto Star* 20 Dec. 1996: C3.

Gessell, Paul. 'Canada's Grand Day on the Booker List.' *Ottawa Citizen* 25 Sep. 2002: C7.

- 'Carol Shields Short-listed for Rich Literary Award.' *Ottawa Citizen* 28 Apr. 1998: B11.

- 'Just One Toronto Writer on List for G-G Book Awards.' *Vancouver Sun* 21 Oct. 2003: C5.

- 'Mistry and Multiculturalism.' *Ottawa Citizen* 6 Apr. 2002: J1.

- 'Toronto Writers Crowd Giller List.' *Ottawa Citizen* 3 Oct. 2003: D1.

- 'Wot's This, Then? Canadian Writers Who Aren't Canadian?' *Ottawa Citizen* 19 Oct. 2002: J1.

- 'Year of the Establishment.' *Ottawa Citizen* 25 Oct. 2000: C21.

Ghosh, Amitav. 'Commonwealth: Misnomer, Not an Award.' *Times of India* 21 Mar. 2001. Nexis UK. Leeds Metropolitan U Lib. 25 Jan. 2008 <http://www.lexisnexis.com/uk/>.

Gibbons, Fiachra. 'Booker Fatwa on Pompous Fiction.' *Guardian* 25 Sep. 2002: 13.

'Giller Winner Tops Bestseller List.' *Calgary Herald* 26 Nov. 2006: C9.

Godard, Barbara. 'Notes from the Cultural Field: Canadian Literature from Identity to Hybridity.' *Essays on Canadian Writing* 72 (2000): 209–47.

- 'Sleuthing: Feminists Rewriting the Detective Novel.' *Signature* 1 (1989): 45–70.

Goellnicht, Donald C. 'A Long Labour: The Protracted Birth of Asian Canadian Literature.' *Essays on Canadian Writing* 72 (2000): 1–41.

Goff, Martyn, ed. *Prize Writing: An Original Collection of Writings by Past Winners to Celebrate 21 Years of the Booker Prize*. London: Hodder & Stoughton, 1989.

Goldman, Marlene. 'Introduction: Literature, Imagination, Ethics.' *University of Toronto Quarterly* 76.3 (2007): 809–20.

– 'Representations of Buddhism in Ondaatje's *Anil's Ghost*.' Tötösy de Zepetnek 27–37.

– 'War and the Game of Representation in Michael Ondaatje's *The English Patient*.' Ondaatje and Lacroix 181–93.

Gombu, Phinjo. 'Canada Boasts Three Booker Finalists.' *Toronto Star* 25 Sep. 2002: A23.

Gordon, Charles. 'Once Canada Finishes Reading, the CBC Has Other Suggestions.' *Ottawa Citizen* 25 Apr. 2002: A18.

– 'Why Cultural Canada Has Yet to Come of Age.' *Maclean's* 11 May 1998: 11.

Goring, Rosemary. 'Carol Shields: Prize-winning Canadian Author Who Never Lost Sight of the Home, Husband, and Children She Adored.' *Herald* (Glasgow) 18 Jul. 2003: 20.

Govani, Shinan. 'Dress Casts a Spell.' *National Post* 4 Nov. 2003: AL2.

'The Governor-General's Awards.' *Canadian Forum* Jun. 1970: 126–7.

Grainger, James. 'Theatre of Memories.' *Toronto Star* 14 Apr. 2002: D12.

Griffin, John. 'Uneven Acting Grounds Swann.' *Montreal Gazette* 7 Mar. 1997: D4.

Gussow, Mel. 'Artisan of Quiet Crises and the Little Things.' *New York Times* 10 May 1995: C13, C18.

Guttridge, Peter. 'Mistry: Carpenter and a Man of Iron.' *Independent* 19 Oct. 1991: Weekend Books 29.

Guy, Chantal. 'Les hauts et les bas de l'année littéraire 2002.' *La Presse* 29 Dec. 2002: F2.

Hall, Judith. 'Clueless.' *Los Angeles Times* 5 Oct. 1997: Book Review 10.

Halliburton, Rachel, and Peter Guttridge. 'Best of British.' *Independent* 27 Mar. 1997: Section 2, 8–9.

Halliwell, Martin. *Images of Idiocy: The Idiot Figure in Modern Fiction and Film.* Aldershot: Ashgate, 2004.

Hammill, Faye. 'Carol Shields's "Native Genre" and the Figure of the Canadian Author.' *Journal of Commonwealth Literature* 31.2 (1996): 87–99.

Hancock, Geoff. 'Mystery That Truly Mystifies.' *Toronto Star* 18 Oct. 1987: C9.

'Hands off the Booker.' *Guardian* 5 Jun. 2002: 12.

Hanson, Cheri. 'In Battle of the Books, Readers Are Victorious.' *Vancouver Sun* 24 Feb. 2007: C8.

Harrington, Anthony. 'Bliss for Booker Worms.' *Scotsman* 3 Sep. 2002: 5.

Härting, Heike. 'Diasporic Cross-Currents in Michael Ondaatje's *Anil's Ghost* and Anita Rau Badami's *The Hero's Walk*.' *Studies in Canadian Literature* 28.1 (2003): 43–70.

Hartley, Emma. 'A Reluctant Millionaire.' *Times* (London) 21 Apr. 2003: Times 2, 7.

Hauck, Gerhard. 'Roses on the Rez: Chronicle of a Failure?' *Canadian Theatre Review* 115 (2003): 47–51.

Hawkins, Susan E., and Susan Danielson. 'The Patients of Empire.' *LIT: Literature Interpretation Theory* 13.2 (2002): 139–53.

Heble, Ajay. '"A Foreign Presence in the Stall": Towards a Poetics of Cultural Hybridity in Rohinton Mistry's Migration Stories.' *Canadian Literature* 137 (1993): 51–61.

– 'Putting Together Another Family: *In the Skin of a Lion*, Affiliation, and the Writing of Canadian (Hi)stories.' *Essays on Canadian Writing* 56 (1996): 236–54.

Henderson, Eric. 'Sexual Bluntness Banal.' *Vancouver Sun* 4 Sep. 1993: D19.

Henderson, Lee. 'Wild Imaginings: Yann Martel Has Written a Work of Rare Brilliance.' *Vancouver Sun* 22 Sep. 2001: D17.

Henighan, Stephen. *When Words Deny the World: The Reshaping of Canadian Writing.* Erin, ON: Porcupine's Quill, 2002.

Herbert, Caroline. '"Dishonourably Postnational?" The Politics of Migrancy and Cosmopolitanism in Rohinton Mistry's *A Fine Balance*.' *Journal of Commonwealth Literature* 43.2 (2008): 11–28.

Heward, Burt. 'Canadian Authors; Ondaatje Stays Nonchalant about Prestigious British Prize.' *Ottawa Citizen* 6 Nov. 1992: A2.

– 'Mistry's New Work a "Feast of a Novel."' *Calgary Herald* 20 Jul. 1991: F13.

Higgins, Michael. 'Montreal Author Wins Booker Prize.' *National Post* 23 Oct. 2002: A3.

Hohenberg, John. *The Pulitzer Diaries: Inside America's Greatest Prize.* Syracuse NY: Syracuse UP, 1997.

Honig, Bonnie. 'Another Cosmopolitanism? Law and Politics in the New Europe.' *Another Cosmopolitanism.* Ed. Robert Post. Oxford: Oxford UP, 2006. 102–27.

Hooker, Ginny. 'Review: Christmas Books.' *Guardian* 28 Nov. 2009: Review 2.

Hornby, Gill. 'Daisy Answers for Her Life.' *Times* (London) 26 Aug. 1993: 34.

Horton, Marc. 'Swann Author Takes Movie Changes Gracefully.' *Edmonton Journal* 13 Sept. 1996: E8.

Howell, Peter. 'A Very Long Journey Indeed.' *Toronto Star* 26 Feb. 1999. Nexis UK. Leeds Metropolitan U Lib. 12 Jul. 2008 <http://www.lexisnexis.com/uk/>.

Howells, Coral Ann. *Contemporary Canadian Women's Fiction: Refiguring Identities.* New York: Palgrave Macmillan, 2003.

– 'Larry's A/Mazing Spaces.' Dvořák and Jones 16–29.

Huggan, Graham. *The Postcolonial Exotic: Marketing the Margins.* London and New York: Routledge, 2001.

Hunter, Lynette. *Critiques of Knowing: Situated Textualities in Science, Computing and the Arts.* London: Routledge, 1999.

Hutcheon, Linda. *The Canadian Postmodern: A Study of Contemporary English-Canadian Fiction*. Toronto: Oxford UP, 1988.

Iezzi, Teressa. 'On the Set with Swann.' *Playback* 11 Sep. 1995: 1.

Irvine, Lorna. 'Displacing the White Man's Burden in Michael Ondaatje's *The English Patient.' British Journal of Canadian Studies* 10 (1995): 139–45.

Italie, Hillel. 'Oprah Picks "Corrections" Follow Up.' *Associated Press Online* 30 Nov. 2001. Nexis UK. Leeds Metropolitan U Lib. 4 Jun. 2007 <http://www.lexisnexis.com/uk/>.

'Jack Rabinovitch.' Internet. <www.thegillerprize.ca/pages/history/jack_bio.asp> Accessed 9 Dec. 2003.

Jaggi, Maya. 'No Thanks, Ma'am.' *Guardian* 15 Jun. 2005: G2, 4.

Jeffrey, Robin, ed. *Asia: The Winning of Independence.* London: Macmillan, 1981.

Jewinski, Ed. *Michael Ondaatje: Express Yourself Beautifully.* Toronto: ECW, 1994.

Johnson, Brian. 'Necessary Illusions: Foucault's Author Function in Carol Shields's *Swann.' Prairie Fire* 16 (1995): 56–70.

Johnson, Brian D. 'The Canadian Patient (Why Can't Canada Make Its Own Hit Movies).' *Maclean's* 24 Mar. 1997: 42–6.

Johnson, Daniel. 'Booker Prize Is Shared.' *Times* (London) 14 Oct. 1992: 1.

Johnson, Randal. 'Editor's Introduction: Pierre Bourdieu on Art, Literature, and Culture.' *The Field of Cultural Production.* Cambridge: Polity, 1993. 1–25.

Johnston, Denis W. 'Lines and Circles: The "Rez" Plays of Tomson Highway.' *Canadian Literature* 124–125 (1990): 254–64.

Jones, J.D.F. 'Retreat from the Flames of War.' *Financial Times* 12 Sep. 1992: Books XI.

Jones, Raymond E. 'Metafictional Mysteries.' *Fiddlehead* 157 (Autumn 1988): 114–16.

Jordan, Justine. 'Animal Magnetism.' *Guardian* 25 May 2002: Saturday 10.

Kakutani, Michiko. 'From "Life of Pi" Author, Stuffed-Animal Allegory about Holocaust.' *New York Times* 13 Apr. 2010: C1.

Kalman Naves, Elaine. 'Welcome to the Golden Age.' *Montreal Gazette* 19 Apr. 1997: I1.

Kamboureli, Smaro. 'The Limits of the Ethical Turn: Troping Towards the Other in Yann Martel's *Self.' University of Toronto Quarterly* 76.3 (2007): 937–61.

– *Making a Difference: Canadian Multicultural Literature.* Toronto: Oxford UP, 1996.

– *Scandalous Bodies: Diasporic Literature in English.* Don Mills, ON: Oxford UP, 2000.

Kanaganayakam, Chelva. 'Cool Dots and a Hybrid Scarborough: Multiculturalism as Canadian Myth.' *Is Canada Postcolonial? Unsettling Canadian Literature.* Ed. Laura Moss. Waterloo, ON: Wilfrid Laurier UP, 2003. 140–8.

– ed. *Moveable Margins: The Shifting Spaces of Canadian Literature*. Toronto: TSAR, 2005.

Kant, Immanuel. 'Perpetual Peace: A Philosophical Sketch.' *Kant: Political Writings*. Ed. Hans Reiss. Cambridge: Cambridge UP, 1990. 93–130.

Kee Thuan Chye. 'A Celebration of Optimism.' *New Straits Times* (Malaysia) 9 Jul. 1997: Literary 8.

Kemp, Philip. Rev. of *Swann*. *Sight and Sound* Mar. 1997: 63.

Kernerman, Gerald. *Multicultural Nationalism: Civilizing Difference, Constituting Community*. Vancouver: UBC Press, 2005.

Kirchhoff, H.J. 'The Awards Get Real.' *Globe and Mail* 19 Jan. 1991: C16.

Kirkland, Bruce. 'Journey for the Joy.' *Toronto Sun* 15 Mar. 1999: 44.

Kokotailo, Philip. 'The Bishop and His Deacon: Smith vs. Sutherland Reconsidered.' *Journal of Canadian Studies* 27.2 (1992): 63–81.

Konchar Farr, Cecilia. *Reading Oprah: How Oprah's Book Club Changed the Way America Reads*. Albany: State of New York, 2005.

Kröller, Eva-Marie. 'Why Family Matters.' *Canadian Literature* 178 (2003): 158–60.

Kubacki, Maria. 'Home Is Where the Heart Is . . . Torn Asunder.' *Ottawa Citizen* 14 Apr. 2002: C12.

Laachir, Karima. 'The Ethics and Politics of Hospitality in Contemporary French Society: "Beur" Literary Translations.' PhD diss., University of Leeds, 2003.

Lacey, Liam. 'Michael Ondaatje, in the Skin of a Filmmaker.' *Globe and Mail* 9 Nov. 1996: C2.

Lasdun, James. 'Taxidermy for Beginners.' *Guardian* 5 Jun. 2010: Review 10.

Leggatt, Johanna. 'Comedy Capsized by Confusion.' *Sun Herald* 6 Jun. 2010: Books 12.

Lehmann-Haupt, Christopher. 'Novelist Gave Life to Characters.' *New York Times* 18 Jul. 2003: C11.

Lemos Horta, Paulo. 'Ondaatje and the Cosmopolitan Desert Explorers: Landscape, Space and Comunity in *The English Patient*.' Kanaganayakam, ed. 65–84.

Lepage, Jocelyne. 'Booker Prize: Life of Pi promise à des ventes vertigineuses.' *La Presse* (Montreal) 24 Oct. 2002: C1.

– 'L'écrivain de l'année: Yann Martel.' *La Presse* (Montreal) 29 Dec. 2002: F2.

– 'Yann Martel: Béni des dieux.' *La Presse* (Montreal) 20 Aug. 2003: C1.

Lessard, Valérie. 'L'histoire de Yann.' *Le Droit* (Ottawa) 23 Aug. 2003: A2.

Levin, Martin. 'Canadian Shields: Winning a Pulitzer Prize Has Brought Winnipeg Author Carol Shields the Recognition Many Believe Is Long Overdue.' *Imperial Oil Review* (Winter 1995): 12–17.

Litt, Paul. *The Muses, the Masses, and the Massey Commission.* Toronto: U of Toronto P, 1992.

Longrigg, Clare. 'Shields Lifts Orange Prize out of Ghetto.' *Guardian* 20 May 1998: 3.

Lowry, Glen. 'Between *The English Patients:* "Race" and the Cultural Politics of Adapting CanLit.' *Essays on Canadian Writing* 76 (2002): 216–46.

Lundgren, Jodi. '"Colour Disrobed Itself from the Body": The Racialized Aesthetics of Liberation in Michael Ondaatje's *In the Skin of a Lion.*' *Canadian Literature* 190 (2006): 15–29.

Lyons, John. 'Author Finalist for British Award.' *Winnipeg Free Press* 23 Sep. 1993: A1.

McClelland, Jack. 'A Novel Suggestion.' *Maclean's* 11 May 1981: 8.

MacDonald, Gayle. 'Canada Reads Sparks Bonanza.' *Globe and Mail* 14 May 2002: R3.

MacDougall, Carl. 'The Extremes of Existence.' *Herald* (Glasgow) 16 Mar. 1996: 13.

McGoogan, Ken. 'More on the Future of Fiction.' *Calgary Herald* 14 Dec. 1997: F2.

– '"Patient" Revives Canada's Books.' *Calgary Herald* 13 Apr. 1998: B7.

MacGowan, James. 'A Bluffer's Guide to Ondaatje.' *Ottawa Citizen* 19 May 2002: C12.

MacInnis, Craig. 'Does Anyone Dream of Genie?' *Toronto Star* 11 Dec. 1993: H1, H8.

McLaren, John. 'From Raj to Republics: State and Nation in Fiction from the Sub-continent.' *World Literature Written in English* 36.1 (1997): 39–56.

McLean, Gareth. 'FAQ Orange Prize for Fiction a Novel Idea.' *Scotsman* 31 May 2000: 3.

McLuhan, Marshall. 'Canada: The Borderline Case.' Staines 226–48.

McPhee, Hilary. 'Skin and Bones.' *Australian* 7 Apr. 2010: 16.

MacSkimming, Roy. *The Perilous Trade: Publishing Canada's Writers.* Toronto: McClelland & Stewart, 2003.

Mahoney, Jeff. 'Fans Seek Out Author Yann Martel.' *Hamilton Spectator* 9 Dec. 2002: C14.

'Making Booker on Canadians.' *Toronto Star* 25 Sep. 2002: F3.

Malak, Amin. 'Images of India.' *Canadian Literature* 119 (1988): 101–3.

Malieckal, Bindu. 'Parsis, Emigration, and Immigration in Rohinton Mistry's *Swimming Lessons and Other Stories from Firozsha Baag.*' *Papers on Language and Literature* 42.4 (2006): 360–83.

Malla, Pasha. 'Well Worth the Wait.' *Globe and Mail* 10 Apr. 2010: F8.

The Man Booker Prize: 35 Years of the Best in Contemporary Fiction, 1969–2003. Chatham: Booker Prize Foundation, 2003.

Maracle, Lee. 'The "Post-Colonial" Imagination.' *Unhomely States: Theorizing English-Canadian Postcolonialism.* Ed. Cynthia Sugars. Peterborough, ON: Broadview, 2004. 204–8.

Marchand, Philip. 'The Author as Explorer.' *Toronto Star* 18 May 1996: L10.

– 'Ladies and Gentlemen of the Jury . . .' *Toronto Star* 22 Nov. 1997: J6.

– 'Our Authors Win Top Prizes.' *Toronto Star* 26 Dec. 1992: K13.

– 'A Tale of Moral Conflict in Bombay.' *Toronto Star* 4 May 1991: K13.

Martel, Yann. *Beatrice and Virgil*. Edinburgh: Canongate, 2010.

– *The Facts behind the Helsinki Roccamatios and Other Stories*. Toronto: Alfred A. Knopf Canada, 1993.

– Interview with Sabine Sielke. *Canadian Literature* 177 (2003): 12–32.

– *Life of Pi*. 2001. Toronto: Vintage Canada, 2002.

– *Self*. London: Faber and Faber, 1996.

– *What Is Stephen Harper Reading? Yann Martel's Recommended Reading for a Prime Minister and Book Lovers of All Stripes*. Toronto: Vintage Canada, 2009.

Martin, Ruth. 'The Political Canonization of the Canadian Anglophone Novel: An Examination of the Governor General's Award Winners between 1980 and 2000.' *Culture + the State*, Volume 3: *Nationalisms*. Ed. James Gifford and Gabrielle Zezulka-Mailloux. Edmonton: CRC Humanities Studio, 2003. 102–11.

Martin, Sandra. 'Just One Great Canadian Novel? No Way.' *Globe and Mail* 16 Apr. 2002: R3.

– 'Oprah Selects Mistry Novel.' *Globe and Mail* 1 Dec. 2001: A18.

Maschler, Tom. 'How It All Began.' *The Man Booker Prize* 20–1.

Mason, Jody. '"The Animal Out of the Desert": The Nomadic Metaphysics of Michael Ondaatje's *In the Skin of a Lion*.' *Studies in Canadian Literature* 31.2 (2006): 66–87.

Menzies, Diane. 'Yann Martel Goes from "Yann Who?" to "The Guy Nominated for the Booker."' *Canadian Press Newswire* 26 Sep. 2002. Nexis UK. Leeds Metropolitan U Lib. 9 Jul. 2007 <http://www.lexisnexis.com/uk/>.

Menzies, Robert, Dorothy E. Chunn, and Robert Adamoski, eds. *Contesting Canadian Citizenship: Historical Readings*. Peterborough, ON: Broadview, 2002.

'Michael Ondaatje, O.C., M.A.' Internet. <www.gg.ca/cgibin/oc_details .pl?lang= e&rec_id=3095> Accessed 17 Mar. 2001.

Mignolo, Walter D. 'The Many Faces of Cosmo-polis: Border Thinking and Critical Cosmopolitanism.' *Public Culture* 12.3 (2000): 721–48.

Mishra, Vijay. 'The Diasporic Imaginary: Theorizing the Indian Diaspora.' *Textual Practice* 10.3 (1996): 421–47.

Misra, Ramesh K. 'India during Emergency as Reflected in Mistry's *A Fine Balance*.' *Parsi Fiction*, Vol. 2. Ed. Novy Kapadia, Jaydipsinh Dodiya, and R.K. Dhawan. New Delhi: Prestige, 2001. 188–93.

Mistry, Rohinton. *Family Matters*. 2002. Toronto: McClelland & Stewart, 2003.

– *A Fine Balance*. 1996. London: Faber and Faber, 1997.

– Interview with Geoff Hancock. *Canadian Fiction Magazine* 65 (1989): 144–50.

– Interview with Robert Mclay. *Writing across Worlds: Contemporary Writers Talk*. Ed. Susheila Nasta. London: Routledge, 2004: 198–206.
– *Such a Long Journey*. 1991. London: Faber and Faber, 1992.
– *Tales from Firozsha Baag*. 1987. Toronto: McClelland & Stewart, 2000.
'Mistry Loves Oprah Label.' *Montreal Gazette* 1 Dec. 2001: D19.
'Mistry Miffed at Greer's View of Novel.' *Toronto Star* 18 Nov. 1996: E7.
'Mistry Wins Award for First Novel.' *Kitchener-Waterloo Record* 27 Mar. 1992: F8.
Mojtabai, A.G. 'An Accidental Family.' *New York Times* 23 Jun. 1996: Section 7, 29.
Morey, Peter. *Rohinton Mistry*. Manchester: Manchester UP, 2004.
Morton, Desmond. *Canada at War: A Military and Political History*. Toronto: Butterworths, 1981.
Moseley, Merritt. 'Britain's Women-only Orange Prize for Fiction.' *World and I* 1 Jul. 2001: 291–301.
Moss, Laura. 'Can Rohinton Mistry's Realism Rescue the Novel?' *Postcolonizing the Commonwealth*. Ed. Rowland Smith. Waterloo, ON: Wilfrid Laurier UP, 2000. 157–65.
– 'Canada Reads.' *Canadian Literature* 182 (2004): 6–10.
Mulvey, Laura. *Visual and Other Pleasures*. Basingstoke: Macmillan, 1989.
Myles, Anita. 'Thematic Concerns in *Such a Long Journey*.' Dodiya 85–92.
Nair, Rukmini Bhaya. 'Bombay's Balzac.' *Biblio: A Review of Books* Mar. 1996: 14–15.
Neale, Steve. 'Art Cinema as Institution.' *Screen* 22 (1981): 11–39.
Nelson, Antonya. 'Celebrating the Ordinary.' *Chicago Tribune* 12 Oct. 1997: 8.
New, W.H. Afterword. *Tales from Firozsha Baag*. By Rohinton Mistry. Toronto: McClelland & Stewart, 2000. 263–9.
'New in Paperback.' *Washington Post* 28 Jun. 1992: Book World X12.
Nichols, John. 'Novel on India's Woes Touches Universal Nerve.' *Capital Times* (Madison, WI) 11 Apr. 1997: 15A.
'Nigerian-born Author Wins Booker Prize.' *Kitchener-Waterloo Record* 23 Oct. 1991: F3.
Novak, Amy. 'Textual Hauntings: Narrating History, Memory, and Silence in *The English Patient*.' *Studies in the Novel* 36.2 (2004): 206–31.
'Obituary of Carol Shields.' *Daily Telegraph* 18 Jul. 2003: 31.
Oliveira, Michael. 'Yann Martel's New Book Gets Some Brutal Reviews but Sells.' *Fredericton Daily Gleaner* 1 May 2010: D8.
Ondaatje, Michael. *Anil's Ghost*. Toronto: McClelland & Stewart, 2000.
– *The English Patient*. 1992. Toronto: Vintage, 1993.
– *In the Skin of a Lion*. 1987. Toronto: Penguin, 1994.
– Interview with Catherine Bush. *Essays on Canadian Writing* 53 (1994): 238–49.
– Interview with Eleanor Wachtel. *Essays on Canadian Writing* 53 (1994): 250–61.

- Interview with Maya Jaggi. *Wasafiri* 32 (2000): 5–11.
- 'Remarks by Michael Ondaatje, Laureate for English-language Fiction, Governor General's Literary Awards 2000.' Internet. <www.canadacouncil .ca/news/ pressrelease/cosp05-e.asp.> Accessed 23 Oct. 2002.
- *Running in the Family*. 1982. McClelland & Stewart, 1993.
Ondaatje, Michael, and Atom Egoyan. 'The Kitchen Table Talks.' *Globe and Mail* 8 Apr. 2000: D6-D7.
Ondaatje, Michael, and J.-M. Lacroix, eds. *Re-constructing the Fragments of Michael Ondaatje's Works / La diversité déconstruite et réconstruite de l'oeuvre de Michael Ondaatje*. Paris: Presses de la Sorbonne, 1999.
'Ondaatje Shares Booker Prize.' *Globe and Mail* 14 Oct. 1992: A1, A2.
'Ondaatje's Honor.' *Toronto Star* 15 Oct. 1992: A22.
Ong Sor Fern. 'Booker Goes Mainstream.' *Straits Times* (Singapore) 7 Oct. 2000. Nexis UK. Leeds Metropolitan U Lib. 25 Jan. 2008, <http://www .lexisnexis.com/uk/>.
- 'Hear Booker's Roar.' *Straits Times* (Singapore) 24 Oct. 2002. Nexis UK. Leeds Metropolitan U Lib. 25 Jan. 2008 <http://www.lexisnexis.com/uk/>.
Oppel, Kenneth. 'The English View on the English Patient.' *Quill & Quire* Dec. 1992: 13.
'Order of Canada.' Internet. <www.gg.ca/honours/order_e.html> Accessed 17 Mar. 2001.
Pacific Rim Voices. 'The Kiryama Prize.' Internet. <http://www.kiriyama prize.org/index.shtml> Accessed 27 Aug. 2009.
Pandit, M.L. 'Fiction across Worlds: Some Writers of Indian Origin in Canada.' Dodiya, ed., The Fiction 14–22.
'The Panel.' Internet. <www.cbc.ca/canadareads/shortlists/measha.htm> Accessed 18 Dec. 2003.
Parameswaran, Uma. 'Landmark.' *Floating the Borders: New Contexts in Canadian Criticism*. Ed. Aziz Nurjehan. Toronto: TSAR, 1999. 184–7.
Pateman, Carole. 'Equality, Difference, Subordination: The Politics of Motherhood and Women's Citizenship.' *Beyond Equality and Difference: Citizenship, Feminist Politics and Female Subjectivity*. Ed. Gisela Bock and Susan James. London and New York: Routledge, 1992. 17–31.
Payne, Tom. 'The Weird Bunch: This Year's Booker Prize Shortlist Is Full of Strange Books by Non-English Writers.' *Daily Telegraph* 28 Sep. 2002: 12.
- 'When Greatness Is Thrust upon Them.' *Daily Telegraph* 26 Oct. 2002: 9.
Perrick, Penny. 'Plots at the Dead Poet's Society.' *Sunday Times* (London) 26 Aug. 1990: 6, 6
Pesch, Josef. 'Post-Apocalyptical War Histories: Michael Ondaatje's "The English Patient."' *ARIEL* 28 (1997): 117–39.

Philip, M. Nourbese. *Frontiers: Selected Essays and Writings on Racism and Culture.* Stratford, ON: Mercury, 1992.

Poe, Edgar Allan. *The Narrative of Arthur Gordon Pym and Related Tales.* Oxford: Oxford UP, 1994.

Posner, Michael. 'The Giller Prize: Shortlist 2005.' *Globe and Mail* 29 Sep. 2005: R1.

– 'Giller Prize Tea Leaves Are the Toughest to Read of All.' *Globe and Mail* 5 Nov. 2005: R1.

– 'No Giller Picks on G-G Short List.' *Globe and Mail* 18 Oct. 2005: R1.

Prasannarajan, S. 'Bleak House Journal.' *India Today* 6 May 2001: 66.

Prokosh, Kevin, and Linda Rosborough. 'Shields Belongs to History.' *Winnipeg Free Press* 19 Apr. 1995: C8.

Rajghatta, Chidanand. 'US, Canada in Immigration Spat.' *Economic Times* (India) 6 Nov. 2002. Nexis UK. Leeds Metropolitan U Lib. 1 Jun. 2007 <http://www. lexisnexis.com.uk/>.

Ramaswamy, S. 'Local Colour in *Tales from Firozsha Baag.*' Dodiya, ed., *The Fiction* 54–60.

Ramon, Alex. *Liminal Spaces: The Double Art of Carol Shields.* Newcastle upon Tyne: Cambridge Scholars, 2008.

Rengger, Patrick. 'Doin' the CanLit Hustle.' *Financial Post* 1 Jun. 1996: Review 24.

Renzetti, Elizabeth. 'Fighting Words.' *Globe and Mail* 28 Oct. 1998: C1–C2.

'Republican Carey Offers Royal Snub.' *Evening Standard* (London) 6 May 1998: 10.

Resnick, Philip. 'Civic and Ethnic Nationalism: Lessons from the Canadian Case.' Beiner and Norman 282–97.

Reynolds, Nigel. 'Bookie's Accidental Favourite Is Awarded £50,000 Booker Prize.' *Daily Telegraph* 23 Oct. 2002: 8.

Richard, Robert. 'Hubert Aquin, best-seller au Canada anglais!' *Le Devoir* 9 Jun. 2003: A7.

Richler, Noah. 'Not Much Ado about the Giller: Where Was the Usual Fuss over This Year's Short List?' *National Post* 17 Oct. 2002: AL1.

– 'Ondaatje on Writing.' *National Post* 1 Apr. 2000: B1, B4-B5.

– *This Is My Country, What's Yours? A Literary Atlas of Canada.* Toronto: McClelland & Stewart, 2006.

– 'We Are Looking for Leaders.' *National Post* 24 Oct. 2002: AL1.

Robbins, Bruce. 'Introduction Part I: Actually Existing Cosmopolitanism.' Cheah and Robbins 1–19.

– 'The Village of the Liberal Managerial Class.' *Cosmopolitan Geographies: New Locations in Literature and Culture.* Ed. Vinay Dharwadker. New York: Routledge, 2001. 15–32.

Roberts, Gillian. 'Spectacle Matters: *Titanic, The Sweet Hereafter,* and the Academy and Genie Awards.' *Canadian Review of American Studies* 30 (2000): 317–38.

Roberts, Michèle. 'Man or Manikin.' *Independent on Sunday* 17 Aug. 1997: Review 34.

'Rohinton Mistry in Line for $20,000 Prize.' *Globe and Mail* 2 Nov. 1997. Nexis UK. Leeds Metropolitan U Lib. 25 Jan. 2008 <http://www.lexisnexis.com/uk/>.

'Rohinton Mistry Signs New Book with McClelland & Stewart Ltd.' *Canadian Press Newswire* 5 Dec. 2003. Nexis UK. Leeds Metropolitan U Lib. 4 Jun. 2007 <http://www.lexisnexis.com/uk/>.

Rosborough, Linda. 'Award Expected to Spur Sales.' *Winnipeg Free Press* 1 Mar. 1995: D8.

– 'She's One of Ours.' *Winnipeg Free Press* 23 Apr. 1995: D8.

– 'Time to Celebrate.' *Winnipeg Free Press* 8 Nov. 1996: C1.

Rosello, Mireille. *Postcolonial Hospitality: The Immigrant as Guest.* Stanford: Stanford UP, 2001.

Ross, Val. 'Awards Now Have a Positive Impact.' *Globe and Mail* 3 Dec. 1991: C1.

– 'Governor-General's Awards.' *Globe and Mail* 30 Nov. 1991. Nexis UK. Leeds Metropolitan U Lib. 1 Jun. 2007 <http://www.lexisnexis.com/uk/>.

– 'Heads-up on Two Literary Horseraces.' *Globe and Mail* 23 Oct. 1999: D10, D11.

– 'Mistry's Dark World Vision.' *Globe and Mail* 19 Dec. 1995: C1.

– 'Mistry's Journey Reaches Its Goal.' *Globe and Mail* 4 Dec. 1991: C1.

– 'Striking It Rich in Canada's Literary Sweepstakes.' *Globe and Mail* 19 Oct. 1996: C10.

– 'A Tale of Two Prizes.' *Globe and Mail* 29 Oct. 1994: C7.

Sackville-West, Sophia. 'Slaves to Misfortune.' *Evening Standard* (London) 30 Apr. 1992: 42.

Samantrai, Ranu. 'States of Belonging: Pluralism, Migrancy, Literature.' *Writing Ethnicity: Cross-Cultural Consciousness in Canadian and Québécois Literature.* Ed. Winfried Siemerling. Toronto: ECW, 1996. 33–50.

Sanghera, Sandeep. 'Touching the Language of Citizenship in Ondaatje's *Anil's Ghost.*' Tötösy de Zepetnek 83–91.

Schäfer, Uwe. '"Both/And" and/or "Either/Or": Syncretism and Imagination in the Novels of Wilson Harris and Bessie Head.' Stummer and Balme 41–7.

Schapiro, Nancy. 'Inspired Stories of Sympathy and Tolerance.' *St. Louis Post-Dispatch* 12 Mar. 1989: 5C.

Schechner, Mark. 'Doofus and the Menopause.' *Jerusalem Post* 5 Dec. 1997: 21.

Scott, Jennifer, and Myka Tucker-Abramson. 'Banking on a Prize: Multicultural Capitalism and the Canadian Literary Prize Industry.' *Studies in Canadian Literature* 32.1 (2007): 5–20.

Sedgwick, Eve Kosofsky. *Tendencies.* London: Routledge, 1994.

Serres, Michel. *The Parasite.* Tr. Lawrence R. Schehr. Baltimore: Johns Hopkins UP, 1982.

Shah, Nila. 'A Critical Appraisal of *A Fine Balance.'* Dodiya, ed., *The Fiction* 115–18.

Shields, Carol. *Larry's Party.* New York: Viking, 1997.

– Personal interview. 18 July 2001.

– *The Stone Diaries.* London: Fourth Estate, 1993.

– *Swann.* 1987. Toronto: Vintage, 1996.

Showalter, Elaine. 'Coming to Blows over the Booker Prize.' *Chronicle Review* 28 Jun. 2002: 11.

Shrapnel, Norman. 'Books: New Fiction.' *Guardian* 23 Aug. 1990: 22.

Siemerling, Winfried. *Discoveries of the Other: Alterity in the Work of Leonard Cohen, Hubert Aquin, Michael Ondaatje, and Nicole Brossard.* Toronto: U of Toronto P, 1994.

Simons, John. *Animal Rights and the Politics of Literary Representation.* Basingstoke: Palgrave, 2002.

Simpson, D. Mark. 'Minefield Readings: The Postcolonial *English Patient.'* *Essays on Canadian Writing* 53 (1994): 216–37.

Simpson, Jeffrey. 'The Giller Prize Has Come of Age for Canadian Writers.' *Globe and Mail* 12 Nov. 1996: A18.

Singh, Rashna B. 'Traversing Diacritical Space: Negotiating and Narrating Parsi Nationness.' *Journal of Commonwealth Literature* 43.2 (2008): 29–47.

Slater, David. *Geopolitics and the Post-colonial: Rethinking North-South Relations.* Malden, MA: Blackwell, 2004.

Slethaug, Gordon E. '"The Coded Dots of Life": Carol Shields's Diaries and Stones.' *Canadian Literature* 156 (1998): 59–81.

Smith, A.J.M. Introduction. *The Book of Canadian Poetry.* Revised ed. Ed. A.J.M. Smith. Chicago: U Chicago P, 1948. 3–34.

Smith, Ali. 'Consolation Prized.' *Scotsman* 12 Feb. 2000: 10.

Smith, C. Lynn. 'Is Citizenship a Gendered Concept?' Cairns 137–62.

Smulders, Marilyn. 'Mistry Discusses Family Matters in Metro: Oprah-picked Author Launches Third Novel.' *Halifax Daily News* 10 Apr. 2002: 29.

Smyrl, Shannon. 'The Nation as "International Bastard": Ethnicity and Language in Michael Ondaatje's *The English Patient.'* *Studies in Canadian Literature* 28.2 (2003): 9–38.

Sokoloff, Heather. '"She Had So Many Books Left to Write," Daughter Says.' *National Post* 18 Jul. 2003: A2.

Solecki, Sam, ed. *Spider Blues: Essays on Michael Ondaatje.* Montreal: Véhicule Press, 1985.

Spinks, Lee. *Michael Ondaatje.* Manchester: Manchester UP, 2009.

Squires, Claire. 'Book Marketing and the Booker Prize.' *Judging a Book by Its Cover: Fans, Publishers, Designers, and the Marketing of Fiction.* Ed. Nicole Matthews and Nickianne Moody. Aldershot: Ashgate, 2007. 71–82.

– *Marketing Literature: The Making of Contemporary Writing in Britain.* Basingstoke: Palgrave Macmillan, 2007.

Staines, David, ed. *The Canadian Imagination: Dimensions of a Literary Culture.* Cambridge, MA: Harvard UP, 1977.

Stoffman, Judy. 'Bombay with a Canadian Twist.' *Toronto Star* 13 Sep. 1998: B1.

– 'Canadian's Novel Wins Endorsement from Oprah.' *Hamilton Spectator* 1 Dec. 2001: D5.

– 'The Life of Larry.' *Toronto Star* 10 Jan. 2001: D1, D2.

– 'Vassanji Wins 2nd Giller.' *Toronto Star* 5 Nov. 2003: F1.

Stone, Jay. 'Does a Grant Mean It's Really Art?' *Ottawa Citizen* 17 Feb. 1992: C7.

Stratton, Florence. '"Hollow at the Core": Deconstructing Yann Martel's *Life of Pi*.' *Studies in Canadian Literature* 29.2 (2004): 5–21.

Striphas, Ted. *The Late Age of Print: Everyday Book Culture from Consumerism to Control.* New York: Columbia UP, 2009.

Stuckey, W.J. *The Pulitzer Prize Novels: A Critical Backward Look.* 2nd ed. Norman: U of Oklahoma P, 1981.

Stummer, Peter O., and Christopher Balme, eds. *Fusion of Cultures?* Amsterdam: Rodopi, 1996.

Such a Long Journey. Screenplay by Sooni Taraporevala. Dir. Sturla Gunnarson. Prod. Paul Stephens and Simon MacCorkindale. Keystone, 1999.

Sutherland, John. 'The Bumpy Ride to Booker, 1981.' *Times Higher Education Supplement* 31 Oct. 1981: 11.

Swann. Screenplay by David Young. Dir. Anna Benson Gyles. Prod. Ann Scott and Christina Jennings. Norstar, 1995.

Taylor, Noel. 'Swann Film Probes Journey of Discovery.' *Ottawa Citizen* 14 Feb. 1997: F3.

Thomas, Bronwen, '"Piecing Together a Mirage": Adapting *The English Patient* for the Screen.' *The Classic Novel from Page to Screen.* Ed. Robert Giddings and Erica Sheen. Manchester: Manchester UP, 2000. 197–232.

Thomas, Joan. 'Pleasures of Self Lie outside Emotional Hold.' *Globe and Mail* 15 Jun. 1996: C20.

Tiffin, Helen. 'Foot in Mouth: Animals, Disease, and the Cannibal Complex.' *Mosaic* 40.1 (2007): 11–26.

– Introduction. *Five Emus to the King of Siam: Environment and Empire.* Ed. Helen Tiffin. Amsterdam: Rodopi, 2007. xi–xxviii.

Todd, Richard. *Consuming Fictions: The Booker Prize and Fiction in Britain Today.* London: Bloomsbury, 1996.

Todorov, Tzvetan. *On Human Diversity: Nationalism, Racism and Exoticism in French Thought*. Tr. Catherine Porter. Cambridge, MA: Harvard UP, 1993.

Tokaryk, Tyler. 'Keynes, Storytelling, and Realism: Literary and Economic Discourse in Rohinton Mistry's *A Fine Balance*.' *Studies in Canadian Literature* 30.2 (2005): 1–31.

Tonkin, Boyd. 'The Real Prize.' *Independent* (London) 26 Apr. 2005: 33.

Topalovich, Maria. *A Pictorial History of the Canadian Film Awards*. Toronto: Stoddart, 1984.

'Toronto Book Awards.' Internet. <www.city.toronto.on.ca/book_awards/index.htm> Accessed 14 Jan. 2004.

Tötösy de Zepetnek, Steven, ed. *Comparative Cultural Studies and Michael Ondaatje's Writing*. West Lafayette: Purdue UP, 2005.

Tracey, Elisabeth. 'Last Chance for Commonwealth Literary Stardom.' *South China Morning Post* (Hong Kong) 5 Apr. 1997: Saturday Review 9.

Trilling, Daniel. 'Notes from a Small Island.' *New Statesman* 18 Jun. 2007. Nexis UK. Leeds Metropolitan U Lib. 25 Jan. 2008 <http://www.lexisnexis.com/uk/>.

'Trillium Book Award.' Internet. <www.culture.gov.on.ca/english/culdiv/cultind/trillium.htm> Accessed 14 Jan. 2004.

Turbide, Diane. 'A Prairie Pulitzer.' *Maclean's* 1 May 1995: 299.

Turner, Barbara. 'In the Skin of Michael Ondaatje.' *Quill & Quire* May 1987: 21.

Turner, Bryan S. 'Foreword: From Governmentality to Risk, Some Reflections on Foucault's Contribution to Medical Sociology.' *Foucault, Health and Medicine*. Ed. Alan Peterson and Robin Bunton. London: Routledge, 1997. ix-xxi.

– 'Liberal Citizenship and Cosmopolitan Virtue.' *Citizenship and Democracy in a Global Era*. Ed. Andrew Vandenberg. Basingstoke: Macmillan, 2000.

Umrigar, Thrity. Rev. of *Family Matters. Boston Globe* 5 Jan. 2003: D7.

Uppala, Sam. 'What India Is Like.' *Charleston Gazette* 13 Jul. 1997: 2E.

Urquhart, Jane. 'Author's Generosity of Spirit Enriched Lives of Her Readers.' *Globe and Mail* 18 Jul. 2003: A1, A6.

van Herk, Aritha. 'Publishing and Perishing with No Parachute.' *How Canadians Communicate*. Ed. David Taras, Fritz Pannekoek, and Maria Bakardjieva. Calgary: U of Calgary P, 2003. 121–41.

Vauthier, Simone. 'A Story of Silence and Voices: Michael Ondaatje's *In the Skin of a Lion*.' *Multiple Voices: Recent Canadian Fiction*. Ed. Jeanne Delbaere. Sydney: Dungaroo, 1990. 69–90.

Vowles, Andrew. 'An Intimate Portrait.' *Hamilton Spectator* 13 Apr. 2002: M18.

Wagner, Vit. 'Book of Negroes Just Keeps Winning.' *Toronto Star* 7 Mar. 2009: E6.

Wallace, Bruce. 'Critics Carp at "Canadianness" of Booker Nominees.' *Montreal Gazette* 19 Oct. 2002: D5.

- 'Montrealer's Pi Wins Booker: $120,000-Prize Winner Yann Martel Extols Virtues of Canada for Writers.' *Vancouver Sun* 23 Oct. 2002: A7.

Wallenstein, Sven-Olov. *Biopolitics and the Emergence of Modern Architecture.* New York: Princeton Architecture Press, 2009.

Walsh, John. 'Six Characters in Search of a Booker.' *Sunday Times* (London) 29 Sep. 1991. Nexis UK. Leeds Metropolitan U Lib. 1 Jun. 2007 <http://www.lexisnexis.com/uk/>.

Walter, Natasha. 'The Week in Reviews: Books.' *Observer* 24 Aug. 1997: Review 14.

Weaver, David. 'Genies: Showcase in Search of an Audience.' *Globe and Mail* 15 Dec. 1997: C1.

Weaver, Robert. 'The Governor-General's Awards.' *Saturday Night* 2 Apr. 1960: 29–31.

Weeks, Jerome. 'Author Has a Woolf-ishness about Her.' *Dallas Morning News* 27 Feb. 1998: 43A.

Whiteside, Shaun. 'Music of What Happens.' *Guardian* 29 Jun. 1993: Features 11.

Whittell, Giles, and Dalya Alberge. 'British Wartime Romance Scoops Oscar Nominations.' *Times* (London) 12 Feb. 1997: 1–2.

Whitworth, Damian. 'American Wins Prize for Female Fiction.' *Times* (London) 20 May 1998: 6.

Wigod, Rebecca. 'Yann Martel's New Novel Is No Life of Pi.' *Vancouver Sun* 10 Apr. 2010: C6.

Williams, David. 'Cyberwriting and the Borders of Identity: "What's in a Name" in Kroetsch's *The Puppeteer* and Mistry's *Such a Long Journey*?' *Canadian Literature* 149 (1996): 55–71.

Williams, Melissa S. 'Toleration, Canadian-Style: Reflections of a Yankee-Canadian.' Beiner and Norman 216–31.

Winder, Robert. 'Booker Prize Judges Opt for Passion in Youthful Shortlist.' *Independent* 23 Sep. 1993: 3.

Wolf, Werner. 'Migration towards a Rewarding Goal and Multicutluralism with a Positive Centre: Yann Martel's *Life of Pi* as a Post-Postmodernist Attempt at Eliciting (Poetic) Faith.' *Canada in the Sign of Migration and Trans-Culturalism.* Frankfurt: Peter Lang, 2004. 102–24.

Woodcock, Connie. 'Celebrating a Good Canadian Read.' *Toronto Sun* 28 Apr. 2002: C5.

Woodcock, George. 'Ondaatje, Hospital; Measure of Maturity.' *Quill & Quire* Oct. 1992: 22.

Wordsworth, Araminta. 'Curious Contenders for Britain's Booker.' *Financial Post* 9 Oct. 1993: S8.

'A World in One Room.' *Economist* (U.S. ed.) 27 Apr. 2002. Nexis UK. Leeds Metropolitan U Lib. 4 Jun. 2007 <http://www.lexisnexis.com/uk/>.

Yanofsky, Joel. 'Don't Bet That Merit Will Win.' *Gazette* (Montreal) 19 Jan. 1991: I3.

– 'From the Authentic Chaos of Life.' *Toronto Star* 9 Oct. 1993: J15.

– 'Picking G-G Winner Can Be Perilous Chore.' *Gazette* (Montreal) 15 Nov. 1997: J3.

York, Lorraine. *Literary Celebrity in Canada*. Toronto: U of Toronto P, 2007.

Young, Judy. 'No Longer "Apart"? Multiculturalism Policy and Canadian Literature.' *Canadian Ethnic Studies* 33.2 (2001): 88–116.

Younis, Raymond Aaron. 'Nationhood and Decolonization in *The English Patient*.' *Literature / Film Quarterly* 16 (1998): 2–9.

Zajac, Ronald. 'Chat with the Queen among Hill's Highlights.' *Brockville Recorder and Times* 4 Feb. 2009: A3.

Index

CULTURAL SPACES

Cultural Spaces explores the rapidly changing temporal, spatial, and theoretical boundaries of contemporary cultural studies. Culture has long been understood as the force that defines and delimits societies in fixed spaces. The recent intensification of globalizing processes, however, has meant that it is no longer possible – if it ever was – to imagine the world as a collection of autonomous, monadic spaces, whether these are imagined as localities, nations, regions within nations, or cultures demarcated by region or nation. One of the major challenges of studying contemporary culture is to understand the new relationships of culture to space that are produced today. The aim of this series is to publish bold new analyses and theories of the spaces of culture, as well as investigations of the historical construction of those cultural spaces that have influenced the shape of the contemporary world.

Mark Coté, Richard J.F. Day, and Greg de Peuter, eds., *Utopian Pedagogy: Radical Experiments against Neoliberal Globalization*

Michael McKinnie, *City Stages: Theatre and the Urban Space in a Global City*

David Jefferess, *Postcolonial Resistance: Culture, Liberation, and Transformation*

Mary Gallagher, ed., *World Writing: Poetics, Ethics, Globalization*

Maureen Moynagh, *Political Tourism and Its Texts*

Erin Hurley, *National Performance: Representing Quebec from Expo '67 to Céline Dion*

Lily Cho, *Eating Chinese: Culture on the Menu in Small Town Canada*

Rhona Richman Kenneally and Johanne Sloan, eds, *Expo 67: Not Just a Souvenir*

Gillian Roberts, *Prizing Literature: The Celebration and Circulation of National Culture*